# HOPE AND HISTORY

# Hope and History

## A Memoir of Tumultuous Times

### William J. vanden Heuvel

### Foreword by Douglas Brinkley

Cornell University Press
Ithaca and London

First published 2019 by Cornell University Press

Printed in the United States of America

Library of Congress Cataloging-in-Publication Data

Names: Vanden Heuvel, William J. (William Jacobus), 1930– author.
Title: Hope and history : a memoir of tumultuous times / by William vanden Heuvel.
Description: Ithaca : Cornell University Press, 2019. | Includes bibliographical references and index.
Identifiers: LCCN 2018060441 (print) | LCCN 2019000907 (ebook) | ISBN 9781501738180 (pdf) | ISBN 9781501738197 (ret) | ISBN 9781501738173 (cloth : alk. paper)
Subjects: LCSH: Vanden Heuvel, William J. (William Jacobus), 1930– | Ambassadors—United States—Biography. | Statesmen—United States—Biography. | United States—Politics and government—1945–1989. | United States—Foreign relations—1945–1989.
Classification: LCC E840.8.V36 (ebook) | LCC E840.8.V36 A3 2019 (print) | DDC 327.2092 [B]—dc23
LC record available at https://lccn.loc.gov/2018060441

In memory of my parents,
Alberta and Joost vanden Heuvel
and my sister, Jennie vanden Heuvel Hoechner
and in loving dedication to my family:

Melinda
Katrina, Stephen & Nika; Wendy, Brad & Lila; Ashley, Alex,
Nicholas, Felix & Isabelle; John, Marie-Noelle, Annabelle &
Olivia; Carol, David, Megan & Daniel; Bruce, Judy, Bryan &
Bobby; Carol, John & the Rochester clan

History says, don't hope
On this side of the grave.
But then, once in a lifetime
The longed-for tidal wave
Of justice can rise up,
And hope and history rhyme.

—Seamus Heaney, "The Cure at Troy: A Version of Sophocles' *Philoctetes*"

# CONTENTS

Foreword by Douglas Brinkley     xi

Acknowledgments     xv

Introduction     1

1. Growing Up in the Age of Roosevelt     3

2. Heroes and Mentors: Roger Baldwin and
   William J. "Wild Bill" Donovan     14

3. RFK, Prince Edward County, and the Revolution for Justice     60

4. Prisons and Prisoners     95

5. The Carter Presidency and the United Nations     126

6. America and the Holocaust     162

7. The Roosevelt Legacy     190

8. Reflections on Years to Come     237

Notes     245

Bibliography     249

Index     255

# FOREWORD

Something about Bill vanden Heuvel always inspires me to do better, to care more deeply about American politics, the United Nations, human rights, and the eternal fight for social justice. The former ambassador, a brave and openhearted American patriot, has spent decades working to stamp out racial bigotry, solve refugee dislocation problems, and curtail systemic poverty all over the world. Vanden Heuvel has been a close friend of mine and mentor for over thirty years. We weekly share laughs about the absurdity of life, family dynamics, headline news, and academia, sometimes becoming our own two-person book club. Every time vanden Heuvel tells me a fresh story about leaders like Adlai Stevenson and Bill Clinton, or recounts being in the diplomatic trenches with William "Wild Bill" Donovan in the fifties, I lean forward. You will, too, when reading this elegant and riveting memoir of this diplomat extraordinaire. For vanden Heuvel is a brilliant raconteur, never flashing his cuffs, able to write in pitch-perfect prose about the constant pendulum swings of history and his own stellar contribution to the never-ending American parade.

The child of working-class European immigrant parents, raised in Rochester, New York, where the ghosts of Susan B. Anthony and Frederick Douglass loomed large, trained in the art of self-sufficiency in the California desertscape around Deep Springs, and minted in law at Cornell University, vanden Heuvel embodies the time-honored Horatio Alger tradition in spades. Handsome, debonair, whip-smart, fearless, physically fit, and a marvelous extrovert with a constant twinkle in his eye, vanden Heuvel's calling cards are personal loyalty and bedrock integrity. He served in the US Air Force, ran for Congress, crusaded for prison reform, created the Roosevelt Study Center in the Netherlands, helped Thailand remain a democratic nation, marched with Martin Luther King Jr. in Mississippi, advised Robert F. Kennedy as he ran for president in 1968, and served as Jimmy Carter's ambassador to the United Nations in Geneva and New York—and all of this while maintaining a career as an international lawyer and investment banker. Always wanting to give back to the country he loves, a philanthropist and impresario of his time, vanden Heuvel is the most Rooseveltian person I know, always consumed with dynamic ideas about making America a more durable and equitable place. Aiming to fulfill Theodore Roosevelt's sense of environmental stewardship, Franklin Roosevelt's belief in the Four Freedoms, and Eleanor Roosevelt's plea for the UN Universal Declaration of Human Rights, vanden Heuvel has traveled far and wide in the name of societal reform and global reconciliation.

As this memoir makes clear from the outset, a compassion for the underdog and down-and-outers has been steadfast throughout vanden Heuvel's life. Not that he hasn't lived the high life of a New York City cultural arbiter and foreign policy establishmentarian. But he has never let his professional success undermine his core New Deal philosophy of helping those most in need. In any given situation he offers an outstretched hand. In a time of crisis, he is a reliable counselor. In public forums his soliloquy is electrifying. There is nothing detached or cookie-cutter about him. With his shock of silver hair, horn-rimmed glasses, and hearty chuckle, he is the consummate Dutch uncle to scores of his friends. His intellectual greatness comes from cavernous caring, omnivorous reading, and daring real-life experience. Even though he epitomizes cosmopolitanism, he is at heart down-home. Witty without ever being caustic, sharp as a knife without the instinct to jab, he is an impressive reservoir of historical knowledge willing to be tapped when asked. Writing letters of recommendation comes easily for vanden Heuvel because he wants to see young people—and thereby America—succeed. Often he assumes the role of the gentleman spur, pushing friends and associates out of their cocoons to embrace the better angels of their nature. True liberty, he knows, from Valley Forge to Gettysburg to Selma, has been earned with blood and sweat. Attaining the promise of the Declaration of Independence is the primary civic duty, he insists, that righteous citizens must embrace.

So readers of this memoir are in for a treat. The prose is smooth yet direct, just like the ambassador himself. His eulogy for Roger Baldwin—founder of the American Civil Liberties Union—is worth the price of admission alone. There is an appealing onward thrust in these pages, superbly edited by the historian Jill Kastner, a PhD in history from Harvard University, that exudes a quick-minded nobility and hard-earned wisdom. In this Dark Age of Trump, the ambassador is a beacon of light. His ceaseless compassion is a rare commodity these days in the public arena. At every turn, he reminds us that the Bill of Rights and the Civil Rights Act must endure.

John Kenneth Galbraith once wrote: "I have often thought as to who should be voted the best citizen of the United States—diligent, effective, intelligent and completely likable. It's a hard question. But of one thing I am sure: a truly leading candidate is Bill vanden Heuvel. Who do you know that does so much that is good while inviting such affection? There may be others but my vote, however many times repeated with whatever legality, is for Bill."

What impresses me most about this memoir, in the end, is that our storyteller isn't afraid to have sustainable heroes. With meticulous care he recalls Eleanor Roosevelt's love of children, Jimmy Carter's no-frills demeanor, and Bobby Kennedy's fearlessness. Franklin Roosevelt is as alive here as the evergreens on his tree plantation at Hyde Park on the Hudson. The legacies of the New Deal and Great Society are championed with fresh appreciation from our urbane eyewitness. In our fast-paced, twenty-first-century world, laced with invective and snark, it's lovely to read a wise voice of reason, decency, and genuine insight. If there is such a thing as an elder statesman, Bill vanden Heuvel is the all-seasons personification.

Douglas Brinkley
July 17, 2018

# Acknowledgments

Always quietly, always with clear vision and focus, and with an abiding belief that whatever my public legacy was worth, our children and family deserved a telling of it, Melinda encouraged the writing of this book and thereby enabled me to thank her for the love, support, and inspiration that brought it about.

Katrina vanden Heuvel was the architect. Deeply established in the media world, and the publisher and editor in chief of *The Nation* (America's oldest political journal, established in 1865), she drew the blueprint. Her unfailing encouragement and participation made it happen—with sensitivity, generosity, and determination. Her aging father became her student and did his homework with the joy of love.

I first knew Jill Kastner as a brilliant doctoral candidate in history working with Ernest May at Harvard. I think of her as the executive director of this project, organizing it as though General Eisenhower asked her to handle the details of the D-Day invasion. She has been an extraordinary collaborator. For five months, our days would begin with a phone call from London setting the day's work agenda, reviewing and editing drafts, encouraging the weary, drawing the blueprint that emerged from our deliberations, reading the endless oral histories that allowed the refreshment of memory. And then there is her personality—so thoughtful, effervescent, so kind, so capable of resolving obstacles, such a wonderful sense of humor. Praise is not enough. Thank you, dear Jill.

Barbara Nienaltowski, my personal assistant at Allen and Company, kept me mindful of my other responsibilities while completing *Hope and History*. I am not a master of the computer, but fortunately Barbara is—and further, she has a searching intelligence that made her a pivotal player in our project. Thoughtfulness and common sense are traits of Barbara that brought everything together. I am most grateful.

I acknowledge with profound appreciation the following friends and colleagues whose friendship and encouragement, one way or another, made this book possible:

Abe Beame, David Blum, Cornelis Boertien, James MacGregor Burns, Schuyler Chapin, Leo Cherne, John C. Culver, Colgate Darden, Arend de Ru, Norman Dorsen, Angier Biddle Duke, Robin Duke, Henry Fisher, John Kenneth Galbraith, Robert F. Gatje, Phil George, Richard Goodwin, Reverend Francis Griffin, Milton Gwirtzman, Ambassador Stéphane Hessel, Richard Holbrooke, Alistair Horne, Jacob and Marian Javits, Elmer Marker Johnson, Edward M. Kennedy, Miriam Kennedy, Robert F. Kennedy, John V. Lindsay, Gordon Moss, Sir James Murray, L. L. Nunn, Edgar de Picciotto, Maxwell Rabb, Camille Remacle, Roger Leon Remacle, Franklin D. Roosevelt Jr., Arthur Ross, Stephen J. Ross, Arthur Schlesinger Jr., Rudolph Schlesinger, Stephen E. Smith, Theodore Sorenson, Jean Stein, Lilian J. Stoneburg, Neil Sullivan, John V. Tunney, Cyrus Vance, John Whitehead, Simon N. Whitney, Milton A. Wolf, William Wolgast.

Herbert A. Allen, Bill Arnone, Wolfgang Aulitzky, Howard Axel and the Staff and Directors of the Four Freedoms Park Conservancy, Donald Beldock, Joan Bingham, Allida Black, Conrad Black, Janneke Boeser, Randolph Braham, John Brickman, Douglas Brinkley, Bartle Bull, Amanda Burden, Brian Burns, Joseph Califano, President and Mrs. Jimmy Carter, the Children of Prince Edward County, Robert Clark, Furio Colombo, Clark Copelin, David Cotner, Bert Cunningham and the "Fighting 69th" Infantry Regiment, Matilda Cuomo, Timothy DeWerff, Peter Duchin, Susan Dunn, Robert Dyson, Fred Eychaner and the Alphawood

Foundation, Anne Ford, Robert Forrester, Peter Georgescu, Toni Goodale, Fredrica and Jack Goodman, Doris Kearns Goodwin, Vartan Gregorian, Jane and Lindsey Gruson, Howard and Consuelo Hertz, Kate Hughes, Nancy Ireland, Steven Isenberg, Denise Kahn, Nathaniel Kahn, Susan Kahn, Ethel Kennedy, Joseph Kennedy III, Kerry Kennedy, Victoria Kennedy, Youida Kerr, Susan and William Kinsolving, Dr. Henry Kissinger, Carolyn Klemm, Barbara Shattuck Kohn and Eugene Kohn, Sarah and Victor Kovner, Jay Kriegel, Ray Lamontagne, Bill Leuchtenburg, Richard Levy, Dan Lufkin, Priscilla McCord, Tom McGrath, Ambassador Donald F. McHenry, David Miliband and the Staff and Trustees of the International Rescue Committee, Sally Minard, Charles Moerdler, Robert Morgenthau, Bill and Judith Moyers, Kenneth Nochimson, Charles O'Byrne, Sidney Offit, Walter O'Hara, David Paterson, Eduardo Moises Peñalver, Katrina Pence, Robert Pennoyer, Charles T. Pinck and The OSS Society, Gina Pollara, Han Polman and the Roosevelt Foundation (The Netherlands), John Postley, Jennifer Raab and Harold Holzer and the Staff and Directors of Roosevelt House, Ene Riisna and James Greenfield, Anna Eleanor Roosevelt, Mrs. Franklin D. Roosevelt Jr., Elihu Rose, Janet Ross, Howard Rubenstein, Stephen Schlesinger, Caroline Kennedy Schlossberg, Herbert and Judith Schlosser, Stan Shuman, Seth Yossi Siegel, Elisabeth Sifton, Dean John Smith, Jean Kennedy Smith, Daisy Soros, Paul Sparrow and the extraordinary Staff and Trustees of the Franklin Delano Roosevelt Library, Elizabeth and George Stevens, Kathleen Kennedy Townsend, Cyrus Vance Jr., Enzo Viscusi, Robin Vrba, Lacy Ward Jr. and the Staff of the Moton Museum, Farmville, Virginia, Miner Warner, Warren Wechsler, Felicia Wong and Directors and Staff of the Roosevelt Institute, Andrew Young, Marlene Hess and James Zirin.

# HOPE AND HISTORY

# INTRODUCTION

We live in a world in which "delete" is far too easy. This fact compels us to be deliberate in what we save. What survives may not be important, but it is who we are. Memory fades, events unwind, the inevitable stamp of new generations covers over what we have built. Duff Cooper, the British statesman, entitled his memoir *Old Men Forget*. They do, but they also remember.

I am the son of immigrant parents. My mother was Belgian, already twenty-five when World War I began. Her schooling ended in the second grade. She had two sons whom she raised in the shadow of war. She lost her husband. Her dream was America. With her sons, four and six years old, she borrowed the fare for steerage, and with a courage and optimism that never left her, she landed at Ellis Island, en route to Rochester, New York. There she worked as a cleaning woman in an orphanage, never having time to learn English with the fluency that her young sons mastered in a matter of weeks. She opened a boardinghouse for Dutch workers who had also immigrated. She married my father, who worked as hard in a factory as any man I have ever known.

For my parents, to be American was the pinnacle of achievement. They never thought in terms of what they did not have. They always embraced the miracle of good fortune that allowed them to create a family deeply rooted in their new country.

My parents understood that education was the key to opportunity. I never forgot the teachers in our public school who removed the restraints of poverty and helped us realize our dreams. I stayed in touch with them, so they always knew the profound gratitude we felt.

Deep Springs College was the most important intellectual experience of my life. Located in a California desert valley, on the Nevada border not too distant from Death Valley, it isolated twenty-four chosen young men for two years of college education while learning also the responsibilities of labor and initiative. Its students truly ran, organized, and managed the ranch and the school. If you endured, you were welcome in any university. The principal option was one of the world's great universities, Cornell, where the counterpart of Deep Springs existed in the form of Telluride House, which offered access to the opportunities of the university while creating a center of intellectual and cultural life on the Cornell campus. Professors and distinguished visitors often shared meals with us, and some lived at the house as well, including a Nobel Prize–winning physicist, Richard Feynman, and FDR's secretary of labor, Frances Perkins. In due course, Cornell Law School prepared me for the profession I had made my ambition at an early age.

With this educational background, I encountered the world that the following pages describe.

I have been encouraged to believe that some of my public statements are worthy of continued reflection. In these fragments, I have remembered private hopes and public purposes. I hope to illuminate various themes I have encountered in public affairs, knowing that these major problems are never solved, but that each of us can affect them.

Contemporary problems have historic roots. The work of democracy is never finished. Each generation must formulate its own response to the challenges of its times.

Our words and deeds are crucial expressions of what we believe. What lies in the following pages is a select representation of my memories and reflections over a lifetime's journey. Perhaps a new citizen or a grandchild or a dear young friend will find something in this chronicle to help strengthen and renew the possibilities of freedom and democracy that have meant so much to me.

# 1

# GROWING UP IN THE AGE
# OF ROOSEVELT

I was born on April 14, 1930, in Rochester, New York, the son of Alberta and Joost vanden Heuvel, both immigrants to the United States. I was named for my paternal grandfather, William Jacobus vanden Heuvel, who was captain of a fishing boat and a religious zealot, championing the most conservative causes of the Dutch Reformed Church in his village and family.

My sister, Jennie, and I grew up in a boardinghouse owned and operated by my mother at 26 Mayberry Street in Rochester. The boarders were Dutch single men, recently arrived in America and working as gardeners for wealthy families, or as factory workers. The house had four bedrooms and an attic. We lived in close quarters. In addition to the eight boarders, who paid $7 a week for room, board, and access to the living room to listen to the radio, the house was home to me, my two half brothers, my sister, and my parents. Our family lived in the attic, which was badly heated—and Rochester had very cold winters. There was only one bathroom in the entire house.

My father came from Breskens, a village in the province of Zeeland, in the Netherlands. He was one of eighteen children. From the age of eight he worked for his father on a fishing boat in the North Sea. He would tell us stories of being strapped to the mast to avoid being blown overboard during fierce storms. He had a quick mind, a generous spirit, a natural love of children, and an affinity for beer. Essentially unschooled, he worked for twenty-five years as a laborer at the R.T. French Company, a manufacturer of mustard, owned by British interests. A man of slight build, he did the heavy labor of loading and unloading boxcars. For some years, he was a one-man manufacturer of birdseed in facilities so dusty that they resembled a London fog. During the Depression, he was laid off from time to time and was always fearful of losing his job. He never questioned management. When a union-organizing operation began, he asked me to see the British president of the company to explain that he would always be a loyal employee, that he was forever grateful for the opportunity of employment, and that he was a company man. On a summer break from college, I worked in the company laboratory earning $1.25 an hour, which was the wage my father was earning after twenty-five years of employment. The union prevailed that summer. I helped the organizers in every way I could and convinced my father that the company would be stronger if its workers were fairly paid. The union won. Within a year, the workers' wages rose 50 percent.

My mother was born in the Belgian town of Lissewege, about ten kilometers from Bruges and today regarded as one of the most beautiful villages in Flanders. Her father was a farmer, his five children his workers. At age eleven, my mother was sent to work as a servant for a wealthy family in Bruges. Her experience helped me understand the novels of Charles Dickens. Poverty was a way of life. She was born in 1889 and was twenty-five when the German armies invaded Belgium in 1914. My mother, married to a baker, lived on the outskirts of the area later known as the battlefield of Ypres, where a million men would lose their lives before the war ended. She had her first son, Camille, in January of the year World War I began. Her second son, Leo, was born in 1916 and became a victim of rickets as a result of wartime malnutrition. My mother lost her husband, her home, and what little she owned. When the war ended, she borrowed $100 to buy passage in steerage, and sailed to America with her sons in hand. They were kept at Ellis Island for ten days while securing medical clearance. Once cleared, she boarded a bus to Rochester, New York, where her sponsor, an irascible brother, gave her temporary shelter while she looked for work. She found it—as a cleaning lady in a municipal orphanage.

My parents met in Rochester and were married in 1928. They spoke Dutch at home, as did we when we were children.

Part of my living memory was the meaning of immigration. Ellis Island became an epic story of heroism and determination. In later years when I served as the president of the International Rescue Committee, I often recalled the courage of those who, practically penniless, chose to leave their own country and settle in a place whose language they did not speak. My parents were in that last cycle of immigrants who could come to America uneducated and unskilled.

An old German immigrant loaned my mother the money that enabled her to buy the boardinghouse. There were many weeks we could not make the mortgage payments. How it pained my mother. In the end, she made certain that every borrowed dollar and its interest were paid.

For our circumstances, Rochester was a wonderful city in which to grow up. The philanthropy of George Eastman, the founder of Eastman Kodak, was evident everywhere. The university, the hospitals, the music schools, the parks system, made George Eastman the benefactor of all of us. He killed himself in 1932, leaving a note saying, "My work is done. Why wait?" We schoolchildren were taught to remember the extraordinary generosity of his life. The Eastman Kodak Company at its peak employed over 45,000 people in Rochester. It was one of the great stories of industrial success in America.

When President Roosevelt declared a mortgage moratorium, my mother led the cheering. We always thought of FDR as having saved our home. The brutality of the Great Depression began to give way to a government of heart and hope, personified by President Roosevelt.

It is difficult to describe the emotional meaning of Franklin Roosevelt to our household. The New Deal was very personal, and the feeling among working people was that Franklin Roosevelt really cared, that he understood their difficulties and was determined to help solve problems that otherwise were insurmountable. With the advent of Hitler and Nazi Germany, FDR became something else: the shield against war and against the enemies of democracy. In 1936, I sat on my father's shoulders as part of a torchlight parade for Roosevelt's reelection. Rochester was a city that was divided by railroad tracks. On our side of the tracks, everyone was for Franklin Delano Roosevelt.

In 1939, I convinced my mother to take me to an "I am an American" rally. Eleanor Roosevelt was scheduled to speak. As the program concluded, I took my mother to the stage and captured Eleanor Roosevelt's attention. She was tall, and she made you feel that she was really listening and was interested in what you were saying. I told her how much we admired her and appreciated her concern for us. She smiled the smile of someone amused by a young boy being so serious. Years later, when I knew Mrs. Roosevelt as a friend and political ally, I took some pleasure in telling her this story.

We never asked for or received any kind of public assistance. Some of our neighbors did receive "welfare." We never questioned or begrudged their need. My sister, Jennie, and I did not think of ourselves as being poor at all. There was always food on the table. We were always neatly dressed. My parents made certain that we acted with respect and dignity. Time was a precious commodity, and we never wasted any of it in the streets—the playgrounds of our community, where there were fights and drinking and lots of baseball. My mother was very strict about how we used our time. We had to be home by a certain hour. There was a sense of discipline and purpose in our daily lives. Even though my parents were barely literate and knew nothing about classical music, we took advantage of every opportunity to attend concerts at school. We were strongly encouraged to read, study, and "better ourselves." Jennie and I even played in the local Veterans of Foreign Wars drum and bugle corps, marching in the Memorial Day parade as part of the honor guard for James A. Hard, who became the last surviving combat veteran of the Grand Army of the Republic, the Union army of the Civil War.[1]

As a child, I never had racial or religious or ethnic attitudes of bias or discrimination. Mayberry Street was a polyglot neighborhood. There were Italians, Irish, Dutch, Belgians, and Germans among the "American" families. Italians were the largest immigrant group. My best friend, Alphonse Ferrara, lived across the street. He was stricken with polio in the summer of 1938. I could hear his cries across the street at night. When he went to a sanitarium for rehabilitation, I bicycled to visit him as often as I could. A reputed member of the Mafia was our neighbor as well. He drove a Cadillac.

Rochester had prominent and significant African American families. Their children were in the public schools, where we all learned together of the heroism of Frederick Douglass, who had lived in Rochester, as the dramatic spokesman for the abolition of slavery. Jennie and I always accepted the invitation of the local African American church to participate in singing and poetry recitals. William Warfield, the distinguished singer who later married Leontyne Price, came from Rochester. His brother Murphy sat next to me in the orchestra, where we both played baritone horn.

We were brought up to accept people on their own terms. Skin color or religion or place of origin made no difference.

The trauma of my childhood was my parents' separation in December 1938. Incredibly, it was related to the visit of my paternal grandfather, the only grandparent I ever met. He arrived in September, and in the three months that he spent with his children, he made religion the center of his concern. He chastised my father for marrying a Roman Catholic. He was unrelenting in preaching the fundamentalism of his own Calvinist background. I witnessed the searing cost of religious divisiveness.

My father, who became Catholic to marry my mother, was certainly not an observant member of the faith. My mother, a clear and open-minded person, carried the anticlericalism of Belgium to the New World. We attended church with my mother on Sundays, but when the priest insisted that we go to Catholic schools, my mother, without hesitation, rejected the thought, saying, "We are Americans and my children will go to American schools."

In December, the religious storms unleashed by my grandfather's presence became too much to bear. My father moved to a boardinghouse nearby, a few blocks from Mayberry Street. Jennie and I would go over to see him on weekends to take walks with him. One vivid scene that I always remember was the day before Christmas in 1938. My mother—in addition to the boardinghouse, in addition to all her labors—had a job as a cleaning woman in the factory where my brother Leo worked. Every Saturday afternoon she would spend four hours out at the factory, receiving $2 for cleaning up the offices. Leo, who worked six or seven days a week himself, had a 1934 Plymouth. It was Christmas Eve. My father had visited us, bringing little Christmas presents that ironically included a rosary for my mother. It was snowing. As Leo drove us away, I watched my father walking down the street alone as the sound of Christmas carols came from the car radio. I understood sadness on that day.

A week later, on New Year's Eve, an icy, wintry night, my father went to visit his father at a relative's home in Sodus, New York. My father fell on the steps of the porch. He was badly hurt, his skull fractured, and he became unconscious. Knowing nothing of medicine, the family simply carried him inside and laid him on the couch. By morning it was clear that he was very near death. He was taken to the hospital.

When my mother found out about the accident, she immediately took control of the situation. My father was near death, but my mother made it very clear that she was in charge and that he was going to recover. How she did it I do not know. My father slowly regained consciousness. We children kept the boardinghouse functioning. At last, my father came home. We were together again, all of us. I remember the happiness and emotion of that moment to this day. Their separation was never mentioned again.

My grandfather, who had been the source of such discord, returned to the Netherlands predicting that war would engulf the Continent within the year. He was killed in the Allied bombing of Breskens in 1941.

I was interested in government and politics from a very young age. I kept scrapbooks of the historical events that crowded those days. I had very strong feelings against Hitler before I was ten years old. My family did, too, certainly after the invasion of Holland and Belgium.

My parents were not involved in politics at all. When I was ten years old, I actively argued for Franklin Roosevelt's reelection as president, talking to people while handing out literature supplied by the storefront headquarters for the FDR reelection campaign. I can remember, while I was still in grammar school, advocating support for Winston Churchill, who had become prime minister in May 1940. I would ask my mother or father to take me to "America First" rallies, where Charles Lindbergh or Senator Burton Wheeler denounced the president. How those audiences railed against FDR, and how I cheered him!

Franklin Delano Roosevelt was the centerpiece of the world that held me in such thrall.

The arrival of war changed everything. The country was on a defense footing, with a tremendous demand for labor. The boardinghouse was no more. My mother enrolled in a special course as a lathe operator and took a job in a factory two blocks away from home. My father now had a steady job with the R.T. French Company. At the age of twelve, I worked as a machine tool apprentice. I always looked older than my age, so when

**Figure 1.** With my parents, Joost and Alberta vanden Heuvel, 1945.

I applied for the position the demand for labor was so sharp that no one questioned my credentials. My brother Camille joined the navy. My brother Leo moved to New Hampshire to operate a lumber mill. When possible, I walked the streets with my father at night, when he served as an air raid warden. People reported the slightest crack of light through closed curtains, presumably out of fear that enemy bombers might fly over Rochester on a mission to destroy our neighborhood. Our German neighbors, who had lived there for years, seemed to be reported for light violations more often than the others, although I could not see the difference. In any event, all of us were in motion.

America, united in resolve, marched to victory. Looking back, we now know that 67 million people were killed, that cities and villages were destroyed and plundered, but that the forces of democracy joined with Soviet heroism won the war.

Franklin Roosevelt died on April 12, 1945. We felt the loss with such anguish. A year later, marking the first anniversary of FDR's death, Harry Truman came to Hyde Park to receive the Roosevelt estate as a gift to the nation. I was there, too. My high school class had collected funds to buy me a ticket to Hyde Park. My Latin teacher lent me her Brownie camera, and I had some money from working in the factory as an apprentice during the war. I took a train to Poughkeepsie and hitchhiked to nearby Hyde Park. I waited outside the gates as a group of eight young people walked in. I walked in with them. When I got to the house, the Secret Service came out and counted heads. The group were students from Franklin D. Roosevelt High School, there to be ushers during the ceremony. When they saw that I was the ninth person, and that I had a little paper bag with a sandwich, they asked who I was. I tried to explain. At that point, I spied Mrs. Roosevelt, who was walking from the main house with Fala, the president's beloved Scottish terrier, to the Rose Garden. I ran over to her and said, "Mrs. Roosevelt, I've come all this way from Rochester just to be here today. Please let me stay." She not only permitted me to stay but allowed me to join the other students in seating the guests and handing out the program of the official proceedings.

It was an extraordinary day. President Truman led the ceremonies. It seemed as though every memorable personality of the Roosevelt era was present. I captured this historic moment in part with the little Brownie camera.

The first phase of my life was over. I was confident in who I wanted to be. I was fifteen when a telegram arrived announcing my acceptance to Deep Springs College.

Deep Springs was as far removed from my Rochester life as could be imagined. It is a two-year college located in a desert valley in California, close to the Nevada border. It was founded in 1917 by an entrepreneurial genius who believed that leadership and public conscience could be developed in young men by temporary isolation, concentrated study, and the hard work required to run a ranch with 300 head of cattle. The students had self-governance over this domain. To give a sense of the academic level of the college, Lawrence Kempton, the director of Deep Springs, left shortly before I arrived to become chancellor of the University of Chicago. The intensity of this life of growth and responsibility included having every opinion, conclusion, and article of faith challenged. The faculty was superb; many were distinguished academics using their sabbatical to be temporary faculty members. Learning, writing, and listening were daily fare, mixed with governance, farm labor, and being a cowboy if you had the skills. Public Speaking and Debate was the only required course, and I delighted in it.

I left home on a six-day bus trip to Big Pine, California. Cost of ticket: $42. My high school principal, William Wolgast, who had befriended me and who had recommended Deep Springs as my next step, drove me to the bus station after I had said goodbye to my family. Before the bus departed, my mother appeared. It was a moment so emotional that it still brings tears to my eyes when I think of it. My mother never cried, but on this occasion, tears glistened in her eyes. A paraphrase of her remembered words has always remained with me: "Whenever you come back, my Bill, life will be very different. You will have learned so much. You will have new friends. You will have opportunities for which you will always be ready. I believe in you; you must believe in yourself. Make a life of purpose. We will always love each other, but you must think of your life ahead and be free to make it happen."

How often I have thought of that scene. I boarded the bus, choked with emotion, and arrived in California six days later.

Deep Springs was the most important educational chapter of my life. I was so homesick that I asked the labor commissioner, who oversaw work assignments, if I could do something to stay busy. He sent me out with two other students to kill a pig. The procedure was to then put the dead pig in boiling water to aid in the skinning process. In doing that, I slipped, and my left leg was submerged in the boiling water. It took an hour to be driven by car over Westgard Pass and into Bishop, and the local hospital. I spent the next two weeks in a ward with four other patients, all of whom died before I left the hospital. Because of the school's isolation policy, Simon N. Whitney, the president and a distinguished economist, was my only visitor. I insisted that my parents not be notified; my injuries were not life-threatening, and there was nothing they could do. By the time I returned to Deep Springs, I felt a lot older. Despite this inauspicious beginning, I embraced the Deep Springs adventure.

Figure 2. A stone, a leaf, an unfound door. Deep Springs, CA, 1946.

Most Deep Springers chose to continue their college education at Cornell University. The founder of Deep Springs, L. L. Nunn, had also founded Telluride Association, whose mission was to provide young people with educational opportunity emphasizing intellectual curiosity, democratic self-governance, and social responsibility. Telluride House was based at Cornell and was fashioned on an Oxford college. The thirty young men who lived there enjoyed the company of distinguished guests like Hans Bethe, Robert Cushman, Roger Baldwin, Richard Feynman, and Reinhold Niebuhr. I lived there for four years, completing my liberal arts and law school education. I was designated the George Lincoln Burr scholar, which provided me with room, board, and tuition. I held a part-time job in the Law School library that covered other expenses.

I loved Constitutional Law and Robert Cushman, who taught it. Professors like Rudolph Schlesinger and John MacDonald gave unforgettable lectures. Luigi Einaudi, whose father was president of Italy, was a frequent guest at Telluride House. My availability as a faux-Italian opera singer, mimicking Verdi and Puccini arias in a compilation that my brilliant and Israel coordinated an attack on Egypt to regain control of the Suez Canal, which had been nationalized by the revolutionary government of Colonel Gamal Nasser.

The Hungarian Freedom Fighters fought the Soviet army to a standstill. They occupied Budapest and rallied forces throughout the country. The Communist government was ousted; the Freedom Fighters organized an interim government to negotiate the withdrawal of the Russian army. Meanwhile, the IRC moved immediately to supply food and medicines. Leo Cherne flew to Vienna and hired a car to take the first IRC workers directly into Budapest to get a clear idea of what was needed and, logistically, what was possible. Cherne then returned to New York and was invited by television host Ed Sullivan to report on the situation to America through his very popular television show. In response, several million dollars were sent overnight from Americans all over the country. With General Donovan as a prominent speaker, a rally for the Freedom Fighters was organized in Madison Square Garden on November 2. Crowds filled the Garden and overflowed into the surrounding streets. The Hungarians sent Anna Kéthly, who had been appointed temporary minister of state, to tell their story. It was an incredible scene.

Sadly, the situation was transformed forty-eight hours later when the Soviet army reentered Budapest. After days of hand-to-hand fighting, in which hundreds of young patriots were killed, the refugee flow began in earnest. Columns of men, women, and children began heading for the Austrian frontier seeking safety and protection. They were the vanguard of 240,000 refugees who pleaded for international sanctuary.

Among the refugees who crossed the border were two children, aged six and eight, John and Mary Hajdok, whose parents pleaded for my help. Circumstances would not allow them to leave Hungary at that moment. They asked me to take their small children, dressed neatly in national costumes, and place them with an aunt in New York City. How heartbreaking that must have been for them, to hand their children over to a total stranger to embark upon an uncertain voyage. I undertook that responsibility; the children were reunited with their parents within a year, and we stayed in touch for many years thereafter.

Sporadic fighting went on to year's end. The border areas remained open. The Soviets gradually replaced the Hungarian frontier guards—but during those dark and dangerous days, over 200,000 refugees reached Austria. The

**Figure 5.** With John and Mary Hajdok, aged six and eight, on the Hungarian border, November 1956. Their parents, unable to accompany them into Austria, asked me to ensure their safe passage to an aunt living in Queens.

United States led the resettlement efforts, arranging emergency visas, reunify-ing families, arranging for transport, working with the office of the UN High Commissioner for Refugees and countless private groups that arranged spon-taneously to make eating, sleeping, and travel arrangements. Forty thousand of the refugees were granted US admission and proceeded to Camp Kilmer, New Jersey, where a mammoth resettlement facility was organized. Cities and towns, churches and individuals, volunteered to take families, to find them jobs, to provide education and special care for the children, many of whom were tearfully separated from their parents, who for a variety of reasons could not escape. The IRC was involved in all of this. Tracy Voorhees, a close friend of General Donovan's, was appointed by President Eisenhower to direct the government's effort of rescue and resettlement.

Unless the United States intervened with military force, the Revolution would be over. President Eisenhower made it very clear that the United States had no intention of intervening in a conflict we did not sponsor. Donovan supported Eisenhower categorically. If necessity required war with the Soviets, Hungary in October 1956 was neither the place nor the time. The Suez fandango turned out to be illusory, as President Eisenhower again rejected war as a solution to a political problem. Negotiation was the solution, not war. The failed attack on the Suez Canal established Nasser's position and gave Egypt permanent control, a result that has worked well despite fearsome forebodings.

The world's attention was now on Hungary, where the defeated Freedom Fighters were hunted down by the Soviets, while thousands of refugees, leaving everything behind that they could not carry, struck out for the Austrian frontier and sanctuary.

A year before, to the puzzlement of the West, Soviet troops had voluntarily left Austria after ten years of occupation. General Donovan and I were in Vienna shortly after the Soviet departure. As soon as the last tank crossed the border, the Austrians erupted in triumphant joy. We were guests of Ambassador Llewellyn Thompson, one of the giants among American diplomats at the time, who took us to the opening of the State Opera where, amidst tears and cheers, the Vienna Opera under Karl Böhm performed Beethoven's *Fidelio*. It was a transformation, a moment when music spoke the words of freedom.

Now Austria was challenged to be the pathway not to safety but to freedom for over 200,000 Hungarians who were ready for any risks. Austria met this challenge with a heroic response. It was a time that Austrians would always remember with great pride. The democracies of Europe, with America in the lead, opened their doors. College students from a dozen countries came to assist. Governments joined the private sector in meeting every need. It was one of those times when people acted better than they are, where courage replaced cynicism, where hope was shared. That moment in history became an unforgettable vision of what civilization could be.

The roots of the IRC are in the resettlement of refugees escaping persecution from totalitarian governments. In the Hungarian situation, our special efforts included urging liberalization of the laws and regulations for refugees seeking resettlement in the United States. General Joseph Swing was the immigration commissioner, and his special assistant was John V. Lindsay, whom I met for the first time in Vienna and who was later elected mayor of New York, and with whom I had a decades-long political friendship and rivalry.

The dimensions of a significant refugee crisis were now visible. In mid-November, a special committee chaired by General Donovan left for Vienna to undertake a ten-day survey of the situation and what should and could be done about it. Claiborne Pell, Herman Steinkraus, and John Whitehead were members of the Donovan Commission, as was I, who was tasked with the assignment to write the report.[5] Entitled "The Sorrow and the Triumph of Hungary," it was published in January 1957. It was the most intimate, personal, and precise report then available as to what had happened and what had to be done, and it helped to galvanize an astonishing American response to the refugee crisis.

### The Sorrow and Triumph of Hungary
### Report of the Donovan Commission of the IRC to Study the Hungarian Refugee Situation in Hungary, by William J. vanden Heuvel

On November 17, 1956 a Commission of the International Rescue Committee under the Chairmanship of General William J. Donovan and including Claiborne Pell, Herman W. Steinkraus, and William J. vanden Heuvel left for a ten-day survey mission of the Hungarian refugee situation in Austria.

This is the Special Report of this Commission to the Board of Directors of the IRC. It was written for the Commission members by William J. vanden Heuvel. It contains an analysis of the revolution, the refugee exodus, and the significance of these events.

*The Sorrow and Triumph of Hungary*

The Hungarian Freedom fighters have given us the most significant story for liberty since World War II. The thousands of refugees who have sought temporary asylum have come not in the spirit of the vanquished but rather with the pride of conquerors. They know what the Free World has not yet fully realized—that *the Soviet monolith has been irreparably shattered* and that the *wreckage of Budapest has created a spectre that will terrify the*

*Communist oppressors in all lands.* This victory will not be denied, despite the staggering number of Hungarian casualties, despite the continued Soviet occupation of the country, and despite the apparent helplessness of the West to prevent Soviet aggression and barbarism.

The origins of the Hungarian Revolution are not secret. It was a spontaneous outburst by a unified people against both Communist doctrine and Russian domination. It was a revolution without a recognized leader. It began with an orderly protest march and surged into violence because of brutal, unexpected incidents. A brief review of the revolutionary events may help our appreciation of Hungary's struggle.

*I. The Revolution*

In the Spring of last year, the first manifestations of "de-Stalinization" became clear when a meeting of Hungarian writers and poets erupted in strong criticism of Rakosi and the Communist government of Hungary. One of the frequent demands was for the "rehabilitation" of Laslo Rajk, the former Foreign Minister of Hungary who had been executed for the crime of "Titoism" in 1949. This demand was finally granted, and a public burial was ordered. This cynical gesture turned out to be a catastrophic miscalculation. The Rajk funeral was held on October 6th, 1956, but instead of the 5,000 expected spectators, a crowd of more than 250,000 appeared. There were only a few organized groups. Most of the people came individually, many bringing flowers, some only a single carnation. This public defiance of the Communist government galvanized the spirit of resistance in Budapest. For the first time, the depth of anti-Communist sentiment became known. No longer did a student or worker have to fear that he stood alone in his hatred of the regime; the Rajk funeral showed that the profound resentment of Communist oppression was widely shared. Yet, no one would have predicted a violent revolution.

The challenge to Soviet domination in neighboring Poland cannot be underestimated in its effect on Hungary. Gomulka's successful defiance of Khrushchev was immediately known throughout the country, and undoubtedly served to embolden different groups to make new demands. The Soviet threat to use force proved to be bluff in Poland, and *this* lesson was not lost on Hungary. Yet, no one would have predicted a violent revolution.

On October 22nd, a student rally was held in Budapest to give voice to their demands for greater freedom. Several student leaders were chosen to draft these demands. From this meeting came the famous 16 points. The next day, October 23rd, a date now ranked among the greatest of Hungary's 1000-year history, students met in Parliament Square to demand the

reinstatement of Imre Nagy as Prime Minister and the correction of the injustices. Although a promise was given that their demands would be read before
the Hungarian Parliament, the students were dissatisfied. They marched to the
station of Radio Budapest, which was supervised by the dreaded "AVO,"
the Security Police. To quiet the demonstrators, three student leaders were
invited into the Station to discuss the issue. Forty-five minutes later, the bod-
ies of these three spokesmen were thrown back to the crowd. This infamous
outrage was the prelude to battle. As the crowd stormed the radio station, the
desperate "AVO" called upon the Army for help. The Army garrison stood
momentarily as a buffer between the angry student crowd and the "AVO,"
but it refused to fire on the students: There is considerable evidence that at
this point the Army turned weapons over to the students and thus gave them
the means to articulate their feelings with force.

Inflamed crowds walked the streets of Budapest the night of October 23rd.
The next morning thousands of citizens gathered in Parliament Square once
more to register their protests: They fraternized with the Soviet soldiers who
manned the tanks that lined the Square. Suddenly, "AVO" men—thrown into
panic by the threat of the growing crowd—fired several shots in warning. The
Soviet tankmen, mistaking the shots as directed at them, opened fire.

And so began the massacre of Budapest.

As hundreds of innocent Hungarians fell mortally wounded to the pave-
ment, thousands of their countrymen retreated—only to re-group in various districts of the city to begin a savage attack in retaliation. No longer did
the students fight alone. Their ranks were swelled by thousands of workers,
and by Hungarian soldiers who quickly defected to the ranks of the Freedom fighters. Communist brutality had been the siren call of the Revolution.
Now the world witnessed the incredible heroism of a people who shouted
in unison for freedom.

We asked a leader of the Freedom fighters why the Soviets had hesitated
so long before they finally crushed the Hungarian attack. The answer was
that there had been no hesitation. The Soviets intervened immediately, but
many of the Russian soldiers refused to fire on the revolutionaries. Some
joined the Freedom fighters; many sold their weapons for food; others used
the chaos as a screen for escape. The crucial fact is that the Soviet garrison
troops proved unreliable. Those who chose to fight were no match for the
revolutionaries. The extent of the Soviet panic can be seen in the tactical
error which committed tanks to the battle without infantrymen in the narrow streets of Budapest. By the adroit use of street barricades and "Molotov
cocktails," the Hungarians were able to emasculate Soviet armored power in
the first days of battle. The Russians had no alternative but to withdraw from
the city and await the arrival of fresh troops whose loyalty would be certain.

The last week of October saw events spiral madly along unpredictable courses. Imre Nagy was made Prime Minister and the hated Gero was discharged as Communist First Secretary. Nagy was caught in a political maelstrom which was beyond his control. First, he tried to restrain the crowds by harsh threats of punishment; then, when he faced the grim reality that the only unifying force for the nation was anti-Sovietism, Nagy called for the withdrawal of Soviet forces, the end of Hungary's participation in the Warsaw Pact, and even finally that act which no Communist state can survive—free elections.

The days of Hungarian freedom in this decade can be counted on one hand. They began with the withdrawal of the Russians from Budapest on October 31st; they ended four days later with the return of that force, this time strengthened by disciplined barbarians who would not be easily dismayed by the courage of patriots. Those days of freedom were filled with the ecstasy of unrestrained happiness; they were tempered by the sorrow of parents grieving for their children, whose lives had been taken as part of Freedom's monument; they were celebrated by the release of the democratic spirit through the overnight publication of a hundred newspapers and the street-corner shouting of a thousand orators; they were palled by the drumhead justice given the hated "AVO's" who were hunted relentlessly in the gaunt ruins of the city; they rang with the promise of Tomorrow—a Tomorrow which could not be described in detail but which reflected liberty's hopes.

The days of Freedom ended in the bitter darkness of Sunday morning, November 4th. A Hungarian military delegation headed by General Maleter had been invited to the outskirts of Budapest to discuss the details of the withdrawal of Soviet troops from all of Hungary. The delegation was imprisoned upon arrival. This cynical betrayal was the signal for the Soviet armor to return to Budapest. They returned without mercy. Innocent women and children standing in food lines were murdered; entire blocks of buildings were deliberately destroyed by marauding tanks searching out snipers. The terror of Soviet barbarism was never seen more clearly.

The Russian soldiers brought in for the November 4th attack were unbelievably illiterate. Many asked where the Suez Canal was, thinking that they had been sent to fight the invasion there. Others thought they were on their way to Berlin to fight an uprising of the Nazis. Some thought they were going to fight the American Army in Budapest.

The ruthless use of overwhelming armed forces by the Soviets brought a quick end to the military phase of the struggle. Still, the revolt persisted. The Hungarians had other weapons—weapons that the Soviets had never seen before. For instance, a general strike was called by the Budapest Workers' Councils, industry was paralyzed, transportation was inoperative, and the workers refused to be intimidated. For example, the bakers of Budapest in the middle of November distributed notes with their bread to the workers which said, "We will bake bread for you as long as you strike." Hungarian disdain for Kadar and his puppet government was never in doubt. By the time your Commission left Austria, a good part of the outlying provinces of Hungary were still defying Soviet domination. A copy of a newspaper printed on November 24th in Gyor boldly headlined the continuing struggle by asking: "Russians, what have you done with Nagy?"

Cardinal Mindszenty's liberation from prison was hailed by the people because he was a symbol of Communist oppression. The Cardinal showed good judgment in refraining from bitter comment and participating in any government. His speech was an eloquent plea for Hungarian neutrality and it was given without rancor or bitterness. The Cardinal's health is apparently good, although the strain of eight years' imprisonment is obvious. He was in the Parliament at the time of the Soviet attack on November 4th, and barely succeeded in escaping to the American Legation.

An insight into the internal situation of Hungary was given us in an interview with five Hungarian border guards who, on the date of the interview (November 25th), were still on active duty in Hungary. The scene was a refugee crossing point. The bridge that spanned the border had not been rebuilt since its destruction in 1945. The temporary structure used since that time had been destroyed by order of the commanding Lieutenant, a loyal Communist. The refugees were still getting across by means of logs, but there was no doubt that this was a precarious pathway to freedom.

The principal spokesman for the soldiers was a non-commissioned officer, aged 26, whose home was 40 kilometers away, where his wife and two children lived. He had already served six years in the Hungarian Border Guard. The other four were single men aged 21 to 23. All were from the neighboring area and none had more than eight grades of schooling. The pay of soldiers had been doubled by the Nagy government, and Kadar had been careful to pay these men at the new rate.

Every one of these soldiers favored the revolution. Speaking of the 70-man garrison to which they were attached, the spokesman said that 98% of his fellow soldiers would never accept Kadar. (The exception in the garrison was the Lieutenant.) To them Kadar was both a traitor and a dupe being used by the Russians for their own purposes. They spoke of Nagy with confidence, describing him as a patriot with great integrity.

I asked: "Will you flee Hungary?" Their answer was that they would not leave unless Soviet occupation was an absolute certainty. Like so many of the refugees, they stated the opinion that "the Russians will have to kill 9,000,000 Hungarians before they can occupy our country—and still they will not win." They expressed a reluctance to flee because "to begin the life of a refugee is never to end it." Their orders were to stop the flight of the refugees by all means short of shooting. The 70-man garrison covered 7½ kilometers of border area. Russian troops patrolled occasionally and Soviet forces were in charge of the adjoining 7½ kilometers. The only time that refugees had been stopped was when the Lieutenant was present. These refugees were taken to Central Headquarters and their fate from that point is unknown.

Not one of these soldiers was a member of the Communist Party, although all of them had been members of KOMSOMOL, the Communist Youth Organization. They had no alternative to joining this organization if they were to participate in athletic activities. To them, Communism was inseparably connected with Russia. Their hatred was therefore directed both against Communism as a doctrine and Russia as the oppressor.

Echoing the opinions of many refugees, the soldiers made it clear that they did not want to replace the Communists by the pre-war type of government personified by "old style land owners." They were convinced that the Hungarian economy could easily be self-sustaining. It would need help because of the revolution's cost, but they were confident that within two years their economy would have recovered. Politically they hoped for neutrality like that enjoyed by their admired neighbor Austria.

Their attitude towards the failure of the West to intervene was one of disappointment rather than bitterness. They accused the United States and the United Nations of using big words while being incapable of action. And yet they expressed confidence that a way would be found by the United Nations to force the withdrawal of Soviet troops. As one refugee said to us later: "We are not angry at the West because we are still hoping—and the West is our only hope." Almost in sadness, many student refugees recognized America's unwillingness to risk World War III, but they insist military intervention was not necessary because of Soviet weakness. Their faith in America and the United Nations persists.

It is important, we believe, to understand the spirit of Hungary's defiance. These fighters began their struggle without thought of outside intervention. They had listened to the broadcasts of the West which had spoken of Freedom's strength and prospects of liberation. They looked upon their revolution as a gateway to liberation, and their disappointment came because they thought the West had failed to grasp the significance of the event.

No longer is there widespread fighting with weapons of war, but the resistance is carried on by the workers who strike, the students who. publish handbills, and by the widows of Budapest who march unafraid before battle-ready Soviet soldiers to honor by floral tribute the fallen martyrs of the Revolution.

As incredible as it seems, Hungary's revolution continues.

*II. The Exodus*

The IRC Commission arrived in Vienna on November 18th. At that time approximately 25,000 Hungarians had sought asylum. By the time we left, ten days later, over 100,000 refugees had arrived in Austria. Today the total is over 160,000.

What the Commission witnessed was the outflowing of the life's blood of a defiant nation. Of the over 100,000 refugees in Austria at that time, it appeared that at least 60,000 were young men under 30 years of age. They did not leave because they feared death in the streets of Budapest. In our talks with countless refugees, the primary factor given to explain their flight was the deportation by the Soviets of Hungarian young men to Siberia. To these people, the reports of deportation were not just rumors. One refugee told of a friend who was concierge of an apartment house in the neighboring block. On November 7th Soviet troops appeared and indiscriminately removed all of the men living in the apartment house to the railroad station. The concierge had gone immediately to his friends to warn them. Without hesitating to gather possessions, this young couple took their month-old baby and began the 200-kilometer trek to the Austrian frontier.

There is a remarkable sense of integrity among these people. In talking to refugees about the fighting in Budapest, they were proud to point out that the fighting was not accompanied by looting. One person told the story of an "AVO" officer who was shot looting a broken store front. His body lay there undisturbed for three days among the untouched articles in the window. I asked one student whom we interviewed whether he was a Freedom fighter. He replied that he had not participated in the fighting. He was then asked why he did not claim to be a fighter since assistance might be more readily forthcoming. His reply belongs to the greatness of the Hungarian revolution. "I have had to lie for ten years. I do not want to do that anymore."

The fleeing thousands seeking sanctuary in Austria cannot be described in the normal newspaper terms used for refugees. They are not "poor, broken, drifting or wretched." The faces of these people, though exhausted, reflect the joy of victory. They have come to the West confident that their revolution will succeed, perhaps not today nor next week but ultimately—and they are certain that Hungary's spirit will prevail over Communism's brutality.

There is never an exodus of refugees without poignant scenes. None of us will forget the Hungarian father who hesitated at the frontier. The 14-year-old son did not want to leave Hungary because his mother was still in Budapest. The father had the wisdom to know this decision was too profound for anyone to make other than the boy himself. Finally, with tears streaming from his eyes, the young boy became a man and crossed the border to safety.

On Thanksgiving night, we stood on the border of Hungary again. It was a bitter cold evening. A bonfire had been built both for warmth and as a beacon. A small hut was used by a single Red Cross nurse to hand out hot tea and chocolate bars. The IRC had brought a supply of warm clothes and we had ordered a special truck which was available to carry the refugees the last 9 kilometers to shelter. The refugee flow was considerably decreased this day. Soviet patrols had been seen near the border and the sound of shooting was unceasing. We were told that hundreds of refugees were lying in the marshes, waiting for dark, so that they could avoid the Soviet patrols. A young Hungarian Freedom fighter decided to go to the border and tell those hiding in the marsh when it would be safe to come across. We shall never forget the cold, gaunt figures of these fleeing hundreds as they finally reached the bonfire and sanctuary.

On our return to Vienna in the early morning hours, we met a group of 40 refugees who had found their way to freedom by still another path. They beseeched us to find the woman 8 ½ months pregnant who had stopped to rest in a hayloft about a mile away, too exhausted to go on. We found her and took her to the hospital in the nearest town.

Our long day had ended but for these countless refugees, their day had just begun. They would be taken by an Austrian Government bus from the border area to a collecting station probably at Eisenstadt. From there, they would go to any one of a number of camps being administered for the Austrian Government. If they had friends or relatives in Vienna, they might go there—but no one could predict where they would be tomorrow. They might be on their way to any one of the generous nations of Western Europe that offered asylum; or they might be standing in line at the American Consulate seeking a visa. Literally hundreds came to the IRC offices every day seeking assistance. Despite the uncertain future, not one of these people betrayed fear or lack of confidence.

It should be recognized that all of us owe a great debt of gratitude to Austria. Only a year ago that country itself had been freed by Treaty from foreign occupation. Now, without asking the cost, the Austrians had given asylum and met the urgent needs. Clearly, the costs of the Hungarian exodus are too much for a nation of Austria's size to bear.

The Inter-Governmental Committee for European Migration has done an excellent job in making the transportation arrangements for the thousands of refugees who are being given asylum in countries other than Austria. Your Commission discussed these migration problems with Ambassador Harold Tittman, Director of the ICEM in Geneva. The IRC relationship to the ICEM has been one marked by good will and cooperation. The same must also be said of the United States Escapee Program whose Director, Richard Brown, continues to give effective leadership in finding solutions for refugee problems.

It is impossible to project the needs of these refugees for the indefinite future. Much will depend on the determined resolutions shown by the West. Several possibilities exist. Should the United Nations succeed in forcing the withdrawal of Soviet troops, a great many of these refugees will want to return to Hungary. Should the Soviets determine to crush the Hungarian spirit of liberty without regard for World opinion, then we must face the possibility of an extermination campaign which will rival Soviet barbarism in the Baltic States. In that event, we can expect the exodus of refugees to be multiplied several times over. There is the possibility also that inaction and lack of resolution will cause a long interim of camp confinement. If this happens, the normal bitterness and sorrow of refugee life can be expected, and we can also expect the Soviets to resume their techniques of redefection pressures in an attempt to destroy the significant results of the revolution. Your Commission urges that our Government announce promptly its willingness to assume more than a generous share of the ultimate cost. Whatever the cost in dollars and resources, America should accept its portion gratefully. It should be paid, not as an emergency relief measure, but rather as a sign of solidarity with these Hungarian heroes who have given Freedom and the West the most momentous victory since World War II.

### III. The Significance of the Hungarian Revolution

Despite the frustrating inability of the West to aid the Freedom fighters of Hungary, we believe that these patriots have recorded a monumental triumph.

First of all, the Orwellian spectre of "1984" should no longer haunt our Society. In Hungary, we have seen a generation of children trained under the relentless eye of Communist masters rise up in defiance. We can take courage in the knowledge that the tyranny of Communism has been unable to destroy the minds and spirit of its children. Although their access to literature and to unbiased information was throttled, the growing generation of Hungary still learned Freedom's meaning.

We have seen the structure of Communist Society shattered. The two basic cornerstones of Communism—the workers and the students—joined together to deliver a smashing blow. It was upon these groups that the Communists have counted for their future. They now know the students and workers are not their chattels. We have seen the rotten core of Communist institutions; and we have seen the units of family and church sustain the spirit of a people oppressed for a decade by ruthless men.

For the Soviets, it must be a pulverizing blow to realize that the armies of their satellites cannot be relied upon. Not only did the Hungarian Army refuse to resist the revolt; it actually joined the revolutionaries and supplied them with weapons. The Kremlin must also face the defections of the Red Army. Soviet leaders cannot easily forget that their own garrison troops proved unreliable. Only the influx of fresh troops carefully disciplined and propagandized saved the Red Army from complete embarrassment. The Hungarian Freedom fighters performed another service for our world. They tore away the deceitful mask of "co-existence" from the Soviet rulers. The neutral and uncommitted nations were shocked and stunned by the evidence of Soviet brutality and treachery in Hungary. No longer will a smiling Khrushchev be able to tour the uncommitted nations speaking of Soviet respect for self-determination and geographical integrity. If there was lingering doubt about Soviet motives, the Fighters in the streets of Budapest have removed it.

The Soviet monolith has been shattered, along with its propaganda shield of invincibility. The Iron Curtain has been ripped, probably beyond repair. From Budapest to Poznan to Berlin, the principles of human liberty have been re-affirmed.

The World has witnessed the Second October Revolution. The First October Revolution was fought in 1917 and from its chaos came the foundations of international communism. The Second October Revolution has begun the destruction of those foundations.

As the bells toll in Budapest now for Hungary's martyrs, let us remember that they toll for us too. We can lift our hands to ease Hungary's greatest sorrow by giving in the most generous of America's traditions to those who stand in critical need. And let us also stand proudly as free men, confirmed once more in the conviction of liberty's strength—and eternally grateful for the courage and heroism that has brought us Hungary's greatest triumph.

WILLIAM J. VANDEN HEUVEL
*January 2, 1957*

What was the legacy of the Hungarian Revolution? The Soviet empire was dramatically undermined. Never again would the countries of Eastern Europe be regarded as willing satellites of Moscow. It was now clear that the nations behind the Iron Curtain were occupied countries, and their occupiers, the Soviet Union, now had to confront the seething anger of these nations who wanted to be independent rather than colonies of Communism. The Hungarian army had not only refused to do battle against the Freedom Fighters, it had actually joined the revolution by supplying weapons and food to the insurgents; some soldiers even fought alongside their compatriots. The Freedom Fighters had undermined the validity of the Warsaw Pact and achieved a significant victory in the Cold War.

One anecdote has remained with me. Upon our return from Hungary, General Donovan asked me to travel to Missouri to brief former president Harry Truman. "Mr. President," I said as I entered his office, "I've just returned from the Hungarian Revolution. Is there anything more we might have done to help the Freedom Fighters?" I was stunned by his immediate response. "Absolutely not." President Truman, who prided himself on his knowledge of history, then described for me events following the First World War that brought the Communists and Béla Kun, the Fascists and Admiral Horthy, and then the Nazis to power in Hungary. The president continued: "Then when the military action took place in Suez, the Hungarians saw an opportunity to get help in freeing themselves from the Communists." At this point, I politely reminded President Truman that the Hungarian Revolution was a spontaneous event that started on October 23, whereas the Suez crisis began on October 29 with the Israeli invasion of Egypt. The president said: "So they were totally unrelated?" "Yes," I said. "Oh," replied President Truman. "Then maybe we could have done something."

The Hungarian Revolution was the final battle for General Donovan. In 1957, he suffered a massive stroke. He died on February 8, 1959. None had been a greater patriot. Few could match his extraordinary accomplishments. President Eisenhower spoke for the nation when he said that America had lost "the last hero."

As of 2017, the UNHCR lists 22.5 million refugees within its mandate. There are 65.6 million people forcibly displaced. These staggering statistics tell a story of human suffering that is an indictment of our world governance. In my experience, refugees are a special people. It takes extraordinary courage to leave your home, give up your possessions, make a journey that is fraught with danger, to land on shores that are often not welcoming, and then in the process of resettlement often to learn a new language and seek employment where your professional credentials have no relevance.

Those countries that give sanctuary to refugees have been proven to be the ultimate beneficiaries. Hitler's refugees, for example, included the eminent scientists of the world, who played an indispensable role in the Allied victory over the Nazis. So, too, with the Hungarians, the Cubans, and the Indo-Chinese who have resettled in this country. This should be a continuing lesson for all nations to understand that the gift of freedom is a benefit to all involved in its protection.

America's embrace of refugees has been an inspiring part of our country's history. No one expects a single nation to resolve the increasing problem of human flight. But America has been and must be the leader of the international community in seeking solutions. The problem has become so gigantic that it has caused democracy itself to be at risk. The foremost effort that should be made is to stop war, the primary source of refugee creation. We must make special allowances for children, again by example, and certainly through leadership. Refugees and the problems of forced migration leave behind a legacy of fear, both for the person fleeing and for the people being asked to give shelter. Agencies like the IRC are compelling examples of compassion and responsibility. Americans must lead in finding a way to abate the human suffering that refugees represent.

David Miliband, formerly the foreign minister of Great Britain, has been the president and CEO of the International Rescue Committee since 2013. His experience in high-level politics is a valuable asset. The numbers in every aspect of the refugee crisis are staggering, but worse is the absence of the United States as a positive force in seeking international solutions. I read my notes about the Hungarian Revolution and remember the extraordinary response of the democracies. Of course, the problems then and today are fundamentally different, but the spirit of freedom can inspire all of us to do more to bring hope to the oppressed and bring the talents and resources of a very wealthy world to the planning tables where solutions can be considered and adopted.

# 3

# RFK, Prince Edward County, and the Revolution for Justice

If a single date can mark the beginning of the modern African American revolution, it is May 17, 1954, when the Supreme Court handed down its unanimous decision in *Brown v. Board of Education*, finally destroying the constitutional basis of the "separate but equal" doctrine that had compelled African Americans to live in a status of inferior citizenship. In 1955, Dr. Martin Luther King joined Rosa Parks in leading a bus boycott in Montgomery, Alabama. In 1960 came a wave of sit-ins, begun by college students in Greensboro, North Carolina. Beginning in 1961, Freedom Riders began traveling on interstate buses in the South to enforce the nonsegregation policies, often with violent results. Street demonstrations swept Birmingham, St. Augustine, and many other cities. America was ablaze. The civil rights revolution had taken hold and demanded an affirmative response from those who governed America. New organizations, with new methods and leadership, offered competition to the NAACP, which had been the unchallenged spokesman for African American rights for half a century.

All of this signaled a basic change in civil rights strategy. A program of legal action pointed exclusively toward the southern states and directed by an integrated leadership gave way gradually to a social and economic effort, using political techniques, in the North as well as the South, under increasingly black leadership. Probably most significant was the fact that for the first time, the poor of the African American community became involved in civil rights objectives. The message of the "revolution of rising expectations," which government officials were preaching in all corners of the world, had a special resonance for black Americans. The emergence of the independent African states had given them a sense of identification. The slow economic improvement of black Americans since the Depression had raised their aspirations, making them increasingly unwilling to accept a subordinate position in the white man's world. During World War II, Joe Louis, the most prominent African American in the country, could say that he would "rather be a Negro in America than a white man anywhere else in the world," and his compatriots would accept this as patriotic gospel. Now it was not enough.

## RFK and the Revolution for Justice, Part I

One of the five cases consolidated under *Brown v. Board of Education* involved Prince Edward County, Virginia. It became the spearhead of Virginia's "massive resistance" to the federal constitutional obligation to end segregation. In Prince Edward County, the resisters went even further, taking the position that the Constitution did not oblige the Commonwealth of Virginia to provide public education. In 1959 the county board of supervisors voted to close the public schools rather than integrate them.

The Birmingham riots in May of 1963 had caused Attorney General Robert F. Kennedy to send Burke Marshall, assistant attorney general for civil rights, to meet with the protestors and the white leadership to see if a common ground was possible. It was no longer enough to acknowledge the oppressive and humiliating discrimination that African Americans had endured. The new demands of the black community essentially were for power—political and economic—that would allow them to share in the wealth and promise of America.

In the spring of 1963, RFK had a meeting in New York with African American intellectuals and cultural representatives to solicit their ideas for new programs. He was not prepared for what met him. A sharp exchange between him and Jerome Smith, a young man who had been severely beaten while traveling as a Freedom Rider in the South, brought forth a torrent of insults against Robert Kennedy as a representative of the white power structure. His efforts to explain the difficulties of getting civil rights laws through a Congress dominated by southerners were met with derision. Kennedy thought of himself as one who had defended African American interests at great personal and political risk. The leaders who met with him did not dispute his commitment to civil rights. But for the most part, it was irrelevant to them. They were not interested in or sympathetic to the political difficulties of their white liberal allies. They were speaking for a people who were tired of waiting. Lorraine Hansberry, the gifted playwright, told Robert Kennedy that many African Americans were disinterested in integration, preferring their own institutions to participation in a society they felt was hopelessly rotten.

Kennedy was angry. He resented the way he had been treated. But the measure of the man was that he took time in the months ahead to consider what had been said to him, to understand the suffering that was expressed in their truth, and to accept the responsibility of moving forward with greater force and urgency.

I came to know the Kennedys during the election campaigns of 1960. The Democratic Party had nominated me as its candidate for New York's Seventeenth Congressional District, the "silk stocking" district. The 1960 elections went well for Kennedy but less well for me—the race went to John Lindsay, who would later become mayor of New York. But out of a close friendship with Arthur Schlesinger Jr. and John Kenneth Galbraith came a meeting with Robert Kennedy in 1962. It was a turning point.

The Kennedys came to civil rights on the national agenda reluctantly. Congress was dominated in many ways by white southern committee chairmen who exercised dictatorial control through the rules of seniority. Robert Kennedy had come under intense criticism because he had recommended to the president the appointment of Judge William H. Cox of Georgia, who was an out-and-out segregationist. But unless that appointment was made, Senator James Eastland, a Democrat from Mississippi and the powerful chairman of the Judiciary Committee, would block

**Figure 6.** Campaigning with Harry Truman in Manhattan, October 1960.

**Figure 7.** At the Democratic National Convention, Los Angeles, July 1960, after the nomination of John F. Kennedy and Lyndon B. Johnson.

scores of crucial liberal appointments that would enable JFK's progressive reorganization of the judiciary to go forward. Cox became a federal judge, and the obstacle to liberal appointments for the moment was resolved.

The transformation of Robert Kennedy in his years as attorney general is part of his legend. At the time of his appointment, many thought of him as his "father's son"—a man of very strong, often conservative opinions, and one who saw the threat of Communism as the real danger to the world. His nomination to be attorney general was severely criticized as an example of classic nepotism. He was berated because of his youth and inexperience. He was thirty-five years old and had never tried a case in court. FDR's last attorney general, Francis Biddle, was a caustic critic. Yet when RFK resigned the office of attorney general in 1964, Biddle publicly hailed his tenure as perhaps the most outstanding in the twentieth century. RFK was a pragmatic, tough politician. In 1961, his principal concern was to protect and enhance the administration of John F. Kennedy as president of the United States.

RFK was a gifted administrator who selected a team of strong, intelligent, and fair-minded individuals to assist him. They understood the Constitution of the United States and were not hesitant to defend their viewpoint.

At our meeting, the attorney general described the situation in Prince Edward County as one of personal concern to the president, who was outraged that any group of American children would be denied the opportunity of education. In Prince Edward County, black children—and poor white children, in some measure—had not been to school in three years. RFK appointed me as his special assistant, with the rank of assistant attorney general, and asked me to begin by proposing a resolution to the Prince Edward County situation.

And so began my journeys to Prince Edward County. It was a profound experience for me, learning about racism in America. I had lived in the South when I was an air force lieutenant, at Maxwell Field, Alabama, but a military base was a cross section of America, not really the heart of Alabama. In Prince Edward County, I talked to black leaders and to white leaders; they did not talk to each other. The pain of ostracism that was suffered by those who dared speak out or lend a sympathetic ear to the black cause was really difficult to accept, and made you understand what the cost of social progress was in our country. The supervisors of

Prince Edward County were a very tough breed. There was an arrogance to the white point of view. The code word was "states' rights." The language of the Constitution and its history were expressed in the aspiration of freedom, but the ultimate translation was apartheid and black oppression. The bottom line was the choice to destroy the educational structure of Prince Edward County by those who had the responsibility of government.

In terms of desegregation, the focus was on the South. The North had always taken the prideful position that it was different, and it had derided the South for its racist social structure and its denial to blacks of basic constitutional rights. But as the comedian and civil rights activist Dick Gregory, on a visit to Prince Edward County, once told me, "You know, there's not much difference between the North and the South, as far as blacks are concerned. In the North, they don't mind how big we get as long as we don't get too close. In the South, they don't mind how close we get as long as we don't get too big." There was a basic truth in Dick Gregory's humor. The southerners with whom I worked in Prince Edward County would say, "How can you call me prejudiced? I had a black mammy. She raised me. She breast-fed me. Her children were my playmates." And this was true; to a certain age, blacks and whites had lived together, and their lives were intertwined. But as they approached school age, the attitudes of racism became reality.

The North was not immune to these same attitudes. When you observed the social structure of the city where you lived, segregation was as much a reality in New York as it was in Atlanta, if not more so. The racism of the North began to be aroused by the protest movements in the streets. The open housing provision of the Civil Rights Act of 1964 had to be abandoned after Democratic congressmen from urban centers found their constituents vehemently opposed. In 1966, Senator Edward Kennedy and I had dinner with Martin Luther King Jr. in Jackson, Mississippi, where the senator had spoken at an NAACP event. Afterward, as we relaxed with Dr. King, he began talking about his experiences confronting northern segregation. He said that he had never felt more violently threatened than by the hatred of demonstrators in Cicero, Illinois, a suburb of Chicago.

A movie that had a powerful influence on me was *Rashomon*, Akira Kurosawa's 1950 film about a murder in medieval Japan. It tells the story from the viewpoint of four witnesses, and each story is incredibly different.

I've always believed in the *Rashomon* theory of seeking the truth, and of understanding that much of what you see depends on where you stand. My determination was to listen to anyone who wanted to express a point of view. My recommendations to RFK began to form. Could we create a system of free schools, sponsored but not controlled by the federal government? Could we create a model school in Prince Edward County that would attract teachers from all over the country who could provide an intensive remedial experience for those children who had been excluded? Could we close the gap of the three years that had been lost?

RFK authorized me to go ahead. We agreed that what should be done could be done. He asked me to keep him posted on a daily basis so that he would be aware of what progress was being made. His awareness, his judgment, his willingness to break through every obstacle, made success possible.

My first objective was to create a biracial board of trustees for the Free Schools. I had intensive discussions with the Reverend Francis Griffin, pastor of the First Baptist Church of Farmville and a valiant and stalwart ally in this endeavor. He was also state chairman of the Virginia NAACP. We agreed that the involvement of Colgate Darden, a Jeffersonian Virginian who had served as governor and as president of the University of Virginia, would give the project credibility. He was the most respected man in the state. RFK invited him to his office in Washington, where after several hours of discussion, Darden agreed to be chairman of the Prince Edward County Free Schools.

Darden helped organize a board of trustees comprising three African American presidents of universities and three white educators, including himself. We needed to find a superintendent of schools who could hire a minimum of 100 teachers and negotiate with the Prince Edward County Board of Supervisors to take over the abandoned school facilities at no cost. We found such a person—Dr. Neil Sullivan, the superintendent of schools in an affluent district on Long Island, New York, and a talented and nationally respected leader.

We set an opening date of September 17, 1963. In the interim, we had to convince the black families of the county that these schools would meet their promise.

I felt like one of the old circuit riders, making the rounds from the governor's office to Colgate Darden, to the individual trustees, to Reverend Griffin,

**Figure 8.** On August 14, 1963, Albertis S. Harrison Jr., governor of Virginia (*left*), announces the establishment of the Prince Edward County Free Schools at a press conference in Richmond. Seated with the governor are, *from left*, State NAACP President Francis L. Griffin, Assistant Attorney General William vanden Heuvel, and NAACP attorney Henry Marsh. (AP Photo/Richmond News Leader)

**Figure 9.** With former governor of Virginia and retired president of the University of Virginia Colgate Darden welcoming Robert and Ethel Kennedy to Prince Edward County, Virginia, spring 1964.

**Figure 10.** Joining with the children of Prince Edward County at the raising of the American flag on the first day of school, September 17, 1963.

to the white supremacy forces in the county, to the black families, to the white families, to the newspaper editors, to anybody who I felt had to be involved in the thing—I knew that successful negotiations depended upon building a relationship of confidence. By August of 1963, I was able to hold a press conference with the governor of Virginia, Albertis S. Harrison Jr., and Reverend Griffin to announce the creation of the Prince Edward County Free Schools.

The courts of the United States had stood firm in the interpretation and defense of the Constitution. The government was prepared to do its constitutional duty, beginning with the enforcement of desegregation by President Eisenhower in Little Rock, Arkansas, in 1957. Eisenhower was himself a conservative man, and he counted among his closest friends many of the southerners who were segregationists. The creation of the Prince Edward Country Free Schools was the first time the federal government had established a school system since the Civil War.

After the schools opened in September, I stayed in daily contact and helped to resolve problems as they arose. I also stayed in touch with community leaders. I was careful to tell the segregationist leaders, "You're going to have to live as a community. It's time for you to begin talking."

Many of them held onto the old ideas of black intellectual inferiority propagated by the Ku Klux Klan. One of the things we showed them in Prince Edward County was how good these children could be, and how responsive they were to education if given the chance. In the spring of 1964, the Supreme Court ruled 9–0 that the action of the Prince Edward County Board of Supervisors had been unconstitutional and ordered the reopening of the schools.

On the fiftieth anniversary of the closing of the schools, I was invited to give the keynote address at an assembly organized by Hampden-Sydney College as we recalled the painful, difficult years that led to this historic moment. The location was significant. Hampden-Sydney College was a distinguished all-male college founded in the eighteenth century that counted American revolutionary Patrick Henry among its alumni. In 1962 it had no black students. As we gathered in 2009, Hampden-Sydney was preparing to welcome its new president—an African American, Christopher Howard. That evening we listened to President Barack Obama give his first State of the Union address. A majority of voters of Prince Edward County had helped secure his victory. Many students who had graduated from our free schools were there.

Many heroes had made this success of liberty possible. The passage of years had claimed some of them: Robert F. Kennedy, the Reverend Francis Griffin, Colgate Darden, and Neil Sullivan, who had acted as superintendent of the school system. Many tears were shed as the surviving teachers, students, and citizens of the community, white and black, finally came together in recognition of a great victory for human rights. The doors had been closed, but they were now open.

**"Closing Doors, Opening Doors": Fifty Years after the School Closing in Prince Edward County, Virginia Keynote Address by William J. vanden Heuvel A Symposium at Hampden-Sydney College, Prince Edward County, Virginia, February 24, 2009**

The bicentennial of Abraham Lincoln has given our country an opportunity to remember the brutal conflict that almost destroyed the Republic. In its own way, the event we recall today—the closing of the public schools of Prince Edward County in 1959—was a last battle of the Civil War. History marked this county. On April 7, 1865, Robert E. Lee, knowing that defeat was imminent, rested here briefly before his final retreat. On April 8, the next day, Ulysses Grant, in pursuit, was in Prince Edward County. He dispatched a note to his adversary. They agreed to meet at the Appomattox Court House the next day. And so, on April 9, 1865, the Civil War was ended by its most illustrious commanders. Ulysses Grant became president of the United States. Robert E. Lee devoted the last five years of his life to efforts to "lead the young men in peace," and he gave this advice to southern parents: "Forget local animosities. Teach your sons to be Americans."

It took a very long time for that message to reach the white establishment of Virginia and in particular Prince Edward County. The racial, political, economic, cultural struggle that defined the Civil War found its last echoes in the voices of those who invented "massive resistance" to the Supreme Court's decisions on desegregation and who fought bitterly over the role and future of the public schools of this county.

In 1959 Prince Edward County had almost 16,000 residents. More than half of the farm owners were white, but the majority of the 6,000 tenant and farm workers were African American. Twelve hundred farms averaging about 120 acres in size and carved out of the county's heavily wooded hills had tobacco as their major crop. Prince Edward was regarded as part of the "Black Belt," the name given those areas of the South where the African American population approached or exceeded 50 percent. Many of its families dated to pre-Revolutionary times.

On April 23, 1951, the students at Robert R. Moton High School—all African American—went on strike to protest the overcrowded, leaky, badly heated buildings that had been erected as temporary facilities but then had acquired a distressing permanence. The NAACP, in a search led by its counsel, Thurgood Marshall, was looking for situations which could be developed into civil rights cases to challenge the constitutionality of segregation and overturn the doctrine of separate but equal established by the Supreme Court in *Plessy v. Ferguson,* decided in 1896. Barbara Johns, the sixteen-year-old student who led the protest at Robert Moton School, was the niece of Vernon Johns, an early and inspirational advocate of desegregation. The picketing students were insisting on better facilities—and to that, the facts were clear. The Prince Edward County School Board was quick to reply. It promised a new high school, and within two years there was such a school which under the doctrine of separate but equal would have been acceptable, but the argument had already advanced beyond that point. The NAACP lawyers told the students that they would file suit if the students would agree to press for ending segregation, if the students would end their strike, and if their parents would join the litigation. The African American community met to discuss the situation in the First Baptist Church of Farmville, of which the Reverend Francis Griffin was the pastor. The lawsuit was approved. It was filed on May 23, 1951. It was one of the five cases that became *Brown v. Board of Education of Topeka, Kansas.* The Supreme Court of the United States decided the Brown case on May 17, 1954. It ruled unanimously that segregation in public schools was unconstitutional. Freedom in America had a new definition, but enforcement of the court's decision was a different matter. Desegregation was supposed to be accomplished with "all deliberate speed," but in Virginia the ruling establishment responded with "massive resistance," and Prince Edward County made clear that their schools would never be desegregated even if they had to be padlocked to prevent it.

It became a legal war of attrition. The best lawyers of Virginia and of the NAACP fought tenaciously in the federal and state courts. In 1956, the board of supervisors enacted a resolution that prohibited any tax levies that could be used to support public schools at which both "white" and "colored" were taught. In 1959, disgusted by the delays and the legal labyrinth that had been created, the United States Court of Appeals directed the immediate desegregation of the Prince Edward County public schools.

And that is where our story this evening begins. True to its word, the board of supervisors refused to appropriate money for its public schools, resulting in their closing [for four years]. The 1,500 white children attended hastily organized private schools which were privately funded and also subsidized by state tuition grants. The 1,800 African American children in the county were left without formal instruction. Back and forth. Back and forth. Legal arguments, endless motions, federal and state courts intervening, rising anger, demonstrations—then the Virginia Supreme Court upheld the Prince Edward supervisors, essentially ruling that there was no constitutional obligation to have public schools, but if the local authorities did have public schools they had to be desegregated. The federal district court rejected this decision but refused to order the opening of the schools until the United States Supreme Court ruled.

During the course of these events, John F. Kennedy was elected president of the United States. He, and his brother, the attorney general, Robert F. Kennedy, were personally determined to resolve the crisis, hopefully in the courts. Despite the prodding and the pressure of the Justice Department, the legal process malingered. President Kennedy made reference to the Prince Edward situation in his 1962 State of the Union address. After the Virginia Supreme Court decision, he again publicly expressed his dismay. In a 1962 press conference, President Kennedy said there were only four places in the world where children are denied the right to attend school. He named them: North Korea, North Vietnam, Cambodia, and Prince Edward County, Virginia. Privately he told the attorney general that the situation was unacceptable, that the children had been denied education for three years already, and that a way had to be found to have the children in school by September. It was 1963. In May, Robert Kennedy called me to his office, reviewed the legal situation, expressed the president's profound concern, and instructed me to go to southern Virginia and Prince Edward County to see what could be done.

So began countless trips to Richmond and rural Virginia; endless meetings beginning with Francis Keppel, the federal commissioner of education and his colleagues, and interviews and discussions with the leaders of Prince Edward County, and a review of the mass of material that had been written about the closing of the schools and the process of desegregating educational facilities. Burke Marshall, the assistant attorney general for civil rights—and one of the preeminent public servants of his time—told me that there was no possibility that the case would reach the Supreme Court and be decided before its spring term in 1964. If the children were to have school facilities, it would have to be accomplished by an unprecedented effort of public and private forces.

I met at length with the Reverend Francis Griffin, the pastor of the First Baptist Church of Farmville. He was also the state chairman of the NAACP. His children were both litigants and students, deeply affected by the crisis. Reverend Griffin was a wonderful preacher, a modest man of tenacious determination, a leader who worked tirelessly and never spared himself, a minister of God's word who had been bullied, harassed, vilified, insulted, but who never lost his dignity, his patience, and his courage. As I developed the idea with him of a privately funded Free School Association with excellent teachers offering an outstanding educational opportunity to all of the children of the county, he saw as I did the incredible complexities in bringing it about. I asked him: "Reverend Griffin, would you support the effort if only African American children responded and the white families boycotted the schools?" Together we saw the Free School possibility as a bridge to the time we were certain would come when the Supreme Court would order restoration of public education—and Reverend Griffin's affirmation of the effort, indispensable to its possibility, depended on his confidence that his community would support it. The African American community knew that President Kennedy and the Department of Justice would be behind the Free School program and that quality education could help make up what their children had lost and in no way diminish the federal government's commitment to abolish apartheid in America. But the cooperation of the authorities of Prince Edward County was also necessary because we had to lease the school buildings from them. The Free School Association would have to be privately financed, racially integrated, and of a stature to command the approval of the Virginia establishment.

I visited at length with Barrye Wall, the publisher of the *Farmville Herald*. He was the leader of the "close the schools" movement. His attitudes reflected classic white supremacist values, veiled in the parlance of nullification, secession, and states' rights. He was convinced, as he said, "that in the South neither the White race nor the Negro race would be happy in an integrated society." Barrye Wall was five feet two, white-haired, a rather corpulent man in his midsixties, always with a Phi Beta Kappa Key across his necktie, scrupulously polite, easily available for talk and discussion—and convinced, as he warned the community in multiple editorials, that "outside sources are using your children as pawns in a national if not international conspiracy, and we citizens of Prince Edward are not going to pay for integrated schools." As he often said to me, "And that's that." Every editorial ended with the battle cry: "Stand steady, Prince Edward."

There was no possibility in the white community of disagreeing with Mr. Wall without painful consequences, but in the midst of the bullying and harassment there were heroes determined to save the soul of Virginia, as they put it, and keep the Commonwealth in the Union. Such a man was Gordon Moss, the Dean of Longwood Teachers College for Women in Farmville. A kind, soft-spoken gentleman of impeccable Confederate ancestry, Mr. Moss favored integrated public schools and said so in interviews with national media. He was told his academic position was in jeopardy. He was asked to leave his church. Old friends avoided being seen with him. Dean Moss was convinced that major opposition to public education was based not only on racial attitudes but also on economics. Prince Edward was a poor county. Less than 10% of its tax revenues came from the African American community, and more than half of the students were the children of that community. In the private conversations of the powerful, these facts were frequently noted. Professor Moss believed that integration was the excuse that the leaders of the segregationist movement had been seeking for a long time, an opportunity to get rid of the public schools. He publicly stated that the forces behind closing the schools believed that educating the white children in private schools would be much less expensive and would keep the supply of cheap, unskilled Negro labor available in the county. There would be no tobacco without this cheap labor, and tobacco was the only significant money crop in the county. He saw the "white establishment" as feeling threatened by the possibilities of a liberal education for the Negroes. They recognized that they could hardly maintain the status quo of privilege and prerogative if a fully adequate education was given to the African American community.

After reporting my detailed proposal for the Free School Association to the attorney general, I convened the interested parties on July 16, 1963, in the office of Commissioner Keppel, a fearless, articulate, nonbureaucratic leader who had been the dean of the Harvard School of Education before joining the Kennedy administration. The recommended proposal was favorably received, but extreme doubt was expressed that it could be carried out—there remained only two months to organize a school system, raise the necessary funds, hire an integrated faculty, and not least of all encourage the children to come back to school. Robert Kennedy had his doubts, too, but he authorized me to go ahead—if the goal was right, he was not intimidated by obstacles. "All I want you to do," he said, "is to keep me posted. Talk to me every day—a minute will be enough—then I will know where you are and what you are up to." His suggestions and interventions along the way were indispensable to our success. He was a brilliant administrator, unleashing the imagination and energy of those he trusted while having a clear sense of what was happening.

I briefed the governor of Virginia, Albertis Harrison, in his Richmond office about our plan. The first and crucial step was to establish an interracial board of trustees to be appointed by the governor. Albertis Harrison was equal to the challenge. He asked Colgate Darden, a former governor of Virginia and president emeritus of the University of Virginia, to be its chairman.

Colgate Darden was of the quality of our Founding Fathers. He was saddened to see his beloved state waste its resources and its children's lives in racial confrontation, but he had also been a witness against desegregation in the 1951 trial of the Prince Edward lawsuit. He came to Washington and met with Robert Kennedy and talked to the president. I spent hours with Colgate Darden reviewing the complexities of what had to be done. He agreed to serve. On August 14, 1963, Governor Harrison held a press conference with Colgate Darden, Reverend Griffin, and myself at his side. He announced the formation of the Prince Edward County Free School Association with Colgate Darden as its chairman. Also appointed were the vice chairman, Dr. Thomas Henderson, president of the Virginia Union University, and Dr. F. D. G. Ripple, the retiring dean at the University of Virginia Law School, as treasurer. The other members were Dr. Fred B. Cole, president of Washington and Lee University; Dr. Robert P. Daniel, president of Virginia State College; and Dr. Earl H. McClenney, president of St. Paul's College at Lawrenceville. The racial balance among the board members, their eminence, and their dedication to education validated our effort. The *New York Times* ran the photograph of the press conference as a front-page story. Colgate Darden later said: "I have been a Congressman, a Governor, a University President but this—Chairman of the Free School Board of Trustees—is the most important service I will have rendered my native state of Virginia."

The date of the opening of the Free Schools in Prince Edward County was set for September 16. We had a month to organize a school system for 1,900 children. It was a hot and violent summer. The march on Washington was scheduled to be held on August 28. The stakes were high. Failure was not an option. The first task was to find an educator who could serve as superintendent of the school system.

Commissioner Keppel suggested talking to Neil Sullivan, who had written extensively on nongraded education and who was serving as superintendent of schools in an affluent school district in New York. I called Dr. Sullivan on August 16. He knew about the crisis—and wrote later that he felt as though a lightning bolt had hit him with my call. Public education and racial issues were his two driving interests. Neil Sullivan became a close friend and a respected colleague. I told him that the plan for the Free School Association had been approved by both the president and the attorney general, that Colgate Darden had accepted its leadership, supported by five outstanding citizens of the Commonwealth. After meeting with the attorney general and with Governor Darden, Dr. Sullivan agreed to go to Farmville and tell us within forty-eight hours if he would take the position.

Colgate Darden had conditioned his acceptance of the position of chairman on the agreement that picketing by the children would be prohibited. Reverend Griffin said he could not ask the children for that commitment, that it was a matter of freedom of speech, but he believed that there was no desire to be disruptive and that if the schools could be opened and their possibilities properly described the children would not undertake demonstrations. Governor Darden withdrew his demand.

Hundreds of students and parents joined by twenty white citizens who supported their cause met on August 21 at the First Baptist Church and heard Reverend Griffin and myself present the case for the Free Schools. There were questions, there were concerns, there were prayers, there was singing, but by the end of the evening there was a strong affirmation of what we were trying to do. Neil Sullivan spent intensive time meeting with families and children and former teachers and others, like Barrye Wall. On August 27, at a meeting of the trustees in Lawrenceville, Virginia, the position was offered, and Neil Sullivan agreed to take it. The next day was the historic march on Washington and Martin Luther King Jr.'s unforgettable "I Have A Dream" speech. Dr. King had indicated support for our efforts. The leaders of the NAACP were with us every step of the way.

There was a wonderful spirit that touched every part of our effort. There was a feeling that we had broken through some terrible barriers, that there was a possibility of creating a new and different America. On September 3, the county board of supervisors authorized the contract to lease the schools to the Free School Association after meeting with me and Governor Darden. The four school buildings, including Robert Moton High School, had been padlocked for more than three years. There were no books, no teaching materials. The school buildings had to be repaired and cleaned. The library was practically bare, the cafeteria had to be rebuilt. In fact, the buildings were in deplorable condition. Dirt, dust, and rubbish were everywhere. Floor boards were rotting, plaster had fallen, water had penetrated the walls. The toilet areas were cluttered with debris, and the stench was sickening. In two weeks all of this had to be changed. Mr. J. D. Dishman was the gentleman who had the responsibility for building maintenance for the Board of Education. He told Dr. Sullivan that he would undertake the work but would take orders only from him and not from any Negro. But, in fact, he worked around the clock, cleaned the schools on schedule, made all the necessary repairs, and in time came to take orders from Negroes.

We had to hire 100 teachers. The African American teachers who had been part of the faculty of the schools for the most part had left the county when the schools were closed in 1959. The word went out from

Commissioner Keppel's office and from the National Education Association that 100 teachers were urgently needed, teachers of high quality, with experience in nongraded teaching, men and women who would have the flexibility to deal with certain and uncertain challenges that required courage and optimism to withstand. One of the first faculty hired by Dr. Sullivan was Miss Willie Mae Watson, a former Norfolk principal who had returned from two years in Nigeria with the Peace Corps, as our supervisor of elementary education. Miss Watson was a born leader with boundless energy, with incredible spirit and courage. She began contacting former Peace Corps associates. I talked to the leaders of the Peace Corps, leaders of the teachers' unions. The media wrote stories telling of our need. Invitations to qualified teachers to apply for positions went out to every school superintendent of cities with more than 100,000 population and to every college and university of any size which trained teachers. We placed ads in the leading newspapers.

Finding secretarial help was as difficult if not more difficult than finding teachers. Half of the teachers hired were from Virginia, an objective Colgate Darden and the trustees were anxious to bring about. More than 30 percent of the faculty was white—and five of those white teachers were Virginians. Miss Etta Rose Bailey of Richmond, a white elementary school principal who had retired the previous June and who was probably the state's outstanding principal but who had never taught Negro children, readily agreed to become principal of one of the elementary schools. She said: "You are giving me an opportunity that has been denied me during all of my forty-five years in Virginia schools. I have always wanted to work with Negro children." Faculty members began arriving from around the country. The Pledge of Allegiance was spoken at the end of their first meeting. As the final phrase was concluded, Etta Rose Bailey spoke: "I have repeated that oath all of my life," she said, "and only now at seventy do I really understand what it means."

". . . One nation under God, indivisible, with Liberty and Justice for all."

Everyone participated in the cleanup to get the schools ready. Virginia State College arranged to send twenty student teachers so that there would be enough personnel while out of-state teachers were making arrangements to arrive. Housing was a major problem. Dr. Rudolph Doswell was already working for the trustees at the Branch Elementary School. He was absolutely invaluable. He contacted African American families regarding housing. Suddenly the rent on single rooms doubled. Reverend Griffin was a one-man price control system. The new teachers were already absorbing significant financial sacrifices. The salaries of the Free School Association were without exception lower than what they had been receiving in their present positions. The affluent school districts who encouraged individual teachers to take sabbaticals and join with us were also helpful in subsidizing the salaries of those who came, including the East Williston School Board for Dr. Sullivan.

In the midst of threatening mail and phone calls, the families of the county had to be approached to bring about the registration of their children. They enrolled in large numbers. Vaccinations and inoculations began. Long lines formed early every day with parents and their children, who were extremely well-mannered. They stood in line for hours without complaint. But they were silent. They did not laugh or play or talk, they just stood in line. For many of them, they would be entering school for the first time. For most of them, they had not been in touch with educational programs for three years. Many of them lived in isolated rural areas with very little social contact. The stories are endless of the goodwill, of the spirit, of the energy, of the hope, of the courage of all those who participated in opening the schools.

As of August 15, no funds had been raised. The anticipated budget would approach $2 million—in 1963, a very significant sum. The first contribution, privately and with no publicity, came from President Kennedy himself—$10,000. I then began an endless series of conversations with the leaders of the major foundations, finally putting together a consortium, led by the Ford Foundation and the Marshall Field Foundation, which assured us of at least $500,000. Teacher groups around the country made it clear that they wanted to participate. The National Education Association (NEA) was heroic in enabling individual teachers and educational groups to become sponsors of our effort. The children of Cleveland gave $30,000. The teachers of Washington State gave $20,000. Literally hundreds of thousands of dollars were raised from teacher associations, parent-teacher groups, and schoolchildren around America. Students from Long Island even donated their spare uniforms. I approached corporate leaders. For some it was necessary to arrange telephone conversations with Robert Kennedy so they could be assured of the importance of the Prince Edward County project as far as the administration was concerned. The financing of the Prince Edward County Free School Association—all from private sources—was assured. The money was carefully spent, and closely audited.

Michigan State University, under Dr. Robert Green, organized a team to study the implications of the failure to provide schooling to the children of Prince Edward County. The university psychologist who had done the testing found that the mean IQ of the test group of the Prince Edward County students interviewed was only 69—in a representative group of normal children that number would have approximated 100. It was clear that the longer children were out of school, the more significant was the drop in their IQ. Many children did not know how old they were. The extent of the psychological intellectual damage was startling. The majority of the children under 12 had essentially lost their ability to communicate as well as their reading skills. They came from illiterate or semi-literate homes. Very few homes had a daily newspaper or access to magazines or books. The only library in the community was for "whites only." The remedial effort of the Free Schools changed all of that and restored the IQ levels to normal. Three of the 1570 students had IQs of over 150. One was an eight-year-old boy named Beauregard Lee who could trace his ancestry five generations in Prince Edward County. His father was a mechanic, his mother a nurse. At eight years of age he loved Mark Twain, could discuss John Glenn's orbiting the earth with intensity; he knew about Arthur Miller and wanted to know more about James Baldwin.

The Free Schools were scheduled to open on September 16, 1963. The media from all over the country came to Farmville. As the nation looked to Prince Edward County for hope with the opening of the schools, on Sunday, September 15, the day before our opening, a bombing in Birmingham killed four little girls as they attended church. The gloom and despair of the Birmingham murders were felt by all of us. It was a reminder of the hatred and criminality that had attended the lynch mob enforcement of segregation since the Civil War. The story of the Prince Edward County Free Schools was the other side of the coin. The decency of America was its message. A willingness to reach out to a fractured community distorted by attitudes of racial supremacy was the definition of our effort. In less than a month we had enlisted more than 100 faculty members from all over America, black and white, qualified beyond any previous measure to offer the remedial education that was critical to our success. And on opening day we had 15 white children join the 1,550 black children—there was Mrs. William Tew, the wife of a white farmer who owned a small amount of tobacco acreage south of Farmville who came with her eight-year-old daughter. She hadn't sent her daughter to the white academy because they "didn't like that kind of private school." There was Dickie Moss, the son of Dean Moss, who, left completely to his own decision-making process, decided that he wanted to carry on the fight of his father. He was a senior in the high school class. They came—the children came neatly dressed, clean, and touched by fear of what was going to happen. They were met by an educational opportunity that they had never had before. The faculty had nightly orientation sessions to teach colleagues team-teaching and how to operate a nongraded school system. Activities for the students were kept open until 5:30 every afternoon and on Saturdays, too. The library and science labs, the art and the music rooms, all stayed open. Tutorial classes in reading and mathematics were held after school hours. Vocational training and building trades, auto mechanics, agriculture, homemaking, office procedures, beauty culture, were offered in the rehabilitated classrooms. Students elected their own student council and drafted their own rules for governing activities. The older students were treated as adults and given an opportunity to earn money by being cafeteria workers, library assistants, playground supervisors. They became first-class citizens overnight.

The children, who initially were quiet, taciturn, laconic, removed, burst into new demonstrations of energy, vitality, and imagination. The bonding of the teachers and students created a memorable community. There were crises, unexpected crises. The autumn of 1963 produced a severe drought in Virginia and especially in Prince Edward County. Suddenly we were told that the water supply was exhausted. The children were sent home. But a group of students came to see Neil Sullivan. They pleaded with him not to close the schools again. How are we going to get along without water? he asked. How would we handle the toilet problems? Simple, one of the boys replied. We will divide the woods behind the school—the girls can have one side, we will use the other. Fortunately, it turned out that only a new pump was needed and that we could take care of immediately, but what it showed was that everyone was prepared to deal with whatever crisis developed.

The progress in communication and reading was breathtaking, but with the cold weather of early winter, the absences from school became significant because the children did not have proper clothes. Overnight, in response to the appeals we made through the media, tons of warm clothing, heavy shoes, and raincoats were delivered to Prince Edward County. The whole experience of the Free Schools was blanketed with the landscape of poverty. Children fell asleep at their desks because they did not have breakfast—malnutrition was evident. Our schools provided a free lunch program that contributed significantly to the well-being of the students and the school environment.

The schools brought medical care, the polio vaccine, optometric examinations for glasses and vision defects, audio instructors to test hearing, and a full-time dentist who gave many of the children their first toothbrushes and dental care.

In the background was harassment, the midnight phone calls, the driving through Neil Sullivan's property dumping garbage, trees decorated with floral arrangements from local cemeteries, bomb threats and murder threats to the trustees. Nevertheless, the Free School faculty not only worked together but formed close bonds of friendship and association. Morale was very high. The faculty formed a successful basketball team. A choir of mixed voices gave concerts. Art classes and literary groups met. Bridge and chess tournaments were plentiful, and on Tuesday nights there were free movies for students, parents, and teachers. I contacted the Motion Picture Association in Washington. They provided first-run feature-length films free of charge. In response to our request, publishers sent thousands of books. Our high school students took out countless books monthly to read at home. With so many books in hand, we were able to give books to many families to start their home libraries. Leonard Bernstein helped us find musical instruments for the children, and before graduation there was a band that gave full-dress concerts, playing not less than a dozen numbers and proudly wearing the handsome blue-and-gold uniforms presented to them by a Long Island school district. There was special teaching for handicapped children because another Peace Corps volunteer, Madge Shipp of Detroit, whose grandparents had fought their way out of slavery, was a specialist in that field.

Disciplinary problems were almost nonexistent. Absenteeism was a problem. Virginia had repealed its compulsory attendance law in order to protect the Prince Edward County Board of Supervisors from legal liability. If a child was needed on the farm, that was a priority for many poor families. Reverend Griffin and his many friends and colleagues stayed in close touch with families throughout the county and overcame the problems that had caused the absenteeism.

We bought an old army surplus bus and christened it PT 109. Students took trips to Appomattox, to Charlottesville, to Monticello, to the University of Virginia. Some twenty-eight students were brought to New York in a bus chartered by City College students. They were personally greeted by Mayor Robert Wagner. They toured the United Nations and met with Dr. Ralph Bunche, and they had lunch at the home of Jackie Robinson.

The news of November 22, 1963, the death of President Kennedy, had a special and tragic impact on everyone involved with the Free School Association. John F. Kennedy was their sponsor, their friend. He had carried the torch for these Free Schools. Students signed a special book which was sent to Mrs. Kennedy saying: "Your sorrow is very much our own." The president's death had another result. The harassment stopped. There seemed to be a new acceptance by the general community. The integrated faculty of the Free Schools was invited to use Longwood College's library, the first time ever that a white library in Farmville had been opened to African Americans. Thirty students from Hampden-Sydney College volunteered for after-school tutoring coordinated by a wonderful man, the college chaplain, Arthur Field, a young Presbyterian minister who had recently arrived. Several wives of Hampden-Sydney faculty members joined our staff, including the wife of the football coach, who became a guidance counselor. Free School representatives were welcomed at Hampden-Sydney assembly programs, and representatives of the college accepted our invitations to special events such as the recital given one afternoon by the touring Dartmouth College Glee Club at the Free Schools. As the representative of the attorney general and the federal government, I was invited to speak to the student body of Hampden-Sydney College. I welcomed the invitation. On that day almost fifty years ago, I said: "Public education is the means by which our society guarantees all of our children that they shall have the opportunity to learn, grow, and develop. We must not allow the destruction of the fundamental institution of public education which safeguards against innocent children being the prisoners of poverty and social status." I ended by quoting from the essay on liberty by Learned Hand, one of America's great justices—and closed by saying that the spirit of liberty in some form is part of the aspirations of us all. It takes conscience and courage to permit that spirit to be part of the American dream. The spirit of liberty was at the core of what we were doing in the Free Schools of Prince Edward County.

Robert Kennedy, still attorney general, and Ethel Kennedy came to Prince Edward County in the spring of 1964. Colgate Darden met them at the airport and guided them through the schools. There were not many dry eyes among the huge crowds on that day. We lunched with the children in the cafeteria, and the attorney general and Mrs. Kennedy met with the families and parents of the children. The county officials came forward to greet their distinguished visitors.

The Supreme Court decision was imminent. The case had been argued on March 30. Students and faculty of the Prince Edward County Free Schools had been in the courtroom and heard the arguments before the distinguished justices.

On May 25, 1964, writing for a unanimous court, Justice Hugo Black held that the Prince Edward County Board of Supervisors had acted unconstitutionally in closing the public schools and that the African American schoolchildren had been denied equal protection of the laws. Public education and the governmental responsibility for it had been affirmed, and the insidious system of tuition grants to support segregated private education was struck down.

Our hope was that the Free Schools would be a bridge to a reconstructed community and that, most of all, these hundreds of innocent children would not forfeit the opportunities of their lives because they had been denied their constitutional right to go to school. We worked with the county authorities to assist in the preparation for school reopening in September 1964. We transferred thousands of books, excellent audiovisual equipment, clean and modern facilities, and made some wonderful teachers available for hiring.

There is one other event I would mention—the commencement exercises which took place on June 15 in the auditorium of Moton High School. There were twenty-three members of the graduating class. The schools had been certified so college and other educational opportunities were open to them. Grace Poindexter and John Branch, the valedictorians, spoke on the theme of "Education Lights the Torch for Freedom." The Reverend Francis Griffin gave the invocation and the benediction. Colgate Darden introduced me as the commencement speaker. It was an occasion to celebrate the heroes of a long journey—the children of Prince Edward County, African American and white, who made our aspiration a reality, and the parents of those children, who despite years of demeaning sacrifice gave their integrity and courage as an ultimate gift to their children. We all sang Climb Every Mountain—and I think all of us felt that we had climbed every mountain and we were at the peak.

In the few remaining years of his life, Attorney General and later Senator Robert Kennedy and I talked often about Prince Edward County. One of its legacies is an idea that was born of our witness to the extraordinary idealism of America's teachers, who responded to the call almost overnight to build the Free Schools of Prince Edward County. I wrote a memorandum suggesting a National Teacher Corps so that those wonderful teachers around the country who truly wanted to be involved in the struggle for civil rights and against poverty could enlist for a year or two, maintaining their base in their home communities, while traveling to those portions of the country where the brilliance of their commitment could bring hope to American children who might otherwise never have a chance. It became law and survives to this day, not as we had originally proposed it, but nevertheless effective.

Some of the students of the Free Schools may be here tonight. I know that Mark Warner when he was governor of Virginia passed legislation that honored your sacrifice and your achievements and made scholarship assistance available even at this late date. As we finish our evening together, the forty-fourth president of the United States, Barack Obama, will be going before Congress to give his first State of the Union Address. How extraordinary.

How appropriate that a nation in crisis looks to its first African American president who was not even born at the time that the controversy we discussed here tonight began. How we look to him for confidence and leadership, relying on his dignity, his intelligence, his integrity, and his commitment to the Constitution of the United States. In some way, the struggle of Prince Edward County planted seeds that have allowed this flowering of our nation to come to pass.

I am honored to be with you this evening, as I was honored to work with you in those days, now long ago, when we struggled to define and defend the soul of America.

## RFK and the Revolution for Justice, Part II

The Prince Edward County Free Schools opened on September 17, 1963. It was a triumph of courage and ingenuity on the part of those citizens determined to benefit fully from the laws of the land. But our joy was bittersweet. The occasion was overshadowed by the murder the day before of four black children attending services at the 16th Street Baptist Church in Birmingham, Alabama. In reporting the school opening, the media suggested that our work in Prince Edward County showed an alternative to what happened in Birmingham. The schools were open! And a year of continued progress gave evidence of substantial accomplishment in the field of human rights.

The assassination of John F. Kennedy a few weeks later was a devastating blow to the world, to the nation, and to each of us.

I was lunching that day at the Army-Navy Club in Washington, DC, when my secretary called and said I should come back immediately to the Justice Department. The news that the president had been shot traveled like a lightning bolt. By the time of my return to the Justice Department, the reality of the death of the president had been confirmed. We gathered in the office of Nick Katzenbach, who was then deputy attorney general. RFK was at Hickory Hill, lunching that day with Bob Morgenthau, the US attorney in New York, when the phone calls came from J. Edgar Hoover, first of the shooting and then of the death of the president.

As we were gathered in Nick's office, RFK telephoned to say that Lyndon Johnson wanted the precise wording of the constitutional oath of office. Nick read aloud the words from the Constitution that were then relayed to Air Force One in Dallas, where President Johnson was sworn in. That was a moment of truth.

On Saturday, November 23, we went to the White House, the beginning of three days of obsequies honoring John F. Kennedy. We entered the East Room, where the president's coffin had been placed on the catafalque where Lincoln's body had lain almost 100 years before. RFK stood with his sister at the head of the receiving line, his face etched with grief I will never forget. It was a grief he would live with all the days of his life.

In the months that followed, we all sought to come to terms with the tragedy. RFK counseled his close associates to plan their departures, to know that the new administration would not be hospitable to those with a personal Kennedy association. Arthur Schlesinger and Ted Sorenson were the first to leave. I elected to stay with RFK as long as he remained as attorney general, which turned out to be some eight months. Often, he would go by his brother's gravesite at Arlington Cemetery. Occasionally I would accompany him after working late at night in the Justice Department. We would climb over the wall and walk up to where the president was buried. The guards all knew Robert Kennedy, and they saluted him.

The question of what was next for RFK was almost immediately a subject of public discussion. His relationship to President Johnson was a difficult one. He offered to be the US ambassador to Vietnam, to commit all of his energies to the cause of peace. The vice presidency was frequently mentioned, a Johnson-Kennedy ticket thought to be assured of victory in the November election. The governorship of Massachusetts was a possibility, as was the US Senate seat in New York. In the spring of 1964, President Johnson and RFK met, and the president quickly quashed any thought of RFK on the national ticket by ruling out all members of the Cabinet as possible vice presidential candidates.

LBJ later invited several reporters to his office and mimicked Robert Kennedy offering himself as a candidate for vice president. What had been a relationship of personal dislike was now elevated to one of mutual contempt.

The US Senate seat in New York became the focus. It was held by Kenneth Keating, a former congressman from Rochester, New York, my hometown. Keating was a well-liked, experienced middle-of-the-roader—but Republican. The only potential obstacle to RFK's nomination for the seat was the ambition of New York City's mayor, Robert F. Wagner. The manager of the political interests of the Kennedy family was Steven Smith, RFK's brilliant brother-in-law, married to his sister Jean. Steve advanced a meeting between Mayor Wagner and Bobby that ended with the mayor's endorsement—and Bobby's certain nomination.

The saga of Senator Robert Kennedy was very much a part of my life. I was the senior New Yorker on his staff at the Department of Justice and had been deeply involved in New York politics. I had returned to the practice of law, but I saw him frequently and was his counselor and friend. We traveled together often during a very important part of his life—the transition from his brother's protector to a person in his own right, on his own.

The Democratic convention that nominated LBJ for president convened in Atlantic City in August 1964. Fearing a convention that might stampede and nominate RFK, President Johnson's organizers invited Robert Kennedy to speak at a memorial tribute to President Kennedy *after* Johnson and Hubert Humphrey had been nominated. Their instinct was correct. When Bobby rose to speak, a mighty roar rose from the delegates and lasted for twenty-three minutes of uninterrupted applause. It was perhaps the most emotional and powerful moment of convention history that any of us had ever seen. RFK stood at the podium with the spotlight upon him, tears in his eyes, as an enormous wave of emotion swept over the convention floor.

If the nomination had remained open at that point, it was certainly possible that the convention would have demanded his candidacy. The highlight of the convention was the unexpected appearance of Jackie Kennedy, who despite her reluctance to participate in massive political events stood with Robert Kennedy for two hours, personally greeting all of the delegates. After that, there was no doubt of his nomination for the Senate.

His first public appearances after the nomination made it clear that this was going to be a campaign unlike any other. The crowds were immense. The tragedy and trauma of the past year were now to be overcome by this opportunity to begin the Restoration.

My role was that of deputy to Steve Smith, with the responsibility for speeches, scheduling, and issues analysis. RFK was attacked as a "carpetbagger," as claiming New York as a residence for his opportunistic convenience. In fact, he had been born in Bronxville in 1925, and he reaffirmed his identity as a New Yorker by taking three-year-old John Kennedy Jr. with him to the house in Riverdale where he had lived. The facts did not matter. The carpetbagger charge had some resonance, and we were forced to confront it throughout the campaign.

Scheduling his campaign appearances was a difficult assignment. The crowds were so enormous that lateness was part of the script. It did not seem to matter. In Glens Falls, New York, for example, a town of 18,000 in the foothills of the Adirondacks, 4,000 citizens waited until 1 a.m. to hear him speak. Physical contact between the crowds and Bobby was intense. His hands were made raw, cuff links disappeared, as countless thousands insisted upon touching him.

At the same time, however, the polls began to show a weakness, with voters saying he was not talking about the issues. He was, of course, talking about the issues, but the crowds were so large that he could hardly be heard. Schedules were reorganized, and more television appearances were planned so that substantive stories could appear every day.

On September 28, the Warren Commission report was published. Bobby could not bring himself to read it, but he was briefed on its findings and issued a short statement accepting them. He canceled his schedule that day and stayed in his hotel. Several days later, answering questions from students at Columbia University, he was asked whether he agreed with the commission that Lee Harvey Oswald had acted alone when he assassinated President Kennedy. The question paralyzed him. For almost five minutes he could not bring himself to speak. He turned his back to the audience, so they would not see his tears. Finally composed, he spoke hesitantly and softly: "I agree with the conclusions of the report that the man they identified was the man, that he acted on his own, and that he was not motivated by Communist ideology."

RFK appealed to a broad cross section of America. African Americans identified with his grief. They had come to see in him someone who understood their cries of injustice and who was determined to rectify those problems. Being Irish American, he had a very real appeal to other Irish Americans and Catholics. The working-class people of the state of New York had a strong affinity for him. To the young, he was glamorous and a wonderful new personality on the scene with whom they could identify. He was, after all, only thirty-nine years old when he ran for the Senate.

On election night, RFK won the Senate seat by over 700,000 votes. It was the greatest victory since Herbert Lehman won the governorship in 1936. President Johnson's margin of victory over Senator Goldwater in

New York State, however, exceeded 2 million votes, a point that Johnson referred to on several occasions, much to RFK's displeasure.

Bobby was never accepted as someone whose career would play out in the Senate. He was always seen as a possible, probable president. The issues he chose to embrace had national and international implications. His determination to have the war on poverty be successful reflected his personal passion against inequality, blocked opportunity, discrimination, and injustice. His first trip abroad as senator was to Latin America. His brother had authored the Alliance for Progress, and RFK wanted to recognize Latin America as an equal partner in the defense and development of the Western Hemisphere. We went to Peru, Venezuela, Chile, Argentina, and Brazil. He wanted to give substance to the Good Neighbor Policy that Franklin Roosevelt had pioneered. In Concepción, Chile, he traveled to coal mines, located under the sea, to express his concern about working conditions. He endured abuse from young Communists eager to label him a symbol of the heartless, capitalist West. He invited the Communist leaders to join him in dialogue on the stage, but instead he was spat upon and pelted with eggs. He continued to extend the hand of goodwill and understanding. His trip was a great success.

In February 1968, he embarked on what his critics called a "poverty tour" of America, to eastern Kentucky, the Mississippi Delta, the fields of California, the Indian reservations. He had a very personal and respectful relationship with Cesar Chavez, the leader of the California farmworkers, who had affirmed Kennedy's belief that one man could galvanize a movement. When Chavez broke his hunger strike, RFK flew out to share Communion with him. His travels across America left him with unforgettable images of the deprived children he met. He regarded their condition as a scar on the nation's ideals.

Vietnam had evolved into a major issue; it consumed the nation because of the tragedy it represented—a war that could not be won and seemingly could not be ended. RFK was a voice of dissent; he did not hesitate to challenge college students in particular, who he felt had stood apart from the issue until it affected them personally in the draft. As the domestic debate on the war intensified, RFK was embroiled in grueling personal and political conflicts. Needing respite, he called me one day in January 1967 and said, "Let's go to Europe."

Our trip allowed RFK to address America's image in the world. He spoke to college students, challenging them to engage politically with the Vietnam crisis. At Oxford University, he endured taunts and protests to make his point. Meeting with British prime minister Harold Wilson, he pressed him to convey to President Johnson British opposition to American policy. In Paris, he exchanged views with Valéry Giscard d'Estaing (then finance minister), Jean Monnet, and other French leaders.

In a discussion with Etienne Manac'h, the director of Asian affairs at the French Foreign Ministry, RFK received his detailed appraisal of the willingness of Hanoi to negotiate with the United States, predicated primarily on a halt to US bombing in Vietnam. John Dean, the State Department official accompanying RFK, thought the discussions important enough to forward a summary as a confidential memorandum to the State Department. When news of this meeting was depicted by the press as a "peace feeler" from Hanoi to RFK, Johnson was furious. A heated exchange between the president and Bobby at the White House sealed RFK's conviction that Johnson's course would not lead down the path to peace.

The most important event of the trip was RFK's meeting with Charles de Gaulle. Escorted into the Elysée Palace, they were seated directly facing each other to allow a frank exchange of ideas. "As I told your brother, you cannot defeat a swamp," de Gaulle said of Vietnam. "The United States has always had a special role in the world that has commanded the respect and admiration of other countries. . . . This is now being destroyed. History is the force at work in Vietnam, and the United States will not prevail against it." As the meeting ended, de Gaulle took RFK aside and spoke to him very personally. "Both of us have been deeply scarred in the struggles of our lives," he said. "But my time is almost over, and you have a large role ahead of you as a leader not only of your country, but of the world." De Gaulle warned against letting Vietnam become an issue that RFK's enemies could use to destroy him.

As the year 1967 advanced, the possibility of Robert Kennedy running for president dominated public and private conversations. There were many who urged him to confront LBJ directly and seek the nomination. Many others, including RFK himself, knew that such a race would be profoundly divisive for the Democratic Party, and probably destroy whoever was nominated. He was acutely aware that when he spoke of Vietnam, the positions and actions of his brother's administration were part of the

**Figure 11.** Walking along the Seine with Senator Robert Kennedy immediately after meeting with French president Charles de Gaulle at the Elysée Palace, Paris, January 1967. (Photo: Gilles Caron/Fondation Gilles Caron—Clermes)

dialogue. He absolutely did not want to compromise President Johnson's ability to make peace, but he was increasingly of the opinion that Johnson's strategy was self-defeating.

As hundreds of thousands of Americans became an expeditionary force to the jungles of Vietnam, RFK personally felt Johnson's strategy could not prevail. The anti-Johnson forces who wanted to challenge the president in the Democratic primary offered their support to Robert Kennedy if he would be their candidate. RFK felt it wasn't the appropriate time to do battle. On November 30, 1967, Senator Eugene McCarthy announced that he would run for the Democratic nomination.

Two months later, the Tet Offensive made American military victory in Vietnam almost impossible. But it was the explosive event of the New Hampshire Democratic primary on March 12, 1968, that compelled RFK's decision to run. Senator McCarthy won 42 percent of the vote, but the press portrayed the results as a major defeat for Johnson. RFK decided he could not lose control of the situation. On March 16, he announced his candidacy.

Figure 12. Final meeting at Hickory Hill before RFK's announcement of his candidacy for president, March 1968. *Left to right:* RFK's brother-in-law and campaign manager Stephen Smith, RFK, Senator Ted Kennedy, Ted Sorenson, myself. (Photo by George Silk/The LIFE Picture Collection/Getty Images)

At my urging, RFK's brother Edward M. Kennedy traveled to Wisconsin to extend an overture to Senator McCarthy to coordinate the two campaigns as a strategy for challenging Johnson for the nomination. McCarthy rejected this and maintained a combative attitude that did not change despite the tumultuous times that lay ahead. McCarthy's spiteful absence from the campaign was certainly a factor in Humphrey's defeat in November.

On March 31, in a nationwide television address, President Johnson announced that he would neither seek nor accept renomination as the candidate of the Democratic Party. A large group of friends gathered at RFK's apartment at UN Plaza that evening to hear Johnson's speech. No one expected that Lyndon Johnson, whose entire lifetime was a political scenario, would voluntarily withdraw from the presidency. The crowd was exultant—except for Robert F. Kennedy. He immediately understood that his campaign would be much more difficult with Hubert Humphrey absorbing the Johnson wing of the party, as well as being a strong force in his own right. The real campaign began in earnest, but during the primaries, the struggle was between McCarthy and RFK as to who would lead the anti-Johnson forces at the convention.

It was an immense and very costly logistical problem to put the campaign together. But for RFK it was catharsis. He told a friend that he didn't know what was going to happen, but at least he was at peace with himself.

Those weeks were interrupted by extraordinary events. On April 4, Martin Luther King Jr. was assassinated. Dr. King categorically told one of his closest advisers that he had decided to personally endorse Robert Kennedy for the nomination. It was a decision that was totally at variance with Dr. King's public stance that he would endorse policies but not politicians. Such an endorsement would have had a deep influence on the Democratic convention. In May, the first talks between the United States and North Vietnam encouraged people to believe that the Vietnam War was going to be resolved by Johnson.

As the campaign rolled forward, it became clear that the race would be decided in California. The outcome was far from certain. The California primary was scheduled for June 4. The intensity of the campaign had exhausted RFK. He spent election day with his family. By 9:00 p.m., the result was clear. Robert Kennedy had won. In the exuberance of victory, he reminded the nation of his commitments—peace, social justice, a renewed America.

**Figure 13.** With Martin Luther King Jr. in Jackson, Mississippi, August 1966.

None of his hopes were fated to be. Robert Kennedy can be measured by what he did, and what he inspired the nation to do. Like many great and complex leaders, he meant different things to different people. Radicals claimed him as their own, but so did the coal miners of West Virginia and the schoolteachers of New York. He knew the country was living through revolutionary times. He was a radical and a revolutionary, but foremost he was a practical idealist. Because he was of a younger generation, he was free of the fears of older men, of fears of Munich and the Great Depression. He could see the way to new directions of domestic justice and international restraint.

RFK's politics turned out to be prophetic. A year after his voice was silenced, the bombing of North Vietnam had stopped, the president of the United States had offered the Vietcong a chance to participate in elections, the plight of the California grape pickers was on the cover of *Time* magazine, and a Native American had been chosen to head the Bureau of Indian Affairs.

RFK believed his greatest achievements in government had been his role in the Cuban missile crisis and his management of the 1960 election. But his unique contribution to American politics was his dramatization of the plight of the poor. In placing his power behind their aspirations, especially those of African Americans, he alienated a large segment of the comfortable middle class. He believed the quality of a nation's government should be judged by what it did for those who were the most powerless to help themselves.

By all, he will be remembered as a generous, wise, and passionate man. At a time of life when most accede to the pressure of convention, he used his last years to change himself and all who knew him and to show his country what it could and ought to be.

# 4

# PRISONS AND PRISONERS

In this great country we must never forget that America brings hope to the world through its commitment to democracy and to justice and to freedom. But in the criminal justice system, and especially its prisons, we find the darker side of our country. The facts about America's prison system are shocking. The United States has 4 percent of the world's population but roughly 25 percent of the world's prisoners. Federal and state prisons hold more than 2.3 million inmates; nearly 5 million people are on parole or on probation.[1] The prospects of reforming a system that produces such statistics are daunting. There are times in every generation, however, when the brutality of America's prisons pushes its way onto the national agenda and is addressed, albeit briefly, by people of goodwill and political power who call for change.

In 1970, Mayor John Lindsay of New York City was faced with an epidemic of riots and disturbances in the city's prisons. Racial justice had become the rallying cry across America. The cities were the frontline in the struggle, and New York's streets became a battleground. Alienated from the community and from the criminal justice system itself, jails and prisons had become warehouses of human anguish and mirrors of social injustice. In August 1970, detainees at the pretrial detention center known as the Tombs rioted and held correction officers hostage for five days. On October 16, Julio Roldan was discovered hanged in his cell, also in the Tombs. On the same day, Jose Perez was found hanged in the infirmary at Riker's Island; he was held because he could not make bail of $500. Mayor Lindsay was determined to achieve change without violence. In October, he called me to ask if I would accept appointment as chairman of the New York City Board of Correction.

The Board of Correction before that time was a moribund organization without influence. It had had a purely monitoring responsibility and was rarely if ever critical of the Department of Correction. The board had no funding and no staff. Mayor Lindsay asked me to make it relevant. Although greatly interested in criminal justice, I had no prior experience in the prisons. I asked the mayor to give me an assurance of support, telling him that if ever we were in basic conflict I would resign without embarrassing him, but my chances of success depended upon our working together. My intention was to make the board a catalyst for reform.

John Lindsay and I had first met in Austria during the Hungarian Revolution in 1956. An attorney in the Justice Department, he had been assigned by Attorney General Brownell to assist Joseph Swing, the commissioner of immigration, in handling the resettlement of Hungarian refugees in America; I was there as a director of the International Rescue Committee and executive assistant to General William J. "Wild Bill" Donovan. In early December 1956, Lindsay and I shared a flight home from Vienna. We had hours of intense conversation about New York's Seventeenth Congressional District. John made it clear that he intended to challenge the Republican establishment and become its representative in Congress. In 1958, he won the Republican primary and went on to win the general election. Overnight, he became one of the most highly visible young political leaders in the country and was frequently mentioned as a future presidential candidate. We were opponents in the 1960 congressional election, and although he won handily, it was a hard-fought campaign with over a dozen debates that attracted national attention. In 1965, he was elected mayor of New York City, with Governor Nelson Rockefeller's strong support.

**Figure 14.** With Mayor John Lindsay after my appointment as chair of the New York City Board of Correction, October 1970.

I accepted the appointment and served for three years as chairman of the New York City Board of Correction. Our task was to restore humanity to criminal justice. In my office at the Board of Correction, I hung a translation of the words of Goethe, the great German philosopher and writer: "The way you see people is the way you treat them, and the way you treat them is how they become."

To my observation, the most important person in the system should be the victim. The victims not only suffered from crime; they also suffered from the dysfunction of the system, in which the delay tactics of defense attorneys involved seemingly endless appearances before the courts without resolution of the case. I was aware that the accused were also subjected to unacceptable disparities in the way they were treated in the system. Several years before, I had observed a sentencing proceeding in a federal courtroom in which an African American who had been convicted of stealing a television set from a public property was sentenced to two years in prison. In the next case, a Wall Street broker who had defrauded clients of $25 million received parole and community service. I accepted the mayor's appointment with these stories in mind.

Reform would be challenging. I was aware that candidates for public office most often advocate tougher laws, tougher confrontation, tougher sentencing, and look upon prison reformers as easy targets. But when opportunities come for reform, I deeply believe we must seize them, confident that our Constitution and our laws will be stronger because of it. Reform is the work of justice.

On October 18, 1970, Mayor Lindsay announced my appointment with a public mandate to resolve the threatening crisis. My first step was to approach ten major law firms and ask them each to assign a young lawyer for six months to work on our investigations. The generous response to this request was a great encouragement. The nine members of the board served without compensation. By 1971, for the first time in its history, the Board of Correction had an office, a modest staff, and a budget of $54,283[2]—a grant from the Federal Law Enforcement Assistance Administration, a pittance compared to our needs. It was the extraordinary contribution of voluntary services by countless citizens that made the board's accomplishments possible. My colleagues on the board were a wonderful group, coming from backgrounds of law, medicine, business, academia, and the churches. Everyone knew that very difficult work was ahead of us. Whatever our disagreements, we resolved them, and our decisions were always unanimous, a rare record of activity for men and women whose careers and interests ranged across the political spectrum. In the course of our work, one of the volunteer lawyers, John Brickman, showed exceptional talent and conviction—and he became executive director.

The death of Julio Roldan sparked a demand from many quarters for a public investigation. On the day of my appointment, a group of Young Lords, the radical Puerto Rican liberation movement to which Roldan had belonged, armed themselves with rifles and shotguns, took his coffin from the funeral home and occupied the First Spanish Methodist Church to demand that an independent committee of clergy investigate recent deaths in city jails. They announced that their guns would be used only for self-defense, but it was clear we risked reaching a new level of violence. Time for negotiation and discussion was running out.

A month to the day from my appointment as chairman, I held a press conference and released our first report, *The Death of a Citizen: A Report on the Investigation into the Death of Julio Roldan, an Inmate of the Manhattan House of Detention for Men (The Tombs)*. When I brought it to the mayor for discussion before release, he was astonished that a report so complete could have been written in such a short time. I explained that we had used the *Rashomon* approach, so that every aspect of the case was considered thoroughly by teams headed by volunteer lawyers. The graphic story of the life and death of Julio Roldan, with its detailed description of the labyrinth of criminal justice as told in *The Death of a Citizen*, had a stunning impact. The *New York Times* published the entire report, giving the board immediate credibility. Joseph Morgenstern of *Newsweek* lauded it in his weekly column as a new form of public report, "more often than not written clearly and candidly by people who want to be understood." Morgenstern described it as a "model of the old-fashioned tale told simply and dramatically through the experience of a single man," its "seductive" passages depicting the conditions of Roldan's arraignment, in which the judge was so overwhelmed by the caseload that he devoted "an average of 102 seconds to each defendant that day." Morgenstern called the situation "objectively insane," and noted that the "cool, persuasive text" showed that "suicide can be induced by a judicial and detention system of sufficient inhumanity." Such a suicide was "very little different than murder."[3]

Roldan's gang, the Young Lords, took a militant approach to social change. One of their strategies was to set rubbish fires to draw attention to the poor services of the sanitation department in tenement areas. Roldan had been arrested and charged with attempted arson for allegedly setting fire to a newspaper at the entrance to an East Harlem tenement. Consigned to the maze of the criminal justice system, where no one knew or understood anything about him, Roldan became increasingly desperate. At his arraignment hearing, he created such a disturbance that he was dragged out of the courtroom in a headlock. After two days of increasingly erratic behavior, he took his own life.

As described in the board's report, the guards discovered "a completely limp body hanging by a belt from the rear cell bars . . . approximately over the center of a shelf-like stool. . . . Three officers remember seeing Roldan's feet extending beyond the top of the stool." The officers entered Roldan's cell. One "held Roldan by the waist while the other cut the belt. The sudden shift in weight caused Roldan to ease onto the stool. . . . Roldan was then put face-up on the bunk."[4] Efforts to resuscitate him proved futile.

The report had such resonance because it gave graphic details of Roldan's unfortunate procession through the criminal justice system, ending with his death. People are generally unfamiliar with how prisons work. The report created an indelible impression on the public imagination.

Within three weeks of the death of Julio Roldan, Raymond Lavon Moore died in a solitary confinement cell on the eighth floor of the Tombs. The report on his death, "Shuttle to Oblivion," was also reprinted in the *New York Times* in significant detail. Its fifty-nine pages were distributed to prison administrators, correctional groups, colleges, libraries, and other interested parties around the country. The board's reports and recommendations moved the prison crisis to the forefront of public attention. New Yorkers were beginning to get a sense of what prison life was really like.

Lavon Moore had committed suicide in a solitary confinement cell in the Tombs that was essentially a steel box, five by seven feet, with a small window in the steel door. The only amenities were a steel bunk and an institutional toilet, with no other running water available. Mr. Moore had been a prisoner in the detention facility for more than ten months. He had made twenty-four different appearances before the court without coming to trial. Moore had been subjected to solitary confinement after a confrontation with correction officers over the distribution of medication; he regularly had been given a cocktail of drugs administered to narcotics addicts, along with anticonvulsion medication despite having no history of epilepsy. When he was given the wrong medication, he became embroiled in an altercation with guards, who beat him and locked him in the solitary confinement cell. He hanged himself with a rope made of braided mattress strips. After this incident, the board insisted that solitary confinement cells be forbidden in the prison system of the City of New York, and the mayor agreed.

The Board of Correction had only one real power—the right of its members to go into any prison at any time. It was clear to me that this could be a powerful instrument to achieve reform. We would apply a variation of Heisenberg's Uncertainty Principle—the observer effect—that a body observed behaves differently than one whose activities go unseen. Several times a week, I would appear at various prison facilities around the city at unpredictable times. It gave me an honest picture of what was happening.

I believed strongly that the enormous costs of the prisons could be justified only if they made the community safer and more secure, while at the same time encouraging rehabilitation as well as punishment. I wanted to ensure that victims were not forgotten in the system. I also believed that we should regard our prisons as a place of opportunity, a place where we could identify those who were mentally or emotionally disabled and help them return to a society where they could live without further violence.

I could see that health was an enormous problem, both mental and physical. We organized courses on fundamental hygiene. Dental care was nonexistent; the simple response to a toothache was to pull the tooth. One prisoner confided in me that he feared seeking dental treatment because he was afraid of resembling a jack-o'-lantern afterward. I learned of a group of army reserve dentists providing their required weekend service at the Seventh Regiment Armory on Park Avenue. I met with their commanding officer and suggested that their weekends were being wasted while there was a tremendous amount of need they could fulfill in the prisons. We set up a dental program in the Brooklyn House of Detention where prisoners could be treated by these well-trained dentists. It was spectacularly successful. For the first time, prisoners began to feel there was somebody who really cared about how they were treated and how they looked. It was an opportunity to show respect and consideration to individuals who were not able to help themselves. The dentists benefited as well, pleased that they were assisting where there was genuine need.

It was important to get influential citizens to come into the prisons. I regularly brought in business leaders and academics and elected officials. Once they saw conditions there, they understood the inhumanity of it. No one could visit a prison without being affected by it. The restaurant critic for the *New York Times*, Ray Sokolov, joined me for a dinner of mutton in the Brooklyn House of Detention. He liked the ice cream, but not much else. His subsequent critique was influential in achieving changes in the prisoners' diet.

Overcrowding was the greatest immediate problem. There were over 25,000 inmates in the system, more than half of them detainees awaiting trial or other disposition. It was not unusual for an individual to wait more than a year for his case to be resolved. At the time of Julio Roldan's death, the Tombs held 1,980 men in cells designed to hold 908. The cells themselves were no more than cages, designed for one or two adult men, but more often containing three. Overcrowding forced a reduction in all the services necessary for the administration of the prisons. The correction officers were severely handicapped in their work. Food and health facilities were strained to the breaking point. I told the mayor that if we caged animals the way we did human beings in prison, there would be a major protest march down Fifth Avenue demanding reform.

We finally confronted the problem of overcrowding directly and asked the courts, both state and federal, to intervene. In the course of time, a brilliant judge, Morris Lasker, of the federal district court, took responsibility and administered recommendations that have truly made a difference.

Publicity was the major resource available to us, both to educate the public about what was happening in the criminal justice system and to build a consensus for reform with those working within it. On Christmas Day, 1970, I took several reporters into the prison. Their unrestricted conversations with the prisoners highlighted their loneliness and lack of family support. History has taught us of the danger in any system where the freedom of one individual is given over to the complete control of another. One way of overcoming that danger was to have increased press access to the prisons. The disparagement of human values and the infringement of legal rights were a constant source of concern. My point was to remind all of us who were involved with this system to accord respect and dignity to those in our charge.

Four months after my appointment, I presented Mayor Lindsay with fifty-one recommendations that could be implemented within ninety days. Many of them had been discussed and studied for a long time. Most of them did not require resources beyond those already committed. Some of the actions recommended were fundamental, such as establishing legal limits on the amount of time a human being could be held in detention awaiting trial, or obliging clerks of courts to report unusual or disturbed behavior of prisoners in a courtroom. Others seemed relatively insignificant, such as hiring an additional plumber in the Tombs to allow detainees to help maintain showers and toilets, or repairing the movie equipment. We also wanted to ensure that greater emphasis was placed on helping prisoners return to the community after their incarceration. In the past, they had been discharged with as little as $1 and a subway token. We wanted them to be able to gain experience they might use to aid them in living a law-abiding life, to be trained by people who knew something about cooking, carpentry, or other skills.

We sought all kinds of measures to reduce the atmosphere of tension. Many prisoners had great talent in music or acting. All kinds of groups of young people in the city were delighted to come into the prisons and organize concerts, all on a voluntary basis. Coretta Scott King spent several hours speaking to groups in the prison. James Brown and Harry Belafonte performed at the facilities; Willie Mays stopped by to talk baseball. Such performances were open to correctional officers as well as prisoners. Of course, much remained to be done after ninety days, but it was extraordinary to see how much could be accomplished if the light was properly focused on what had to be done.

One area of continuing concern was narcotics. The problem affected everything, especially overcrowding and medical resources. With the rise in narcotics-related crimes in the early 1970s, and increasingly stringent penalties for the possession of narcotics, the prison population began to swell. There were practically no programs or medical care available to help the addicts, who now made up at least half of the prison population. Dr. Vincent Dole and his wife, Dr. Marie Nyswander, of Rockefeller University, pioneered the use of the synthetic narcotic methadone to ease the withdrawal from heroin addiction. I met with them for lengthy discussions about introducing methadone programs into our prison system, to assist addicts to withdraw safely. Their efforts were heroic. Mayor Lindsay and Commissioner of Corrections Ben Malcolm agreed to an experimental program. As success was recorded, programs were enlarged. The adoption of methadone was one of the important and successful programs to humanize the treatment of prisoners.

Any success in diminishing overcrowding depended in large measure on the courts, which themselves were victims of the increase in arrests and more draconian sentencing. Alternatives to imprisonment had to be encouraged; groups like the Vera Foundation played a significant role. Its director, Herb Sturz, made major efforts to provide alternate programs, such as addiction programs to treat drug offenders outside of the prison system, and work opportunities for released inmates.

The bail system was unjust, inequitable, and a needless source of anger in the city's prisons. What protection is afforded the community when one defendant charged with a crime is released on $100 bail while another defendant in practically identical circumstances is jailed because he does not have $100 to make bail? The legal profession has created an extraordinarily complex and technical system of laws and procedures that can be navigated only if competent, experienced lawyers are available. For those who had the financial resources to engage counsel, the system could almost work. The poor, however, were the bulk of the clients of criminal justice. For them the legal system was a maze, a grand game called Ransom, which began with an auction where bail was set and ended with a "plea-bargaining" conference where years of one's life and the integrity of justice were frequently bartered in such a way that all of us lost. The bail system was a major grievance of the prisoners. We recommended that the state legislature study the recent federal bail reform measures and adopt those that were relevant.

We consulted with both correctional personnel and prisoners about their grievances. That paid dividends. For example, one evening I met with Angela Davis, the African American activist and possibly America's best-known alleged terrorist, who had been confined in the Women's House of Detention. She invited me to look at the prison library. In January 1971, the prison library of the Tombs contained 500 copies of *Dining Out in Any Language* and 200 copies of the *Coin Collector's Guide*, but not a single book about Dr. Martin Luther King Jr., nor a single book in Spanish. Within weeks we had changed the nature of the library, gathering books and publications that reflected the interests of the population of the prison. Working with an independently formed group called "Libraries for Prisons," the Board of Correction assigned a volunteer to help create a bibliography for a model prison library, and then obtained copies of the books for each of the city's jails and prisons. Illiteracy was a major obstacle, so we started a program in basic literacy. The boredom of prison life could be confronted through these efforts.

Many of those incarcerated in the prisons were victims of fate, whom fate could also redeem. One night, while walking the corridors of the Tombs, I stopped to question a man in one of the cells. "What are you in for?" I asked. The man, named Robert Apablaza, explained that he had been sentenced in Louisiana to fifty years of hard labor without parole for selling $5 worth of marijuana. He had escaped from the New Orleans Parish Prison, where he had been awaiting appeal, and made his way to New York. He was being held for extradition to Louisiana. With the board's intervention, and after intense discussions with legendary Manhattan District Attorney Frank Hogan, the New Orleans DA recommended that the matter be dropped. On November 16, 1971, forty-two months after Mr. Apablaza's arrest for the $5 marijuana sale, a New York County Supreme Court justice ordered the charges to be dropped. Mr. Apablaza was a free man.

We sought to improve conditions and training for the correction officers as well. One of the things that makes prisons ineffective is the lack of training. Detention center staff often need special training to understand that the individuals within their charge are innocent until proven guilty. Detention centers are often more turbulent than prisons because they hold individuals arrested for a wide variety of offenses, from stealing a car to white-collar crime to murder. Handling this sometimes-unruly population takes special skill.

Correction officers worked in a system that was depressing and dangerous, where violence was always possible. They often came from the same rough environments as those behind bars. I made a continuing effort to communicate with the correction officers and their union. We held several meetings where grievances were invited from the correction officers against the Board of Correction; this was taken up with enthusiasm by the correction officers themselves. I met with union leaders and tried to encourage them to think in terms of all of us working toward common objectives rather than remaining mired in hostility. At times, I had to approach the situation with humor. Leo Zeferetti, head of the correction officers' union, habitually mispronounced my name—"vander Hoivel." I did a half-hour TV interview in which I referred to him by every possible permutation of mispronunciation—"Zeferelli," "Zeferini," "Zeferotti." It worked; from then on, it was "vanden Heuvel." Mr. Zeferetti chose not to run for reelection for president of his union. He ran instead for Congress—and was elected!

On September 9, 1971, rioting broke out at the Attica Correctional Facility in western New York State. Forty-two members of staff were taken hostage. Negotiations broke down. Despite pleas from the prisoners and their hostages to continue those negotiations, Governor Nelson Rockefeller sent in state troopers to end the standoff. The resulting melee left forty-three people dead, including ten correctional officers and thirty-three inmates. It was the deadliest prison confrontation in the history of the country.

The official announcement indicated that the ten correction officers had been killed by the prisoners. A young coroner in Rochester, New York, performed the autopsies. His finding shocked the nation—he found that all the correction officers being held hostage had been killed by guns fired by the state police.

The history of prison riots is generally a pattern of immediate concessions to the prisoners, to regain control of the facilities with minimum violence, followed by excited public attention that concerns itself with the noise of the riot explosion rather than the legitimacy of the grievances expressed. Then a few symbolic gestures of reform—and then a return to the old way of doing things, with a few cosmetic touches added to mark the event of the disturbance.

On September 19, 1971, I spoke before an audience at St. George's Church in New York City to keep alive the public demand that the grievances at Attica be confronted.

**Address by William J. vanden Heuvel, Chairman, New York City Board of Correction, Attica Prison Service of Concern, St. George's Church, Stuyvesant Square, New York City, September 19, 1971**

I have come to the House of the Lord today to speak of the tragedy of Attica. I begin by expressing my profound appreciation to your rector, Dr. Miller, and to all of you, for setting aside your prime church time for this Service of Concern. I am sure that all of you who have reflected upon this subject have formed many differing feelings and conclusions.

I come because I have had an experience that may have been denied you: I have been in prison for over a year—this past year. As the voluntary chairman of New York City's Board of Correction, at the request of Mayor Lindsay after the riots in our own city, I went into a prison for the first time last October. And so the best way I can introduce this subject is to tell you what a prison is. I hope that none of you will ever be in one, except as a parishioner of this church, doing God's work.

Let's take the Manhattan Detention Pens—"The Tombs." The Tombs is a detention prison, unlike Attica which is a place where we consign men who have been sentenced—many of them for their lives. The Tombs is an institution which our community has erected to hold those who have been arrested on a charge of crime, pending the resolution of that charge by the processes of the law. It was built to hold 908 men. On this day, there are 1,460 men in it. On August 5, 1970, when the first riots broke out in the Tombs, there were 1,980 men incarcerated.

The Tombs is a labyrinth of cages. There are so many euphemisms in the correctional world—I wish that we might begin by ripping them all apart and throwing them aside. Attica is not a "correctional institution for men." Attica is a prison, a penitentiary. It has practically no facilities for rehabilitation. The Tombs does not have "cells"—it has cages, where we put men and make them animals. In the Tombs—on this Sunday—in each cage, which measures six by eight feet, there are two adult human beings. When the riots began last August, there were three adult human beings in each six-by-eight-foot cage.

Now you may think: "Well, that's for a brief period of detention." But that is not so. There are many, many citizens in this community who are held in detention prisons for well over six months; some for over a year; some for more than two years. The entire institution begins to crack and fold and dissolve when it's faced with this kind of overcrowding. The feeding facilities that are designed for 900 cannot feed 1,500 adequately. The correction officers who are hired to administer a prison of 900 cannot begin to discharge any compassion in their work when overwhelmed by the bureaucratic and custodial obligations of their work.

A prison is a place where we take a number of citizens who are in trouble with the law and who have developed or who have demonstrated antisocial behavior. It's the beginning of a process through which we dehumanize and depersonalize them to an extent that, if they survive the prison process, they return to the streets of our community more violent, more filled with rage, more filled with hatred, more determined to wreak havoc upon each and every one of us than at the moment they went into that prison institution.

I have tried to say one thing from the beginning of my administration as chairman of the Board of Correction, and I have said it every day: a prison must be a community facility. It must serve our purposes. If our purpose is only to punish men, then we should construct a totally different kind of place and spend much less money on it. But in the City of New York, where we spend eighty million dollars a year on our city prisons, and in the State of New York, where we have spent over a billion dollars during the administration of Nelson Rockefeller—who, in the course of spending a billion dollars, has not yet found fit to visit a single state prison—the time has come to understand what we are spending that money for.

There are some people in our society who have to be confined, who are a threat to us and to our person and to our property and to our tranquility and to themselves. There are people in our society whom neither this community nor any other community has either the experience or the resources to help in their lifetime. They face a lifetime of confinement because of failings, not only theirs, but ours; tragically, they have to be confined if we are to live at peace. For these limited numbers of people, our civilized society should be able to construct an area of confinement that will have at least minimum human standards.

But the overwhelming bulk of men and women who go into our prisons come out again. They come out in a year, they come out in six months, they come out in six years, they come out in ten years, but they do come out again. And I am telling you that the men and women who go in as burglars often come out as robbers, and those who go in as robbers may well come out as murderers.

When we talk about prison reform with the passion and conviction that your rector and I bring to you today, we are talking about it for the benefit of a well-ordered, civilized society that is concerned about the victims of crime, a society which understands that nothing is going to be done about the control of crime until we look into the ultimate ghetto of our society—the prison.

The prison is the home of the poor: the home of the white poor, to be sure, but predominantly the home of the black and Puerto Rican poor. I have never seen a wealthy man in the Tombs. I have never seen the real criminals of narcotics traffic in the Tombs. I have seen them arrested, but I have seen them bailed out overnight for $100,000 or $200,000. Bail means nothing for the real criminals; it's easily available. But I have seen in the cages of the Tombs, in cage after cage, men who may well be criminals by our legal definition, but who in their faces and in their eyes reveal the desperation, the loneliness, and the isolation that doom them to come back again and again to a life of crime.

We talk about prison rebellion as though rebellion were something new. What would have happened to George Washington, or to Thomas Jefferson, or to Benjamin Franklin? Were they protesting or rebelling? By the laws of their time they were certainly traitors, the worst of all heinous crimes, and would certainly have been executed if they had been found. I often say that the prisoners of Attica or the prisoners of the Tombs have no more right to rebel than did the prisoners of the Bastille. A well-ordered society must provide a channel for the expression and resolution of legitimate grievances, or it is doomed to rebellion.

We are free men, and the highest values of our society should be human life and human dignity, even for men and women temporarily confined in our prisons. Unless we provide means for the expression of legitimate grievances in our institutions, unless government is responsive, unless those who have the power to change are willing to listen and use that power, Attica will not be the last of prison rebellions. It is just another of those that we have seen throughout the course of 150 years of penitentiary life.

I stood on the frontiers of Hungary in 1956 and helped and watched 200,000 people fleeing the prison of Communism after a decade of horrible repression. They had found no legitimate outlet for their grievances. Then came the spontaneous spark that ignited a revolution. All of us stood up and hailed their courage and wept at their death and destruction. We remembered what the struggle for human liberty involves. That struggle for human liberty is going on in our country, and it can and must be won if we are to be true to the heritage of America.

Nobody in the community listens to prisoners today, and nobody in the criminal justice system listens. The prisons are a product of our system of criminal justice, a major part of it, and the prison crisis cannot be resolved until the courts understand their responsibility. I was delighted this morning to hear Dr. Miller speak of the responsibility of the courts and question the validity of the governor's appointing the highest judges of this state to select the investigators of what went on in Attica. Much of what is wrong in the prison system of America, and of New York today, reflects what is wrong with our courts; one of the most important things we have to do is to remind the courts that their job is not only to enforce the law, but to administer justice. When a man is picked up, he is caught in the throes of the police; he is put into a judicial system overcrowded and overburdened; he is finally junked in the labyrinth of the prisons. And all through that journey, nobody listens.

I remember a judge in Bronx Criminal Court last year who resigned because he couldn't take it any longer. I asked him what had happened. He said that one day a man in overalls came before him on the charge of stealing a car. He said it was one of 250 arraignments that had come before him in that single day. If any of you have seen how courts operate, you can hear it: the district attorney reciting a litany of the charges in garbled language that nobody can understand; the Legal Aid Society lawyer, whom the prisoner has rarely or never seen—except for perhaps ninety seconds before his arraignment before the judge—saying something quickly that the prisoner doesn't understand; and the court clerk intoning something the prisoner doesn't understand. Then the judge imposes bail, and the prisoner still doesn't understand that he has been remanded to prison.

In Bronx Criminal Court, this prisoner planted his feet squarely in front of the judge at that point and said: "What the hell you doin' to me?" The judge said he suddenly stopped and asked himself: "What am I doing to him?" He asked the district attorney to read the charges carefully so that the prisoner could understand them; he asked the Legal Aid lawyer to take some time so that the prisoner would understand how he could be helped.

Then the judge imposed bail and explained what it meant, and how the man could raise it, and how he could be released from the detention center. The prisoner turned to the court and said: "Thank you, your honor," and walked quietly away.

There has to be some place in this social structure, some place in this procedure of criminal justice, where someone is going to stop and ask who it is that is standing at the bar of justice, what he did, and what can be done to help him as he faces the greatest single trial of his life—an incident that may take his life or deprive him forever of freedom.

So we come to Attica—a long journey through the terrible tragedy of a correctional system that has rarely, if ever, stopped to listen. The grievances that were so quickly agreed to by the State of New York on Friday a week ago were not grievances that the state was hearing for the first time. I received them in the mail in June. They were sent to the state commissioner of correction in May. They were sent to the governor in May, in June, in July, in August. But not a single one of those grievances was heard and resolved. I don't know what the investigators are going to find, but I doubt that they will discover evidence that this was a highly organized rebellion that moved in cadres, and suddenly seized people. What happened, in my guess, is what frequently happens in the prisons: a spark of anger touches off a situation of dynamite and blows up. And, as often happens when injustice ignites, the innocent are the victims.

At Attica, a number of citizens called "observers" were asked for by the prisoners and invited by the governor to go and see what could be done to quell the disturbance and to free the hostages. In my judgment, in any prison disturbance you have to move quickly before it gets out of hand. Then, hopefully, you will have a prison administration that will do something quickly to redress the injustices that caused the disturbance. But once the prison authorities fail to move quickly, once hostages are taken, it seems to me the highest obligation of the state or municipal authority—your highest obligation and mine—is to see that the lives of all the innocent are spared, both hostages and prisoners.

Even if our state officials had refused to give more time for negotiations, where were the prisoners of Attica going to go? "Over these prison walls I would fly," says the old song. Over walls thirty feet high, cordoned off by 1,000 state troopers, National Guardsmen, and correction officers with the highest weaponry that can be imagined, including dumdum bullets, shotguns, and hunting rifles? Where were the prisoners going to go?

And why were their demands agreed to so quickly? I hate to say it, but I don't really think the state meant it when they agreed to those demands, because the man who signed them didn't have the authority to grant them. A number were demands that required legislative action. Prisoners are intelligent and realistic. They understand the reality of the criminal justice system. They knew that those demands were being signed and copied, and that they'd be forgotten just as quickly as when they were originally presented six months ago. That's why the presence of the governor was so crucial. Not in the prison yard, as most other governors in this country have seen fit to be, but inside Attica, convincing the prisoners that the chief executive, with the political power available to him, will support their demands and fight for them in the legislature.

Last January I asked the governor and the legislature for seven simple legislative proposals, including, for example, giving former prisoners the right to work—to work in a restaurant that has a liquor license, as a dishwasher. Do you know what it's like for a man who has spent ten years in prison, who has been taken from his family and uprooted from his community and put into the maximum-security prison at Attica, to come out and be given forty dollars and told to begin his life again? Having gained no employment skills that could possibly help him survive, he is sent back to his urban community where he cannot get a job even as a dishwasher in a restaurant that has a liquor license, because a state law prohibits it. That reform did pass—it was the only one of the reforms that passed that legislature—and it was vetoed by the governor.

Now what are the prisoners going to demand of a state authority which was so callous in disregarding what was asked of them in peaceful times? The governor sent his message: "No, I will not grant you amnesty because I do not have the power to do so. But, furthermore, even if I had the power to do so, I would not grant it." All of these men knew that under the law, as it presently works and as it would work if they were indicted in Wyoming County where the feelings were so intense and emotional, every one of them, if convicted of participating in that prison riot, would have spent the rest of his life in prison. They weren't asking for amnesty in terms of being forgiven for hurting or murdering correction officers. They were asking for the amnesty that would not have punished them for beginning the riot; they were asking to be spared excessive punishment which would have meant they would have to spend the rest of their lives in those prisons. It's not as unreasonable as you think.

The men who made the final decision for that assault were men who have never been in a prison. Nelson Rockefeller and Robert Douglass, his principal aide, the men who really made the decision, had never been inside a prison. That is a fact which does more than anything else to explain why Sparta defeated Athens on the Plains of Attica in upstate New York.

Is it conceivable that men who had been in a prison would think that prisoners would murder hostages, knowing that they would be held guilty for that, when in every major prison riot in this nation where hostages have been held, hostages have never been murdered by those prisoners? Hostages have been killed by those who have invaded the prison yards. But prisoners, in the history of American prison riots, do not murder hostages.

Did they listen to the hostages? Could anyone but weep when one of those guard-hostages stood before the television cameras and pleaded with the governor of this state to come to Attica to save their lives? Did anyone listen to the hostages after they were released, as they talked about how well they were treated by the prisoners, and described the humanity of the prisoners? Did anyone listen as those hostages said: "We learned a great deal in that experience. We know now what the prisoners were talking about."

Does anyone possibly believe that it was necessary to take in all those weapons, bound to unleash a torrent of hate and violence? The role of government is to stand between polarized forces of our community, to build bridges of reason, to stem violence, to save life. To unleash those forces of armed hatred could have had no result other than the indiscriminate and random murder of guilty and innocent alike.

In all of this it has not been said but remember it: The so-called leaders of the Attica Prison riot are alive today. Nobody has asked who the prisoners were that were killed, but you can bet that they were, for the most part, men who had practically no role in that riot or disturbance, but who were running for their lives. Would a man who was scheduled to be released next week from Attica have risked his life by leading that rebellion? Today he lies in a funeral parlor in East Harlem, to be buried by parents who couldn't afford to visit him in Attica.

And so, the men who unleashed that violence committed the greatest crime not only against the prisoners, but against the hostages—yes, against all of us, our decency and humanity, because in a civilized society we must look to our elected representatives to hold back the reins of violence and to use their power to control it.

What is the cost of it all now? The budget-makers will calculate the cost by an addition to the eighty-four million dollars that this state has spent in the past year for its state prisons—eighty-four million dollars in a prison system that spends 72¢ a day for food for 12,000 prisoners. Isn't it time that someone began to ask where that money is being spent? There is not a single rehabilitation program in the entire state prison system that is worthy of the name. Seventy percent of the prisoners in this state's prisons are men and women who suffer from the affliction of addiction, who may be in prison only because they are guilty of the crime of which they are the victim—possession of narcotics. Or they may be involved in other crimes where addiction is a part. Yet in not a single state prison is there a program of narcotic treatment and rehabilitation.

When I went to Napanoch State Prison last March, where 1,000 prisoners are kept who would normally be in city penitentiaries, the warden admitted that at least 70 percent of those men are narcotic addicts. And when I asked about rehabilitation programs, there was not a single program in that prison that was designed to help a person return to the community free of the affliction of narcotics. What if they had been diabetics? What if, in the arbitrary exercise of our executive powers, we had decided that insulin was illegal, and yet a diabetic desperately needed insulin to live? Suppose the black market and criminal price of insulin had risen to $100 or $1,000—to what limits would we go to steal the money to buy it? What have we done by sticking men and women into prison as narcotic addicts, and then pushing them back onto the streets where, within twenty-four hours, they have to commit another crime in order to survive?

It's a system of such irrationality. When I had the New York City commissioner of correction before a public hearing of the Board of Correction two weeks ago, and he was describing how they handle the mentally disturbed prisoner, I said to him: "Commissioner, don't you think the system ought to be held up for a psychiatric exam? Isn't the system insane?" He said: "Yes, it is." No man should take the responsibility of public administration of an insane system unless he is determined to change it. That's the minimum we must ask of any of those who have the power to change situations.

Attica has scarred our community badly. We have suffered wounds that will not heal easily. I have talked to men who were among the observers, who are among the most effective men in public life, and they have indicated to me that they are seriously considering leaving public life because they do not want to be part of a system that would not only permit but direct the massacre of Attica. I have talked in the minority community to its people and to its leaders, and although the blacks may well accept this as just another of the incredible assaults upon their human dignity and humanity in the course of the history of this country, I don't think they will. What hurts them is that the public officials who were associated with this atrocity were leaders whom they had previously trusted as understanding their problems. What hurts more than anything else is that this assault could be unleashed in the name of humanity.

What will happen to prison reform? I would guess that, if it had not been revealed that the hostages had been murdered by the invading force, the cause of prison reform would have been dead for a generation. But the stunning fact that all but one of the hostages who died was murdered by gunfire, at the hands of law and order, has so startled and shocked the civilized community of this state that we may yet have a chance to bring about desperately needed prison reforms.

The most difficult victim of all, perhaps, is government itself. We who have lived through such turbulent times, and who so often have hung our heads in shame when official pronouncements were revealed to be nothing but public relations releases designed to conceal mistakes and errors that have been made, we now have seen the great authority of the state challenged in a way that exacts a price and a toll that none of us can calculate. A well-ordered society in a representative democracy depends, more than anything else, upon the integrity of government and the credibility of its spokesmen. These virtues also lie in the field at Attica, murdered by careless and negligent men. It will take the goodwill of us all to redeem and revive them.

I could stand for another hour and tell you the things that could and should be done. In this city, through the intervention of Mayor Lindsay, we are now getting some of the things done that have to be done. Slowly, but we are getting them done. I will resign my office the day I believe that the correctional administration of this city presents an insuperable block to their achievement.

I suggest that the first thing to be done is for the governor to go into a prison. Not to Attica, where emotions and feelings are now so deep. But I think he owes it to all of us, and most importantly to himself, to understand what a prison is. He should not go to a prison like Czarina Catherine, with a Potemkin as his guide, because that's the tour given to most community leaders. You haven't been to a prison unless you have had the opportunity to talk frankly, candidly, and privately to prisoners. I suggest to Nelson Rockefeller that he go into the cellblocks alone and not be afraid. No one will harm him if the prisoners feel that he has come to talk with them and to listen. Let him walk into that cellblock alone and invite discussion with the prisoners. Let him hear their grievances, and he will be astounded at the reasonableness of what he hears.

I suggest that this state create a Board of Correction, as we have in this city, of independent, unpaid citizens committed to no political cause except the reform of the prison structure. We have a Board of Correction in New York State, but do you know who is the head of it? The commissioner of correction. This may be a constitutional requirement not easy to put aside, but the governor should recognize the vulnerability of such a position and immediately move to create an independent, impartial, objective Board of Correction, by any title he may choose.

State prisons have been located in isolated areas deliberately, so that the community cannot become involved with prison life. Paradoxically, the prison becomes the town industry, where generations of prison personnel grow up with grandfathers, fathers, and sons as prison guards. We must bring the communities of this state into the prisons, to talk, to listen, and to share.

I ask the legislators, each and every one of them, to go into the prisons of their communities before they return to Albany for the important session ahead. I have never taken a single person to a prison who has not left a different person. I have never known anyone who has any basic sense of humanity to go into a prison without leaving it knowing that injustice was being done and that humanity, to save itself, had to move quickly to reorganize its prison structure. I want every legislator to do this. Then, perhaps, they will appropriate the money.

I'm not necessarily asking for more money. That's the excuse you always hear: "We don't have enough money, we need more money." It's not money! The basic element of prison reform is to change attitudes—the attitude of the governor, the attitude of the legislature, the attitude of the prison officials, the attitude of the correction officers, the attitude of the prisoners, the attitude of the community. The most important reform in prisons today is to bring back a sense of human dignity, of respect. It doesn't cost anything to say "Good morning" to someone in a cage. It doesn't cost any more to cook the food you're serving a man, rather than serve it raw; or half cooked. I asked the head of the correction officers at our public hearing: would he want his son to be housed overnight in any one of the city prisons? He didn't hesitate to answer: "Of course not. No." The correction officers are the first to tell you about the inhumanity of the prisons in which they work, because in the cruelest of senses they too are prisoners of those institutions.

We must take those walls down. We must lift the bars of those cages. We must walk into those prisons again as a community, recognizing that the citizens who are there are temporarily there and will return to us. They have been punished, and they suffer punishments that few of us could endure or even understand: taken from their family and community, deprived of what we Americans value most—our human liberty. We confine them, and they are punished through all of those means and many more. But we must assure them, for our sake as well as theirs, that those prisons will begin to serve a community purpose.

I listened to the hymns we sang this morning, and especially to the words written by James Montgomery, who himself had been in prison for writing a poem celebrating the fall of the Bastille:

Be darkness, at thy coming, light;
Confusion, order in thy path;
Souls without strength inspire with might,
Bid mercy triumph over wrath.

We plead with Divine Providence today to inspire "souls without strength" with might—a might committed to justice, to human life, and to a well-ordered society where human liberty is paramount and indestructible. Perhaps we can return a year from today, recall the struggle on the Plains of Attica, and find that the temporary victory of Sparta has been overwhelmed by forces of humanity and justice, represented by the citizens of Athens.

The following year, I wrote an article for the *Columbia Journalism Review* to highlight the need for engaged reporting on the situation in the prisons. Such coverage, I argued, would serve to prevent circumstances in the prisons from becoming so dire that prisoners had no choice but to riot.

**William J. vanden Heuvel, "The Press and the Prisons,"** *Columbia Journalism Review*, **May/June 1972**

A reporter was given general access to a prison in Maine last autumn. In his wanderings in a cellblock, he met an aged prisoner who had been in the institution for more than forty years. Interested in the story the inmate told him, the reporter conducted his own investigation. The prisoner had told the truth. He had been convicted of a burglary and sentenced to six years. When his time for release came in 1930, no one could find his file. The inmate had neither the resources nor the mental capacity to overturn the bureaucracy. Forty years later, because of a reporter's investigative work, a citizen who had lived his life in the caged sadness of a prison was given freedom.

This is one of countless examples of injustice that depends on the news media for final appeal. The fortress institutions that warehouse our crippled children, our mentally disabled, our aged, and our prisoners are intended to remove their problems from public attention and concern. Officials deny access to "outsiders" and hope that is the end of the story. Such was the case at Attica before last year's rebellion. Newsmen petitioned for entry as early as Spring. Correction Commissioner Russell Oswald, who had taken office only a few months earlier, made a real effort to grant press access for prisoner interviews. On July 15, he announced new regulations to that end—but only one reporter exercised the right before the uprising began on Sept. 9.

For the most part, the press has accepted arbitrary and ridiculous regulations that keep it from reporting the true nature of our institutional tragedies. It has been content to report events such as prison riots. Even then, as we saw at Attica with the killing of hostages, the media were used by officials to report their fantasies rather than the reality of the situation. Prison riots, like cowboy movies, have a quick audience because the "good guys" and the "bad guys" are identifiable, and they meet in violent confrontation. But as reporter Nat Hentoff has pointed out, "Except for brief public interest during a prison rebellion, what happens inside these institutions remains unreported and, therefore, unexamined."

The responsibility of the news media is to lift the veil of secrecy surrounding the nation's prisons, to give voice to both the victims of crime and of the criminal justice system, and to reveal the incredible waste that our jails and penitentiaries represent. The federal courts have been responsive to the First Amendment questions posed by prison secrecy. U.S. District Judge Marvin Frankel, for example, ruled in *Sobel v. Reed* in 1971:

> Whatever may once have been the case, it is not doubtful now that the Constitution, and notably the First Amendment, reaches inside prison walls. The freedoms of conscience, of thought, and of expression, like all the rest of life, are cramped and diluted for the inmate. But they exist to the fullest extent consistent with prison discipline, security, and "the punitive regimen of a prison. . . ." There is weighty authority for the view that only a "clear and present danger" of substantial evils (such as breaches of prison security or discipline) can justify curtailment of First Amendment expression by prisoners.
>
> But if that endlessly debated "test" might inject a note of uncertainty here . . . there seems to be no question that prisoners' First Amendment rights may be cut down only (to cite a range of phrasings) where the restrictions are "related both reasonably . . . and necessarily . . . to the advancement of some justifiable purpose of imprisonment" [*Carothers*]; where there is justification in some "compelling state interest" [*Fortune Society*]; where the authorities "strongly show some substantial and controlling interest which requires the subordination or limitation of these important Constitutional rights, and which justifies their infringement" [*Jackson v. Godwin*]. Alleged infringements, and asserted justifications for them, will be tested by "stringent standards" and subjected to "rigid scrutiny. . . ." And here, as elsewhere, it seems appropriate to recall that speech is to "be unencumbered until the State comes forward with sufficient proof to justify its inhibition."

The gates of the prisons are ajar for the media to enter, but the need is for aggressive initiative and creativity by the press to give substance to the Constitutional right the courts have protected.

Two years ago, the prisons were a media wasteland. Interviews with prisoners were generally not allowed. Prison tours were conducted by Potemkins. Censorship was an accepted fact of institutional life, and criticism of prison administrators was the most censorable of items. There was a vague awareness of overcrowded conditions. The suicide of an inmate was given as much attention as the details of his burial. Administrators would appear at public hearings and request more money, which was dutifully reported. But they had neither the power nor the will to challenge the system that they knew was bankrupt.

An unprecedented turnabout is underway. Clearly, the riots at Attica and New York City's Tombs and other prisons have been a major catalyst in the change. Much was certainly traceable to reporters who not only listened to the prisoners but began the investigative work that showed the truth of what they were saying. In New York, reporters like Jack Newfield made the prisons their commitment. Organizations like the Civil Liberties Union and the NAACP Legal Defense Fund and attorneys like Stanley Bass, Herman Schwartz, and Eve Cary began the prolonged assault on the arbitrary regulations that had reduced the media to public relations spokesmen for the bureaucracy. As the Constitutional rights and obligations of the media were asserted, prison administrators and political leaders were forced to respond. For the first time, the community was compelled to look at the inhumanity of a system that was being administered in the name of justice. Groups of former prisoners, like the Fortune Society, kept reminding us that Dostoyevsky had written: "The degree of civilization in a society can be judged by entering its prisons." In New York City, the Board of Correction released detailed studies of prisoner suicides that won national attention when the *New York Times* reprinted large portions of the texts.

Suddenly it was apparent that the prisons were the mirrors of profound and fateful injustices in our social structure. We had created authoritarian institutions with totalitarian disciplines to be custodians of democratic values. We had deprived citizens of their freedom and self-respect and placed them in the arbitrary control of custodians who were not equipped to respond to their needs.

We had taken the sick and maladjusted, the innocent and the depraved, the poor and the alienated, the angry and the retarded, the homosexual and the vulnerable, the addict and the murderer, and we put them all behind the same wall and pretended something helpful was happening that would deter people from crime. We preached to the world the values of an open society and built closed enclaves in rural areas to house the children of the ghetto.

When the enclaves exploded in occasional rioting, we permitted the administrators to explain the violence as the work of Maoists (Attica) or Trotskyites (Auburn) or Leninists (Dannemora) or militants (Tombs), or hard-core barbarians (San Quentin). But the press coverage was no longer limited to the violent event of the riot. The media began the effort to film the cages, to report the quality of food, to describe the "nigger sticks" of the guards, to tell of rules that permitted one roll of toilet paper every thirty-five days, to show the conditions of confrontation that brutalize the guard and the guarded, to witness the anguish of a former prisoner seeking work, to watch the retching of addicts in withdrawal, to pierce the piety of "rehabilitation," and to reveal the racism and hatred that are magnified behind prison walls.

The quickest way to end the insanity of our criminal justice system is to let the press and broadcasting reveal it. The right to know in a democracy frequently depends on the demand to know by the media. For years, we permitted prison bureaucrats to reject requests for press interviews with inmates on the specious ground of prisoner privacy. When Jessica Mitford sought permission to interview specific prisoners in the federal penitentiary at Marion, Ill., the warden politely rejected her request by writing: "As a matter of policy, we do not permit interviews with federal prisoners. The policy has been in effect since the inception of the Bureau [of Prisons] and is intended to safeguard the privacy of the prisoners. . . ."

Common sense would indicate that no interview would be held if the prisoner did not want it. Miss Mitford and the Legal Defense Fund began legal proceedings to compel federal authorities to permit interviews with prisoners. The *Washington Post* and Ben H. Bagdikian, an assistant managing editor of the newspaper, brought—and won—a similar action after Bagdikian was refused permission to interview members of the prisoner negotiating committees at Danbury and Lewisburg. A few weeks earlier, Bagdikian had written a brilliant series for the *Post* which included an account of his own experience of spending a week in a Pennsylvania prison under an assumed name.

A new breed of Correction Commissioner, like Benjamin J. Malcolm of New York City, did not wait for court orders. He has taken the lead by establishing procedures permitting full and free access by the press to consenting prisoners for interviews. Malcolm, appearing in the *Washington Post* case, testified: "We felt by liberalizing the policy, we would let the public see what we are doing. We find it has been advantageous because it begins to erase, to eliminate doubts people have had. It also eliminates tensions in our institutions." At the same hearing, the director of the California prisons testified that interviews with Soledad Brother George Jackson had "magnified his negative leadership role" and brought a "change in attitudes in California prisons" and "disciplinary problems." I wonder what would have happened if California had permitted not only more interviews but also direct and uncontrolled access of the media to all areas of the prison, including the segregated, disciplinary cellblocks. It is inconceivable that the violence, brutality, inhumanity, and sordidness of the "adjustment centers" would be tolerated by a civilized society that was aware of them. It is possible that the interviews with George Jackson did raise prisoner consciousness and protest, but we can no longer tolerate prison administrative attitudes that would silence the anguish rather than acknowledge and resolve it.

In 1965, Senator Robert Kennedy made an unscheduled visit to Willowbrook, a vast institution in New York City that houses more than 5,000 mentally retarded persons, half of them children. The press did not accompany him. When he came out, he was visibly shaken. The pain and anger of his reaction succeeded in conveying the dismal conditions he had witnessed. His personal commitment caused the state to increase appropriations and promise new and smaller facilities. After the Senator's death, various budget crises caused Willowbrook to lapse to its former condition. Last year, the *Staten Island Advance* carried a series of excellent articles that were followed up by Geraldo Rivera of WABC-TV. Using inside contacts, Rivera avoided the official obstacles that denied him access and proceeded to film the actual conditions, including interviews with staff and patients. The horror that had been denied was suddenly on TV screens across the state. The public reaction was so overwhelming that Governor Rockefeller was literally forced to add millions of dollars to his budget for the mentally handicapped. The courage and ingenuity reflected in the reporting of the Willowbrook story must be duplicated in the media for the San Quentins and Dannemoras and Angolas.

Prisoner interviews in the New York City prisons are now a right of the media. WNET, the public TV station, broke through for the electronic media by insisting on interviews with the Harlem Four, who after eight years of imprisonment were facing their fourth trial to establish their guilt or innocence. Some law enforcement officials protested, but the simple fact was that if the Harlem Four could have afforded their individual $75,000 bail, they would have been free for any interviews of their choice. Being poor and, therefore, detained in the Tombs awaiting trial, were they to be denied the same right? In a major, unprecedented decision, the New York City Correction Department upheld the right of access for the media and the right of free speech for the impoverished defendants. Shortly thereafter, Jack Newfield interviewed Herbert X. Blyden, the eloquent and recognized spokesman for prisoner grievances in both the Tombs and Attica riots. The court decision three weeks later to release the Harlem Four on nominal bail was undoubtedly influenced by the public attention attracted to the case. The policy is established. The media now have the obligation to press for its adoption in state and federal prisons. It would be unfair, however, to interview only those inmates who are sophisticated and aggressive enough to demand media attention. The press must have disciplined but total access to the prisons, not only to record the tours of dignitaries, but more important, to chronicle the emptiness and injustice of prison life, to record the countless examples of failure in the bail and sentencing procedures, to hear the despair of the poor who are represented by court-appointed counsel whose only advice is to plead guilty, and to witness the interworking of the police, the courts, and the prosecutors which have reduced Constitutional rights to a covert administrative hearing called "plea-bargaining," where everyone loses.

Prisons have many security problems and are generally understaffed. It is necessary, therefore, to regulate the access of those who do not have custodial responsibility. Ralph Blumenthal of the *New York Times* has suggested a pooling arrangement. The idea makes sense. The media would agree on alternating representatives who would be accredited by the correctional jurisdiction to have access at any time to any place within the prisons. A knowledgeable group of reporters would emerge who would have both the interest and experience to do in-depth studies of many problems that cannot be touched by superficial observation. There are few things more powerful in restraining arbitrary or excessive action than the sure knowledge of public accountability. There are few things more necessary than for the public to understand the strain of the correction officer's work and the alienation he feels because of the hostility directed toward him.

In a sense, the media would then become the community ombudsman, reporting not only the incidence of crime but the effectiveness of the system designed to control it. Instead of official handouts, the press would be reporting its own independent findings and observations. Even in times of disturbances, such pooled reporting arrangements would be valuable to accurately report the administrative moves taken to control the violence and to give some insight into the causes as well as the effects of the event. Journalists, after all, accompany front-line troops in wars as a matter of course. The correctional community, from the wardens to the guards, has complained forever that its work is not appreciated, and the community really does not care what happens to correctional personnel or what goes on in the prisons. The constant, informed attention of the media can illuminate the whole picture, giving balance to the judgments that must be made and appreciation for the courage and compassion of many of the personnel involved.

The prisons, however, are only part of the criminal justice system. The grievances they harbor are frequently beyond their power to correct. For example, John Hughes, one of the most powerful conservative Republicans in the New York legislature, recently completed a study of the state prisons. He found that approximately 25 per cent of the prisoners had profound and legitimate grievances against a legal system which was "chaotic, inefficient, and frequently corrupt." He verified grievances against courts which had given longer sentences than had been bargained for, against lawyers who were available sporadically but never with time or commitment, against district attorneys who prolonged the time of detention until madness was the only alternative to pleading guilty.

Unless the media can translate these grievances into public understanding, there is little hope for prison reform. The quality of justice must be measured periodically by the press. It must report on the attitude, independence, and caliber of judicial personnel. If the general community could watch the courts on TV, you can be sure that the rude arrogance and injudicious temper displays of some of the judges would disappear. The unequal sentencing decisions of the courts would come into focus. How can a prison be free of anger and grievance when an inmate convicted of selling 1/73 of an ounce of heroin receives a sentence of thirty years, while another defendant in another court guilty of the same crime is sentenced to three months?

The press can no longer be satisfied with only reporting the verdict of the jury and the dramatics of opposing counsel. The time has come to confront the judicial system with its inequities. The various canons that the legal profession has provided to protect the administration of justice and the rights of defendants too often provide a shield for its incompetence and shoddy performance. The integrity of the courts and the professional obligations of lawyers need a dimension of public attention that will insist on the reporting of the reality of justice rather than its rhetoric. The important consequence of more complete reporting of judicial administration will be greater self-discipline by the courts, a return of public confidence, and an affirmative response to the urgent need for more resources.

The simple conclusion is that the reporting of criminal justice has been grossly inadequate to the country's need. Billions of dollars are being spent on a system that does not work. Vigilant observation of the exercise of governmental power is a basic need in a democracy. Yet large sectors of the criminal justice system—from the police power through procedures of the courts into the walled recesses of the prisons—operate practically without objective scrutiny and evaluation. The area should be an assignment editor's fantasy. I sometimes imagine the kind of media assignments that could revolutionize our awareness. They include:

The odyssey of a heroin junkie from arrest to return to his neighborhood.

A comparison of sentences on any given day for defendants convicted of the same crime.

Live TV coverage of a prison council such as in the Women's Prison of New York City, where elected prisoner delegates meet regularly with correctional personnel to discuss institutional grievances.

A study of the correction officer, including an analysis of how he is chosen, his responsibility, training, and personal attitude toward his work.

A feature story on prison chaplains, including prisoner reactions to organized religion and the clergy.

A visit to the court pens where prisoners await court appearances—and an analysis on any given day of the disposition of the cases on the court calendar.

An inside study of the grand jury system.

A transcript of a parole revocation hearing.

A story on the incredible waste of citizens' time as the present jury system operates.

An in-depth analysis of an altercation involving prisoners and a correction officer.

A review of the prison commissary system and an accounting of the monies involved.

The death of a prisoner with documentary coverage of the details of his burial in Potters Field.

A conversation with a man who has spent more than twenty-five years in prison.

A reporter living as a prisoner in a cellblock for a week; then working as a correction officer for another week.

A profile of solitary confinement with a review of the procedures by which prisoners are sent to such quarters.

Televised coverage of the arraignment part of any urban Criminal Court.

A story about the consequences to a family when the father is sentenced to prison.

A look at mental illness in the prisons.

Detailed coverage of how a prisoner spends his thirty-seventh week in pretrial detention.

An evaluation of the rehabilitation programs in any prison.

A question and answer interview with the chief executive of a prison's political jurisdiction about his knowledge of and attitude toward the problems of criminal justice and the prisons.

A comparison of the penal systems in the United States, the Netherlands, Soviet Russia, and China.

A study of prisoner deaths in an upstate prison during any six-month period.

A feature story on the life of a prisoner the day after release.

A story about what happens to children whose mother is sentenced to prison.

An in-depth interview with an adolescent prisoner at the beginning of his sentence and when he leaves the prison.

A productivity audit and itemized analysis of a correctional budget so that an average citizen can understand it.

An analysis of the relationship between courts and the prosecutors.

A comparison of prisons in the same jurisdiction, with special attention to the impact of the individual wardens.

Some of these stories have already been done at least in part by superb reporters in the various media. Too often these reporting efforts are one day stories, unsupported by the kind of editorial pressure that could compel change. There also seems to be a failure in communicating the progress and problems of other communities—an assignment that might be a special responsibility of NET or of an annual network documentary.

The news media must establish responsive relationships with the correctional administrators. In New York City, for example, the Board of Correction invited representatives of all media to an informal meeting with Commissioner Malcolm to discuss and resolve the difficulties in properly reporting the prison scene. Publishers, broadcasters, and editorial associations could help by scheduling such meetings, public forums, and tours of prison facilities. The American Correctional Association should devote part of its annual convention to the problem. The American Bar Association should make the media and the prisons a priority topic on its annual agenda, and its lead should be followed by local Bar Associations across the country. Many ideas for reform require legislative action.

Legislators are notoriously sensitive to good reporting. Most governors could transform the nature of the prison system by their administrative order. The press can point out that the most urgent reform needed in the prisons—a change of attitude—will not cost money. It is for the media to reveal to the governors, the mayors, and the people what the true price of their lack of interest in prisons has been. The press has an obligation to push open the prison gates. In the process of reporting the truth, the media will have put powerful weights on the scales of justice.

Dostoevsky wrote: "The degree of civilization in society can be judged by entering its prisons." I believe Dostoevsky would have regarded what we did in the New York City prisons in the 1970's as a significant effort and achievement. The criminal justice system in America needs profound improvement. The reforms and the improvements we made have undoubtedly been diminished by time, but for me, those years represent hope and history.

No one is given high office as a reward for what they have accomplished in confronting the brutality of prison. John Lindsay, with the willingness to use his power as Mayor, made possible the significant changes we brought about. I continue, through the Correctional Association of New York, to insist that the realities of the prisons be confronted. As I read these words I wrote so many years ago, I take heart that some young person will read them again and find in them inspiration to change the world. When I became the Chairman of the Board of Correction in 1970, the population of prisoners and detainees in New York City jails and prisons was over 25,000. Today it is below 9000. Crime is at its lowest level in a century. The talk is of closing prisons rather than building new ones. This success is the work of many people, but I daresay the Board of Correction had an important role.

Many prisoners are brilliant manipulators. Some are great storytellers, others are extraordinary con men. They are street smart and sometimes determined to get out only to resume the activities that brought them to jail originally. The correctional system knows this. The Board of Correction understood this as well, while acknowledging that individual distinctions have to be made. It is our responsibility to turn confrontation into dialogue in order to bring humanity into brutal places. Money alone will not bring about the necessary change. Common sense is the basic force that redeems our efforts. The political will to make change, along with an attitude of respect that acknowledges the dignity of each person, is the force that will reward us all.

# 5

# THE CARTER PRESIDENCY AND
# THE UNITED NATIONS

The presidential election of 1976 was held in the shadow of Watergate. Richard Nixon had resigned, an unthinkable event in the history of the American presidency. Gerald Ford, a good and decent man, and Nixon's unelected successor, was challenged by Jimmy Carter, a one-term governor of Georgia who was essentially unknown in national politics.

In September 1975, Ted Sorenson, JFK's brilliant speechwriter and counselor, invited me to join him at a special dinner to meet Jimmy Carter. *Time* magazine had identified him as the "Voice of the New South." The *New York Times* had printed a profile emphasizing the heavy odds against a Democratic candidate coming out of the South. But Jimmy Carter was ready for the long march. He truly was the spokesman for that generation of southerners who wanted to end the Civil War. At his inaugural as governor, he said, "The days of racial segregation are over." He had placed a portrait of Martin Luther King Jr. in an honored place in the governor's mansion.

Governor Carter had an unusual background. He came out of a town called Plains, population 540, in southwest Georgia. He was a peanut farmer. He was as intelligent a man as ever sat in the Oval Office. He was a graduate of Annapolis, a protégé of Admiral Hyman Rickover, who had created the nuclear submarine fleet, and he was a born-again, fundamentalist Christian. Ted Kennedy had told me that he himself would not be a candidate. I was prepared to support Governor Carter as a representative of the progressive South, and to help him gain an audience in New York.

It was a small dinner of twenty people, and Governor Carter was superb. He spoke about issues with comprehensive knowledge. He knew all of us by name. He had a tangible intensity about him. He said without hesitation: "I am going to be elected president of the United States."

A small committee was formed, including Gillian and Ted Sorenson, Alice Mason, Richard Gardner, Fritzi Goodman, Bartle Bull, and Midge Costanza, from Rochester, New York, with whom I had gone to high school. Midge was a successful upstate politician. Carter liked her very much. Knowing each other was fortuitous. It was decided that Midge and I would act as cochairmen of the state Committee to Elect Carter. I was invited to come to Atlanta to meet with the governor and be briefed by his staff. Our task was to put together a slate of candidates in every congressional district to run as convention delegates for Carter. There was no prospect of getting established politicians to run as delegates. Carter was essentially unknown, but he made a strong impression on those he met personally. To establish the frugality of the campaign, he never stayed in a hotel, but rather overnighted with his supporters in various cities. He frequently stayed at my apartment. The campaign had no money. We had no staff. But we had a candidate who knew he was going to win.

Carter stood alone as a confident contender, but this was New York, where bare-knuckles politics was the name of the game. In January 1976, the *Village Voice,* a New York City journal with considerable influence beyond its Greenwich Village base of operations, denounced Carter as a true southern segregationist. At last, an important publication was recognizing him as a candidate, but at the same time, Steve Brill, the author, was throwing a dagger at the heart of the campaign.

The governor had me call Georgia congressman Andrew Young to ask him to write a letter rebutting the charges. I had called Andy, an old friend from civil rights days, in September 1975, asking his advice on whether I should accept the New York chairmanship of the Carter campaign. I was fascinated to learn from Andy that he was supporting Mo Udall, his colleague in the House of Representatives. He praised Jimmy Carter and was aware of his record. He then said: "Now if it were his mother [Lillian Carter] running, we would all be for her, because it was she who from an early time stood up for the blacks in Georgia. Carter's father never allowed blacks to come through the front door of his home." Jimmy Carter's mother had been a midwife for poor black families. At the age of sixty-eight, she had gone to join the Peace Corps and worked for two years in a remote village in India. She was an extraordinary woman and was a clear part of her son's success. Andy wrote the letter of rebuttal, giving Carter a campaign missive that established his credentials in the best possible way. It sounded like a ringing endorsement—and that was the way it was accepted.

Another public question had been asked about Carter's relationship to Martin Luther King Jr. Governor Carter had me call Dr. Martin Luther King Sr. to discuss the possibility of an endorsement. He said, "Oh yes, I am for Jimmy Carter. But let me qualify that. If Nelson Rockefeller runs—I will be for him. But I'll support Jimmy Carter against the other Democrats for the nomination." Dr. King in fact became an effective and enthusiastic campaigner for Carter.

There is a tendency in political campaigns to overstate the candidate's credentials and professional history. A threat to our presentation of Governor Carter related to the several descriptions of his work with nuclear submarines, where at various times he was called a nuclear physicist, a nuclear engineer, and more accurately a student of nuclear physics at Rensselaer Polytechnic Institute for one term. I raised this question with Hamilton Jordan. The opposition had begun to discuss this variance at public meetings. Jordan reassured me and said, "Just remember, Bill, that in the South when we go to sell a mule we call it a horse. People understand."

Carter was determined to identify with middle-class America. When I would go to meet him at the airport, he would come off the plane with his suit-bag over his shoulder, waving off any offer of help. He had a brilliant instinct for the right optics. The governor had four or five stock speeches that he delivered according to a grueling schedule we arranged from early morning until late at night. No one worked harder or was more self-disciplined. Each night, he would compose a dozen handwritten notes to key people he had met during the course of that day. He had an obsession about time that sometimes resulted in his arriving at an event before the audience did. He once said to me, as we were driving through the rolling hills of Westchester County, "Bill, I would rather lose $5000 than be late."

Hamilton Jordan, the closest associate of Governor Carter and a brilliant political strategist, had written a seventy-two-page memorandum outlining in detail the steps that Carter could carry out in order to emerge as the candidate of the Democratic Party. Jordan understood that the caucuses scheduled in Iowa were ignored by the media and were therefore a perfect opportunity for Carter to take a chance and establish himself. If Carter could quietly win those caucuses—all the other candidates were looking to larger victories—it would establish him as a major force. Carter's labors included over a hundred trips to Iowa in the course of 1975–76. The results of the Iowa caucus were the first to be announced in the 1976 presidential campaign. Carter came in first. ("Uncommitted" came in second.) The larger victory came in media attention, which propelled the governor to the front page. The Atlanta headquarters organized a "peanut squad" of Georgia citizens to go door to door in New Hampshire boosting the governor. He proceeded to win New Hampshire the following week, a crucial step forward. Money began to flow into the campaign. Suddenly, Carter's name was being mentioned as a growing possibility in the Democratic sweepstakes.

Our task, first of all, was to introduce Carter to politicians and political leaders in New York. When invited to a meeting, they would say, "Jimmy who?" The "Establishment" candidates for the nomination were Senator Henry "Scoop" Jackson, of the state of Washington, and Arizona congressman Mo Udall, who had strong support from liberal Democrats. The peanut squad kept marching. In the background was George Wallace, who had won 14 percent of the vote as an independent in the 1968 presidential election.

On March 17, 1976, Carter came to New York for the St. Patrick's Day parade. I had to plead with the president of the City Council to allow Carter to march beside him. We stationed twenty unpaid volunteers along Fifth Avenue, shouting, "Here comes Carter! Here comes Carter!" The *New York Times* invited him for a "coffee." He was not accepted as a serious enough candidate to merit a luncheon invitation.

Could Carter stop George Wallace in the South? Both Scoop Jackson and Mo Udall chose not to compete with Carter in the primaries of Florida and North Carolina, calculating that if they stayed out of the race, Carter would have a strong opportunity to win, thereby overcoming the threat of Wallace in future primaries. But they underestimated the impact of Carter's victory against the forces of the Old South. Carter knew these states as a neighboring governor. He showed himself to be an intense, effective campaigner. He won in both states.

Governor Wallace dropped his bid for the nomination and acknowledged a new spokesman for the South by endorsing Jimmy Carter. Hamilton Jordan's strategy held together brilliantly. Jimmy Carter now looked forward to the Pennsylvania primary, which would show whether he could win over the powerful labor unions that had carried Scoop Jackson's candidacy to this point.

The Pennsylvania primary scheduled for April 26 now promised to be Waterloo for someone. Carter scored a crushing victory, causing the expected victor, Senator Jackson, to withdraw to reconsider his position. Mo Udall had yet to win a primary.

Two months before, the vast majority of Americans had not known who Jimmy Carter was. A fundamental transformation of American politics was taking place—and Jimmy Carter was the moving force. He had carved out a new coalition of small-town and rural voters, blue-collar ethnic voters, white-collar suburbanites, and inner-city blacks. *Time* magazine described him as one of the most phenomenal politicians to rise in the American political scene in the twentieth century.

Having endured more than a decade of tumult and violence—the assassinations of John and Robert Kennedy and Martin Luther King Jr.; the Cuban Missile Crisis, which brought us all into the nuclear age; the threatened impeachment and pitiful resignation of a president who had been elected by overwhelming majorities for a second term just four years earlier; the tragic humiliation of abandoning the Vietnam War—Americans were now prepared to accept Jimmy Carter's lack of governing experience as an asset. The moral dimension of Carter as a man and as a president promised to restore purpose to the Republic.

New York had a critical role in assuring Carter's nomination and his election as president of the United States. Carter's spectacular victory in Pennsylvania united the opposition and brought new and formidable candidates, Governor Jerry Brown of California and Senator Frank Church of Idaho, into the race. Carter believed that Hugh Carey, the governor of New York, was ready to endorse him, bringing with him a major block of delegates. I disagreed and told him there was only one New York leader whose endorsement would be decisive and who could deliver more than 100 delegates in the process—and that was the mayor of New York, Abe Beame. Beame wanted evidence that Carter understood the urban crisis in

America and that he was prepared specifically and substantially to assist the cities. Carter welcomed this request. He had spent considerable time studying urban problems and was absolutely prepared to make a commitment to their resolution. Working intensely with Howard Rubenstein, Abe Beame's closest adviser, we developed memoranda that were acceptable to Carter and Beame. We scheduled a meeting between them that achieved the results they both wanted.

The mayor was as good as his word. He delivered the crucial delegate votes in support of Carter's nomination. If Beame had chosen to withhold his endorsement, it is certainly possible that Governor Brown or Senator Church could have made a strong case for his support. They proceeded to win significant victories over Carter in the remaining primaries. It was too late. Beame's commitment to Carter held. New York was in the vanguard of the campaign to make Carter the standard-bearer of the Democratic Party.

On election night in Pittsburgh, I was having a late supper with Hamilton Jordan. We discussed the possibilities of the years ahead. Hamilton said that if Zbigniew Brzezinski became national security adviser, Cyrus Vance became secretary of state, and Bob Strauss was chair of the Democratic National Committee (DNC), we would have changed nothing. But that is exactly what happened. I never tried to follow up with Hamilton on this topic, but his logic seemed to be that if important change was expected through the appointment of innovative figures, it wouldn't happen now.

The negotiations with Abe Beame and Howard Rubenstein proceeded to public announcements. Governor Carter and I then met with Governor Carey and David Burke, the governor's principal assistant. Carter continued to believe Carey was prepared to endorse him and give him considerable delegate support. I knew Hugh Carey to be one of the smartest and most principled leaders in government, but I also knew that the astonishing election results that had made Carter the putative front-runner had also encouraged Carey and others to believe in the possibility of a brokered convention where Carey himself might emerge as the candidate. Carey made clear that he would withhold any endorsement until the candidates clarified how they understood New York's problems and what they would do specifically to assist the state. That is just what happened. Carey stated that he would organize a public forum inviting all the candidates to address what they would do for New York. Carter quietly fumed. He now understood that Carey had less than a handful of delegates he could "deliver" and that he had no intention of giving his personal endorsement to Carter—unless he had no alternative.

Because of Beame, New York was decisive in Carter's nomination. The Democratic convention was held in New York City. The mayor and I were cochairs of the New York delegation and stood proudly together when New York's name was called to announce that the state cast its 274 votes for Jimmy Carter as the next president of the United States.

On election night, New York State voted for Carter. If Ford had won New York, he would have been elected president. Jimmy Carter called Abe Beame as soon as the New York result was verified to thank us and New York for being such a positive force in his victory.

No man in modern times has come to the presidency owing less to anyone than Jimmy Carter. His triumph in the 1976 presidential election—astonishing to everyone except Carter himself, who never doubted he would win—is one of the greatest upsets in American political history. Jimmy Carter was the dominating force responsible for his victory. Hamilton Jordan, Jody Powell, Jerry Rafshoon, Stuart Eizenstat, and Jack Watson wrote the script for the journey and carried it out brilliantly. It takes nothing away from their accomplishments to say that Jimmy and Rosalynn Carter had a clear sense of their destiny and were singularly responsible for its fulfillment.

On January 21, 1976, President and Mrs. Carter greeted those who had been part of his miraculous campaign at the first White House reception of his administration. As we greeted each other, he simply said: "Bill, I want you to be part of this administration." "Thank you, Mr. President, I would be honored." Without further word from anyone, I received a phone call from Cyrus Vance, the secretary of state, saying that the president would like to appoint me as the United States ambassador and permanent representative to the European office of the United Nations. Would I accept? Yes, I would, and yes, I did.

After congressional hearings, announcements, and FBI clearances, I was confirmed and sworn in by Judge Marvin Frankel at a ceremony at the UN in July 1977. I was delighted that Roger Baldwin, aged ninety-three, was there. I had first gone to Geneva with him in 1950 as his assistant to promote human rights organizations in postwar Germany.

I arrived in Geneva on July 14, 1977, and before the sun set, we were celebrating Bastille Day with the French ambassador, Stéphane Hessel, who became our cherished friend.

**Figure 15.** Working the phones as cochair of the New York State delegation at the Democratic National Convention, New York City, July 1976.

**Figure 16.** After a meeting at the White House with President Jimmy Carter, July 1977.

At that time, the ambassador to the European office of the United Nations was also the representative to GATT, the General Agreement on Tariffs and Trade. The ambassadorial portfolio included liaison with all of the UN specialized agencies: the World Health Organization, the International Labour Organization, the International Telecommunication Union, the World Intellectual Property Organization, the World Meteorological Organization, and the International Red Cross in Geneva. The CIA reported to me instead of to the ambassador in Bern, which was an unusual arrangement underlining the importance of the Geneva Mission. The UN High Commissioner for Refugees was based there. Much of the substantive work of the UN was done in Geneva. This included the Commission on Human Rights, to which I was the American delegate. There were all kinds of economic negotiations. It was a large and busy embassy. For me, it was almost as though my life had prepared me for this responsibility, because so many of the problems that the UN dealt with in Geneva were ones I had dealt with in my public life.

The International Labour Organization (ILO) demanded immediate attention. The ILO had been formed in 1919 to fight for improved labor standards, higher wages, and social benefits for workers. It was the only international organization devoted to the rights of labor. FDR had supported its creation when he was assistant secretary of the Navy, and the United States became a member in 1934. In 1969, it was awarded the Nobel Peace Prize.

The ILO was under attack by organized labor in America. George Meany and Lane Kirkland, the leaders of the AFL-CIO, wanted to withdraw the United States from the organization. The ILO had an unusual tripartite governing structure representing governments, employers, and workers. The rationale behind the tripartite arrangement was the creation of free and open debate among governments and social partners. Because of the nature of the Soviet Union, the AFL-CIO argued that the Soviet delegates were all representatives of government and therefore there could be no debate with the Soviet private sector because it did not exist. Meany and Kirkland's complaint was not incorrect. But the event that forced the issue was the granting of observer status by the ILO to the Palestinian Liberation Organization. By the time I arrived in Geneva, the decision had already been made for the United States to withdraw. My first major memorandum to the president stressed that it would set a bad precedent for the leading democracy in the world to withdraw rather than resolve the differences that had arisen. The United States had never left an international agency. If we felt the ILO needed reform, we should do it from within, I argued. But the White House, with midterm elections in mind, elected to leave the ILO. I was a reluctant messenger, and I immediately began working to encourage the ILO to adopt positions the United States could accept. In 1980, the United States was restored to full membership.

Meanwhile, the Polish workers in Gdansk had revolted, founding the Solidarity movement in August 1980 under the leadership of Lech Walesa. An observation team from the ILO traveled to Poland to ensure that the Polish government was living up to the ILO conventions it had ratified. It helped Solidarity to survive. Pope John Paul II made a special trip to ILO headquarters to express appreciation for its work.

One of the great successes of the World Health Organization (WHO)—one of the great achievements of the United Nations—was the eradication of smallpox. It was extraordinary that this disease, which had ravaged the world for centuries and claimed countless lives, was finally isolated and destroyed by working through the UN and WHO. Those who complain about America's financial contributions to the UN should remember that before 1978, if you traveled abroad, you had to have a smallpox vaccination. After the WHO announcement in 1978, that requirement no longer existed, and hundreds of millions of dollars were saved over the course of time.

In the summer of 1978, my daughter Katrina, then eighteen, flew from New York to spend some days with us. As I left the residence that morning, I said to the Marine guard, "I'm off to the airport to meet my daughter." He replied, "Well, you'll have a busy time there, because a plane has been hijacked." I didn't think anything of it. When I arrived at the airport, I learned that the plane on which Katrina was a passenger had in fact been hijacked. The "hijacker" had delivered a twenty-one-page typed message to a sleeping stewardess in the darkness of night, so the crew had no idea which of the passengers was the threat. The message stated that the hijacker had a bomb in the luggage hold that he could trigger from his seat. He threatened to detonate it within twelve hours unless Rudolph Hess, along with Robert Kennedy's assassin, Sirhan Sirhan, and five Croatian terrorists were released from prison. Rudolph Hess was the last significant Nazi prisoner of war. He had been deputy chancellor under Hitler, the third-ranking official of the Nazi Reich. He made a dramatic flight in May 1941 to Scotland, presumably believing that he could negotiate

**Figure 17.** With my daughter Katrina immediately after her escape from a hijacked TWA airliner, Geneva, Switzerland, August 25, 1978.

with Prime Minister Churchill to end the British involvement in the war, thereby granting the Nazis an opportunity to invade the Soviet Union without worrying about the Western front. His plane crash-landed, he was arrested and imprisoned, and at the Nuremberg trials, he was sentenced to prison for life. He died in 1987 in Spandau Prison in Berlin, apparently by his own hand.

I had the responsibility for the negotiation. The president of Switzerland came to the airport, and Secretary of State Vance was on the phone. We had continuing contact with the pilot. I told him that Katrina was on that plane. I did not want any special preferences given to her, but I also did not want her to be targeted because she was the ambassador's daughter.

The plane's curtains had been closed as the hijacker's note demanded. We surrounded the aircraft with all kinds of fire-fighting equipment in case of an explosion. As Katrina sat writing in her journal, waiting for something to happen, the passengers' fate remained in limbo while the pilot tried to engage the "hijacker" in discussions. No one came forward. His identity remained a mystery.

After six hours, the pilot informed the passengers that a Red Cross representative and the American ambassador to the UN were prepared to come aboard to negotiate. He invited the hijacker to come forward. No one spoke up. Secretary Vance did not want me to go aboard and thereby risk an American ambassador being held hostage. He suggested that a Swiss government official accompany the Red Cross representative instead. Nearly eight hours had passed, and the airplane fuel had by then been used up. There was no food, and the water was running low. The negotiators entered the plane, looking for anyone willing to discuss the demands. No one said a word. At a signal, the stewardess opened the rear door. The Red Cross representative quietly asked everyone to disembark in an orderly fashion. It had to be the fastest plane evacuation in history. Katrina ran into my arms. It was an unforgettable moment.

We finally returned to the residence. Katrina went to her room and wrote an account of the event which the *Washington Post* published the next day. The FBI trailed the suspected perpetrator for two months. He was a German American who had come to New York before the war and who believed Rudolph Hess had been in Spandau Prison long enough. Having been identified by the typewriter in his apartment in Yorkville on which the demand note had been typed, he was arrested, tried, and sentenced before the end of the year.

As a representative of the United States, I always made a special effort to develop relationships with Third World countries. There is a tendency toward arrogance in the exercise of power, especially when it is unchallenged. It becomes destructive. In addition, in the UN, if the permanent representative or the spokesman for the United States is playing to a domestic political agenda, the international diplomatic objectives can suffer.

It is easy to target the UN because the information received by the public generally comes from critical sources. Furthermore, the UN and its spokesmen are carefully restricted in what they can say or write in response. I advocated that the Security Council proceedings be publicly televised so as to engage the public, but the permanent members did not encourage the idea. That is why the president's support of the UN is crucial—the president must explain to the people why it is in America's interest to be in the UN. It is a continuing educational process. Being a scapegoat for its members is a role the UN has accepted from its beginning.

Andrew Young was President Carter's choice to be ambassador to the UN in New York. Andy had a significant outreach to the international human rights community—and human rights was high on the president's priority list. In August 1979, Andy was about to assume the rotating position of the presidency of the Security Council. In that context, he lunched at his residence with the ambassadors of four Arab nations, who informed him that the PLO was about to introduce a resolution demanding that it be recognized as the head of the Palestinian state-in-exile, with its capital in Jerusalem. In an effort to have the resolution delayed, or even abandoned at this time, the Kuwaiti ambassador suggested that Andy come to his home later that afternoon for an informal cup of tea. The PLO representative would also be there. Such a meeting and its substantive conversation were clearly contrary to US policy, which forbade any contact with the PLO, but Andy thought his responsibilities as Security Council president obliged him to hear the Arab point of view, which was being offered in a constructive, benign manner. Andy immediately afterward reported the meeting in considerable detail to Yehuda Blum, the ambassador of Israel to the UN, who in turn reported to Moshe Dayan, Israel's foreign minister.

By morning, the horses were running wild. Demands for resignation combined with anger, misunderstanding, political jousting, and bureaucratic revenge forced Andy to submit his resignation.

Donald McHenry, already serving as the UN ambassador with responsibility for the Security Council, was appointed as Andy's successor, with everyone's warm approval. McHenry had been in the US Foreign Service and had taught at Georgetown University. He was an excellent negotiator and an expert in international relations.

As part of the reorganization, President Carter appointed me to serve as deputy permanent representative of the United States to the UN mission in New York. Donald McHenry and I worked together wonderfully well and have remained close friends and colleagues.

The last two months of 1979 witnessed chaos, turmoil, and great uneasiness in the world. At home, Ted Kennedy was under significant pressure to seek the Democratic nomination for president in 1980. The polls showed that he would score an easy victory over the incumbent, Jimmy Carter. In my judgment, the pressures on the senator to run were almost exclusively external—he himself was not originating the idea. In the summer of 1969, Ted and I had a long lunch together where, among other things, we

**Figure 18.** Being sworn in as US Ambassador and Deputy Permanent Representative to the United Nations in New York by Judge Jack Weinstein, September 1979.

discussed his future presidential prospects. Ted said to me that practically everyone expected him to seek the presidency, but he had some profound misgivings. He said that when his brother the president was murdered, he thought it a fateful accident. But when Robert Kennedy was assassinated, he believed it would be inevitable that he would suffer the same fate.

I believe that the reservations he expressed never left him. Then came Chappaquiddick, which dramatically changed the political landscape. Ted loved being the senior senator from Massachusetts. He was a brilliant legislator. The voters had reaffirmed their confidence in him as their senator, and his life, always filled with dramatic challenges, had become stable and purposeful. Nevertheless, the clamor for him to run against Jimmy Carter continued unabated.

On October 19, 1979, the John F. Kennedy Presidential Library was dedicated in Boston. It was a great Kennedy occasion. I. M. Pei's magnificent building won general acclaim. The echoes of Camelot were everywhere. President Carter had been invited to speak at the dedication, lending a major dimension of drama. It was an extraordinary event, in part because President Carter gave the best speech I had ever heard him give. It was almost as though Carter wanted to get Teddy into the ring with him. It was always my impression that Carter had been disappointed in 1976, when Senator Kennedy chose not to run. Carter was confident that he could defeat Kennedy, and in the process automatically establish himself as a political giant-killer, giving his candidacy a major boost. It was clear to me as we left the Kennedy library that Carter was ready for the fight. In my judgment, there were several things Carter could have done to avoid the confrontation. Instead, for whatever reason, he deliberately provoked the Kennedys. For example, Congress had voted a medal honoring Robert Kennedy. Carter did not award it—obviously a deliberate decision, but politically inexplicable. The first thing Ronald Reagan did when he came into office in 1981 was to hold a ceremony at the White House presenting Ethel Kennedy with the medal that had been especially voted by Congress in RFK's memory.

Carter did not like Ted Kennedy. In fact, he didn't like the Kennedys. He was a moral and righteous person, and very judgmental. He never saw the Kennedys as allies and made little or no effort to reach a political understanding. Kennedy loyalists saw Carter as a variation of Elmer Gantry. They saw a big Cheshire-cat smile covering a hard, determined,

**Figure 19.** Sailing off the coast of Maine with Ted Kennedy.

opportunistic ambition. He pronounced his righteousness in the ways of the Lord, while his opponents were sinful transgressors.

The polls showed Carter with devastating weaknesses. They showed Kennedy beating him easily. Kennedy felt that Carter was not a strong president, and that the progressive agenda of the Democrats needed strong leadership. In his own mind, the growing pressure for him to run was an ambiguous call to the future.

Our strong personal friendship required a candid statement of opinion. I had several discussions with John Tunney, a former senator from California and a close friend of both Kennedy and myself, and I talked to Senator Kennedy as well. I knew that a vast throng of Kennedy-ites were urging him to run, telling him that the Democrats would have a terrible defeat if Carter was the candidate, and identifying Kennedy as the only hope for the restoration of Democratic power, arguing that there was no strong Republican who could overcome the disaster of Watergate. They argued that this was the time for Kennedy to reclaim the presidency.

I saw it differently. I saw that even a superficial reading of history revealed the vulnerability of challenging a sitting president. I recalled in our discussions the election of 1912, in which Theodore Roosevelt, by far the most popular Republican in the country, sought the GOP nomination from his designated successor, William Howard Taft. The divisions in the Republican Party were deep and personal. Taft won the nomination, but Teddy Roosevelt's challenge served to elect Woodrow Wilson as president. Kennedy had many loyalists, but so did Carter. In my judgment, Teddy could have run in 1968 and won, because an important part of the South would have been with him. In 1980, however, the situation had been transformed. The South was strongly antagonistic, and the Nixon strategy of making the South into a Republican stronghold, based on a policy of silent racism, was well underway.

Teddy announced his candidacy in early November. A television interview with Roger Mudd aired simultaneously, and it was devastating. Mudd asked Kennedy why he wanted to run, and the senator seemed to have no answer. Mudd pressed on: "What are the issues that are causing you to run? Why would you challenge a Democratic incumbent as president?" Teddy had no strong answers.

What the public did not know was that the Mudd interview had taken place several weeks before it was actually shown. At that time, Kennedy was in the process of formulating a decision. The Mudd program had been in response to the CBS request for a friendly family piece, showcasing Hyannis Port and the Kennedy family compound. Instead it became a political interrogation at a time when Kennedy had not yet made up his mind to run. He did not want to discuss such questions until he had made his own decision. But the public reacted as if all of that was a rationale, and that he shouldn't have exposed himself to the possibility of such questions unless he was prepared to answer them. The damage was considerable. Chappaquiddick was in the background, and its tragic days would be relived.

On November 4, a group of Iranian students in support of the Iranian Revolution seized the American embassy in Teheran and held 52 Americans hostage, demanding that the shah be returned to Iran for public prosecution before the hostages would be released. President Carter, under tremendous pressure, had permitted the shah to come to the United States for medical treatment of cancer. That decision prompted a wave of protests that culminated in the hostage situation.

The president had had a warm relationship with the shah, and America had benefited from this friendship. He was quoted in 1978 as asking

Mrs. Carter, "Where shall we celebrate New Year's Eve?" They agreed to accept the invitation of the shah and the shabanu in Teheran. Celebrating the New Year, Carter gave an extravagant toast saluting the shah's achievements. In a country on the verge of revolution, he described the shah as a great force for human rights, and Iran as the island of serenity in an area of violent political storms.

Carter chose to use the Iranian crisis to divert attention from the Kennedy challenge. It was a major story, but it became much bigger by the White House reaction to it. If the Iranian hostage situation had been dealt with outside the context of an American presidential election, Carter would certainly have been well advised to downplay it. The more press attention that was addressed to Teheran and Ayatollah Khomeini, the more reluctant Khomeini was to bring the hostage crisis to a resolution. The Iranian ambassador to the UN told me many months later that he had gone to Khomeini in the summer of 1980 and suggested that Iran's interests obliged the release of the hostages. Khomeini said to him: "Release the hostages and lose the world's concern and attention?" Holding the hostages was a great benefit to the mullahs. The strategy of the White House, to deal with it as the most important issue of our time, made it something that could not be easily resolved.

Much of the Iranian crisis was played out in the UN. Ambassador McHenry and I spent a great deal of time in discussions with the secretary-general and with delegations in the Security Council and in the General Assembly friendly to us and in working contact with the Iranians. But there was no release of the hostages. The UN was paralyzed and dominated by the hostage issue. As long as the situation remained a direct confrontation between the United States and Iran, Iran was the focus of international attention. At the same time, the world was unified around the idea that despite political differences of various countries, diplomats could not be used as political pawns and hostages. This created a strong international front against Iran.

The Soviet Union tried to be helpful to us. Then in December 1979, the Soviets invaded Afghanistan. That was an enormous breach in the possibilities of goodwill that we were trying to engender between the Soviet Union and the United States. Carter had met with Leonid Brezhnev in Vienna in 1977 and had embraced him and sent him a handwritten note. He was totally prepared to work with the Soviet Union, to move in a different direction. But

Brezhnev was too far gone—too old, too much under the control of the Politburo—and he made no response to Carter's handwritten note.

On March 1, an incident occurred in the UN that threatened the presidential campaign. An Arab-sponsored resolution had been proposed condemning all Israeli settlements in the Occupied Territories. It also made reference to "occupied Jerusalem." American policy at that time forbade support of any kind of resolutions referring to Jerusalem. Secretary of State Vance and the president were not opposed to the resolution if the offending language regarding Jerusalem could be excised. An affirmative US vote was approved on the assumption that this would be undertaken, but the language was not changed before the vote. As President Carter later explained, a mistake had been made—but the damage had been done. The Israelis were furious. To complicate the matter, the primary election in New York was scheduled for the following Tuesday. New York's powerful Jewish leaders expressed outrage. The media gave the incident full coverage. The expectation was that Carter would beat Kennedy as he had in Illinois the previous week, and the senator would then withdraw as a candidate. Instead the senator scored a solid victory—for whatever reason—and the painful campaign continued, more negative and bitter than before.

At the same time, polls began showing an increasing American demand that something be done to resolve the hostage crisis. Carter changed direction, and instead of having a steadfast commitment to the fundamental point that the safety of the hostages was our first obligation, he now determined that the interests of the United States required an effort to rescue the hostages.

That effort, on April 24, 1980, which cost the lives of eight servicemen, was a public debacle. At the UN, it played out with a sense of nervous astonishment. Secretary of State Vance resigned. Vance was not consulted on the rescue mission and was informed of it only as its execution began. In order to give the rescue a chance of success, Vance refrained from any public criticism, but he informed Carter of his resignation, to take effect within a week of the rescue effort's conclusion, successful or not.

The White House continued its search for other channels by which the crisis could be resolved, but with no success. After the failure of the rescue attempt, Khomeini distributed the hostages to different areas of Teheran. The Iraqi invasion of Iran on September 22, just weeks before our presidential election, essentially ended negotiating possibilities. It was a painful time for the hostages and for all of us.

On the eve of May Day, April 30, 1980, I was representing the United States in the Security Council deliberations on the unending question of settlements in the West Bank. The Soviet ambassador, Oleg Troyanovsky, and I discussed the agenda for the meeting and then separated to go to our seats. At that moment, I was attacked from behind and covered in red paint. I did not know at the time whether it was paint or blood. I looked over and saw that Ambassador Troyanovsky was being attacked as well. The guards rushed in and tackled the assailants, who turned out to be Trotskyite Maoist Japanese Americans from California, who were attacking the United States and the Soviet Union on the eve of May Day as the two great war-making powers of the world.

I rushed to Troyanovsky to make sure he was all right. I was dripping with paint, but not otherwise physically injured. We were the first ambassadors ever to be attacked within the physical confines of the United Nations.

Troyanovsky later told me that I made him the resident wit of the United Nations and enhanced his career in the Kremlin. As I was walking out of the Security Council chamber, still covered in red paint, one of the reporters shouted, "What did Ambassador Troyanovsky say to you?" I replied, "Better red than dead."

The assailants were tried and found guilty. Some months after their conviction, my daughter Katrina came home wearing a button that said, "Free the UN Two," given to her by an activist in Union Square.

The Cold War prevented the UN from being as effective as it could have been. On the long nights in the Security Council during the Iranian discussions, Ambassador Troyanovsky and I often talked about what the world would be like if the Soviet Union and the United States could be on the same side of issues, instead of constantly in conflict. Of course, that possibility came, but it came with the collapse of the Soviet Union. If the Soviet Union had stayed together and had been led by Gorbachev, the UN would have been a much more significant body, because Gorbachev was prepared to deal with the United States through the UN. With the collapse of the Soviet Union, the United States became the only superpower. The arrogance and isolation of that status no longer had to concern itself with a decent respect for the opinions of mankind. As illustrated in the deceitful invasion of Iraq in 2003, the UN was treated with disdain by the United States.

**Figure 20.** "Better red than dead . . ." Standing outside the UN building after an assault by Trotskyites on Soviet Ambassador Oleg Troyanovsky and myself in the Security Council, April 30, 1980.

During my years of close association with the United Nations, I frequently participated in discussions regarding its importance and its future. One such discussion was a private luncheon in July 1995 with President Clinton. The invitation came about after the ceremonies at Warm Springs, Georgia, in April 1995, commemorating the fiftieth anniversary of the death of Franklin Roosevelt. Arthur Schlesinger was quoted in the *Washington Post* in an offhanded response to a reporter who asked him to compare Presidents Roosevelt and Clinton. Arthur responded by saying that FDR seemed to enjoy the battle and take more pleasure in confronting his political enemies, whereas President Clinton seemed to want to avoid confrontation and resolve differences by consensus. Clinton wrote to Arthur expressing his disappointment that Arthur seemed to doubt his willingness to fight for the cause of progress. Arthur replied that the president might want to occasionally consult with some liberals possessing government experience; he, Ken Galbraith, Joe Califano, Ted Sorenson, and I were available anytime. We subsequently received an invitation for July 7.

On the appointed morning, Arthur and I flew to Washington. Arriving early, we stopped at the Hay-Adams Hotel, got a cup of coffee, and walked across Lafayette Park and then to the White House. There we met Ken Galbraith, Ted Sorenson, and Joe Califano. As a harpist played Handel's "Largo" from the opera *Xerxes*, we had drinks and greeted members of staff, many of whom had served there for years and had known us in our various capacities in the past. At noon the president appeared, and we were escorted into the president's personal dining room.

There followed a frank, wide-ranging discussion about the growing disparity of wealth in America, the increasing burden on the middle class, the coming confrontation over the appropriations bill, and the transformation of the National Rifle Association from an organization primarily promoting gun safety, as it was when the president was a child in Arkansas, to a lobbying force pushing gun rights over common sense.

But the topic that most concerned me that day was the situation with the United Nations. From my seat directly across the table from the president, I made the argument that the presidency is preeminently a place of moral leadership, and that in foreign affairs the president speaks for the nation. I told the president that he seemed to be avoiding making foreign affairs an important part of his presidency. I told him that the UN bashers such as the Heritage Foundation had had an open field day for fifteen years, with no one on the other side standing up and explaining to the American people how the UN serves the American national interest, in practical terms. The Iraqi invasion of Kuwait and the world's response, Operation Desert Storm, was a perfect example. The Arab nations would only have joined in the struggle against Iraq under the auspices of the UN. And because of that, the nations of the world picked up the cost—over a hundred billion dollars—and the United States paid practically nothing. The UN might have bureaucratic problems, but certainly no more than any other government I knew. The surest way to destroy the UN was to attack it for things beyond its control, and then starve it of funds so that it could not fulfill its mission.

The UN needed reform; on this we agreed. But I stressed to the president that if the UN needed reform, it was up to us to lead the way, and up to him to make the case to the American people.

After two hours of lively discussion, the luncheon came to an end. As we were leaving, I handed the president a memorandum I had written for the occasion. He took it and glanced over the first page, which began with the sentence "The rich and the powerful will always take care of themselves." With a laugh, he promised to read the entire document. He later called me to stress that he had indeed read it—twice!

In the memorandum, I had written that the test of our progress, as President Roosevelt said in his second inaugural address, is "not whether we add more to the abundance of those who have much; it is whether we provide enough for those who have too little." This extended to the possibilities of the UN for protecting the world order created in the past seventy years. Machiavelli had written that a great leader must be as brave as a lion and as shrewd as a fox. The American people wanted the UN to succeed; American presidential leadership was the only way to make this a reality.

Sadly, less than a decade after our luncheon, the Second Iraq War gave us an object lesson in the perils of sidelining the UN. The United States, under both President George W. Bush and President Clinton, had made a strong case against Saddam Hussein as not only a tyrant but also someone who had developed an inventory of weapons of mass destruction that gave him immense power. The United States asserted that because he had these weapons, we had no alternative but to depose him. But in the debate in the UN, Iraq denied it had these weapons. The UN devised a process by which its designated inspector could go anywhere in Iraq to discover any weapons of mass destruction, and appointed Hans Blix, the former Swedish foreign minister and perhaps the most renowned diplomat in the field of disarmament, to head up the study. But the administration of President George W. Bush did not want an investigation. It wanted war. As Saddam gave the UN team access to everything he had, on a continuing basis, the United States went ahead with its invasion plans. In 1990, George H. W. Bush had followed the UN's lead, and had had an extraordinary result. But in 2002, the Bush administration's policy was one of deceit and deception. If they really had evidence of the weapons of mass destruction, Hans Blix and the UN gave them the opportunity to prove it.

The vote on October 10–11, 2002, authorizing the president to use force in Iraq was a historic and tragic occasion. I worked closely with Teddy Kennedy in opposition to the authorization. Three weeks before the vote, I sent him a memorandum analyzing the issue. He later told me that his vote against the resolution authorizing force was the most important vote he ever cast.

In my experience, the decision to invade Iraq, based as it was on miscalculation and deliberate deceit, was the most damaging decision in foreign affairs of any president in my lifetime.

Memorandum
To: Senator Edward M. Kennedy
Date: September 19, 2002
Re: Some Thoughts and Reflections on the Crisis in Iraq

1.  War is an intensely deliberate act, often accompanied by unintended consequences. The Senate is a deliberative body. It has to treat the subject of war with greater scrutiny and concern than practically any other subject that comes before it.

2.  If we were proceeding rationally instead of under domestic political pressures and strategies, we would welcome the role of the United Nations in the enforcement of its resolutions against Iraq. We would work with the Security Council to draft a resolution that provides for unconditional, timely inspections with the clear understanding that the failure of this process will have consequences, including possible military consequences. At some point, a President moves from being the leader of his party to being the President of the people of the United States

and the Commander-in-Chief of the Armed Forces. If a President appears to be making military decisions where American interests are put in danger and innocent people are threatened, he runs the risk of being condemned by history and despised by true patriots of the Republic. In 1942, FDR decided to order the invasion of North Africa. We had suffered a brutal series of reverses, beginning with Pearl Harbor, and the Democrats were jittery about the impending Congressional elections. Democratic leaders urged dramatic military action before the election. FDR could have advanced the invasion plans. It was launched on November 8, 1942, four days after the election. It was an immensely successful operation and did represent a significant turning point in the war. FDR never regretted his refusal to pressure the military commanders to advance the date so that there could be political benefits registered in the Congressional elections—an election that was costly to Democratic control in the Congress. The politics of war cannot be maneuvered for partisan advantage.

3.  The extremist ideological advisers of the President want a pre-emptive war on Iraq. It is not altogether clear why they are obsessed by this since it has been so difficult for them to offer evidence as to any imminent threat to the United States, the only grounds in international law that would justify a pre-emptive assault. The President in response to political pressures from the center of his own party decided to go to the United Nations to build an international coalition to support the effort, but his speech to the U.N. was directed to the breach of U.N. resolutions and the failure of Iraq to permit the unconditional inspection that prior resolutions and the 1991 cease fire authorized. The enforcement of U.N. resolutions is a very different objective than regime change or pre-emptive war. The U.N. can respond with a Security Council resolution that defines the requirements of unconditional inspections. It could even provide a precise procedure that might include a police-keeping dimension in support of the inspectors. And, it could ultimately indicate, depending upon the success of the inspections and the weaponry found, that military action might be authorized and forthcoming. But the U.N. is not authorized to undertake regime change as the deliberate objective of its resolution. There is nothing in the Charter that would permit that. If the U.S. is dissatisfied with the Security Council resolution or with the inspection process, it can still consider its own unilateral action, but presumably that action would be based on the imminent threat that Iraq represents to the United States and would require the President to present to the Congress and to the people of the United States

the clear evidence that would justify that kind of action. The Administration has been unwilling to do that. Rumsfeld has refused to offer evidence to either America or to the nations abroad. Senator Hagel of Nebraska has been reported in the press as saying that the CIA has no evidence that would justify this kind of military action. It is not difficult to ascertain whether Iraq has any nuclear capacity—or how close it is to achieving such a capacity. The inspectors could certainly do that. As to bio-terrorism, Peggy Noonan's article which Frank Rich quotes in his column on Saturday, September 14, reminds us that many countries— and many individuals—have access to the weapons of bio-terrorism such as anthrax. Somebody in Trenton, New Jersey with four envelopes of miniscule amounts of anthrax practically paralyzed the government of the United States last October–November. If such weapons are available and the U.S. does attack, there certainly has to be a likelihood that they will be used against our forces or in some way that would be very costly to us as a nation and perhaps to other nations.

4. I did not know the terms of the Iraq Liberation Act that was signed by President Clinton on October 31, 1998. It may register an American commitment to regime change in Iraq, but presumably the question is how to do that short of war. There are certainly many options that should be considered before military invasion, options such as extending the overflight zones, or further assistance to opposition indigenous forces, or rallying Arab and Muslim countries to undertake a campaign against Saddam with the understanding that regime change is our most important objective. Tremendous evidence has been compiled against Saddam and his cohorts regarding violations of international law and international covenants. The Security Council could set up an *ad hoc* international tribunal and indict Saddam as a war criminal, thereby changing his status overnight and causing nations to deal differently with Iraq. We could compel all nations to truly honor and enforce U.N. sanctions which is not being done now. Our satellite and other intelligence facilities presumably can pinpoint buildup areas which can be targeted if the evidence justifies their destruction. Where are the so-called "international police"—the intelligence services like the Mossad, the CIA, the MI6—whatever happened to their capacity to target Saddam as a "wanted murderer?" The U.N. could enlarge the blockade of Iraq. Radio Free Iraq could be established as an outreach to the people to encourage an indigenous revolt.

5. The costs of war are unpredictable—measured not only in the loss of our own troops or significant civilian casualties, but also with the

destruction of the very heart of ancient civilization. Any war involving an invasion of Baghdad could very well be destructive of cultural monuments and historical areas that would represent an infinite loss to the world's heritage. There is also, of course, the possibility of some kind of an assault on Israel, although Sharon has indicated that Israel is quite prepared to take care of itself. The political and economic disruption of Turkey has to be taken into account as well as the immense impact on Saudi Arabia, Jordan and Egypt.

6.  Above all, the Administration has not proved its case for a unilateral military act against Iraq. If such a case exists, the Congress must insist that it be made to the American people. It should insist that the President come before it under the constitutional authority of Article I Section 8 and formally request a declaration of war. America is entitled to a full and public debate of a projected action that would reverse the commitment of our entire history against the very thought of a pre-emptive war. The cost of the threatened military action against Iraq has already been estimated at $100–$200 billion by the President's economic adviser. The cost in terms of casting a heavy shadow over our economic recovery is also something that should be measured. If the war results in a dramatic increase in the price of oil, the economic consequences could be disastrous. Any cost, of course, must be subtracted from America's willingness to deal with its own social needs, a loss that most Americans would probably be unwilling to allow on the basis of the inadequate evidence and arguments presented to it.

7.  Colin Powell has said: "There is not a scintilla of evidence linking Iraq to Al Qaeda . . ." Scowcroft's argument is persuasive that you cannot undertake this action against Iraq without jeopardizing the war against terrorism, and certainly jeopardizing the international coalition which is essential to the war on terrorism's success. How imminent a threat can Iraq be if the Administration has delayed for so long a response to that threat? Every effort must be made to keep reminding the President and his Administration of the so-called war on terrorists. Where is Bin Laden? His deputies? What is the result of the anthrax investigation? There is a need for Americans to regain their sense of confidence after 9/11. Americans are not a fearful people. The most corrosive agent to undermine democratic values is fear. FDR knew that, any great President would know that. To enlarge the specter of terrorism by promising a war that could involve us in a Mideast catastrophe has an aspect of lunacy to it.

8. An American military victory over Iraq is not in doubt, although its length and costs are unpredictable. But what do we do with Iraq after the military victory? This question has been asked for generations by people who have been concerned by the political chaos of the area. A strong President would lead the nation in a debate of this question in a calm, deliberate and rational manner. In that event, were he to bring the Congress with him, he could prevail. But no President could or should lead America into a war that its people do not understand and would not willingly support.

Exactly a year later, in October 2003, I was invited to give the Arthur Ross Lecture for the Foreign Policy Association. I was pleased to accept. By that time, Operation Iraqi Freedom had come and gone, destroying the regime of Saddam Hussein between March and May and unleashing the instability that plagues Iraq to this day. My comments were made in that context, but many of the points are still relevant.

**If the United States Government Truly Supported**
**the United Nations . . . Arthur Ross Lecture,**
**by William J. vanden Heuvel, Foreign Policy Association,**
**New York City, October 30, 2003**

The founding of the United Nations was a singular act of political creativity, certainly the most successful in history's long record of efforts to fulfill mankind's quest for a just, compassionate, and peaceful world. More than anyone else, Franklin Delano Roosevelt was the instrument of that creation. He understood that collective security required the most powerful nations to be responsible partners in this great enterprise.

While the Second World War was being fought, the peace to follow it was being prepared. Even before the US entry into the war, the president addressed the Congress and insisted that the terrible sacrifices that the world was about to endure could only be justified if, in the world to come, all nations and all peoples could be assured of the Four Freedoms, namely, Freedom of Speech and Expression, Freedom of Worship, Freedom from Want, and Freedom from Fear. The declaration of the Atlantic Charter sustained this theme. The Charter of the United Nations itself and the Universal Declaration of Human Rights which was to follow it had this commitment to freedom at their core. The separate responsibilities of the Security Council and the General Assembly were intended to reflect both the power needed for collective security and the democratic participation of all nations in the processes of the United Nations. There were no illusions. FDR understood very well the oppressive totalitarianism of Communism under the Soviet Union. He also understood that the Allied victory in World War II was due in substantial measure to the extraordinary sacrifice of the Russian people who had lost 27 million dead with much of their country plundered and destroyed. He also understood that we were about to enter the nuclear age and that conflicts among nations now required a forum for these conflicts to be resolved by means other than war. The United States, at this point, as Roosevelt advanced the cause of the UN, was unquestionably the dominant power of the world, the singular possessor of nuclear weapons, the overwhelming economic force among nations with a military capacity that had no competitor. The United States was more powerful then in relationship to the rest of the world than it is today. Those who repeat the mantra of our overwhelming power today as though it justifies the flaunting of the opinions of other nations should remember that at no time since the Second World War has the United States been anything but the most powerful nation on earth with military, economic, and political resources essentially beyond challenge. Roosevelt, Truman, Eisenhower, Kennedy, and George Herbert Walker Bush understood how important the United Nations could be as an instrument of governance that could protect American interests and encourage the acceptance of American values. The Cold War delayed and certainly endangered the possibilities of the United Nations that had been envisioned by its founders. Nevertheless, the intervention in Korea in 1950 was under the flag of the United Nations. And, in the most serious crisis of the nuclear age, President Kennedy very effectively used the United Nations as the means of convincing the world of the legitimacy of America's response to the presence of Soviet missile weaponry in Cuba.

As with so many things, the Vietnam War undermined the developing peacekeeping possibilities of the UN. President Johnson chose to Americanize the conflict in every way, manipulating a "coalition of the willing" rather than seeking UN mediation to bring the civil war to an end. The United Nations was made to look weak and irrelevant, but, in fact, it was the United States that paid the price of a profoundly divided nation and a generation of self-doubt.

Before considering the impact on the United Nations of the Gulf War in 1991 and the invasion of Iraq in March of 2003, let me say that one of the problems in our country is lack of knowledge regarding the UN—ignorance of its history, of what it is, of how it operates, and of what it can do. A basic lesson about the UN would tell us the following: the UN is not a sovereign entity. It is an association of sovereign member states. The United

Nations is not a government. It is not an executive, it is not a legislature that can command the peoples of the world. It is not a court that can adjudicate and then enforce its decisions. It has no standing army, no air force; no, not even arsenals kept ready to support its missions. The assessed annual financial obligation of the United States to the UN is approximately $300 million.

The United Nations is a mirror of a very imperfect world; it can only do what its 191 members permit it to do. The national interests of the United States can be advanced if our government has the will and skill to do so but, because of our veto and our power, nothing significant can happen in the UN that adversely affects us.

Now that is the reality.

Most Americans are fair-minded and willing to listen and learn but in the complicated field of international relations where the president has primary power, it is the president and his spokesmen who must explain American interests in encouraging the success of the UN. Absent that powerful advocacy—and it has long been absent—the enemies of the UN, well financed, well organized, and unencumbered by any need, desire, or responsibility to make balanced presentations to their audiences have done great harm to the relationship between the United States and the United Nations.

When Saddam invaded Kuwait in August 1990, George Bush Sr. made it very clear that this aggression would not be allowed to stand. He set out to organize the United Nations in such a way that Saddam was confronted by a united world resisting his fundamental transgression of the Charter. George Herbert Walker Bush led both the United States and the United Nations brilliantly in the Gulf War, a struggle where France as well as the United Kingdom, where Germany as well as Japan, where Arab nations as well as Israel, where Turkey as well as Mexico, stood with us and even paid the financial burden of $100 billion.

In his 1998 memoir, *A World Transformed*, George Bush Sr. wrote the following to explain why he did not send American forces to Baghdad—a decision in which he was supported by General Colin Powell and General Schwartzkopf and by every senior member of his government:

Trying to eliminate Saddam . . . would have incurred incalculable human and political costs. Apprehending him was probably impossible. . . . We would have been forced to occupy Baghdad and, in effect, rule Iraq. . . . There was no viable "exit strategy" we could see, violating another of our principles. Furthermore, we had been self-consciously trying to set a pattern for handling aggression in the post-Cold War world. Going in and occupying Iraq, thus unilaterally exceeding the United Nations' mandate, would have destroyed the precedent of international response to aggression that we hoped to establish. Had we gone the invasion route, the United States could conceivably still be an occupying power in a bitterly hostile land.[1]

How painful it is to hear those words in the light of what has happened and is happening in Iraq today.

American policy relating to Iraq as determined by this administration was profoundly influenced by a group of ideological radicals who have made careers out of bombastic nationalism and vicious, well-funded attacks on the United Nations. I cite as an example Richard Perle, who as chairman of the Pentagon's Defense Policy Board led the demand for war and the invasion of Iraq.

On March 21, 2003, in the *Guardian*, Mr. Perle wrote: "Saddam Hussein's reign of terror is about to end. He will go quickly but not alone—he will take the U.N. down with him. Thank God for the death of the U.N." If we believe in internationalism, if we believe that America has tried to play a constructive role in leading the world toward democratic values, if we believe that the United Nations is an important instrument in this age-old struggle to control the greed and corruption of mankind, we must realize that we are jeopardizing the ideals of America that great generations of Americans have sustained in the last seventy years as the responsibility of world leadership has come to us.

It is the obligation of our leaders to give the nation and the world a vision of hope and confidence and courage. The Great Depression and World War II were much greater crises, much greater threats to the existence of our nation than anything we face now. President Roosevelt, who understood the corrosive nature of fear, strove to restore the nation's confidence in itself. "We have nothing to fear but fear itself," he said in his first inaugural—and Americans believed him. "Freedom from fear is an objective that should be sought for all nations and all peoples"—and the world believed him. September 11, 2001 was an overwhelming and terrible crime. Terrorism emerged in a new form and with a new name, Al Qaeda. It is the responsibility of our political leaders to identify our enemy and to mobilize the resources to defeat it. Al Qaeda is not an enemy that threatens the existence of our nation; it threatens the soul of our people. Our response should be one of determination, of courage, of confidence—not feckless fear that undermines the very values that define America for ourselves and the rest of the world.

I wondered during the course of the Iraqi debate: could there be any doubt that America's national interests would best be served by America's challenge to Iraq being legitimized by UN approval and support? Did not our leaders understand the meaning, opportunity, and value of the UN's immediate support of the American response to the terrorist crime of September 11th? It was said during the Senate debate—and I repeat it now—the war was the easy part—the world's finest, most powerful military force was contending against a country of 24 million people, a country with no comparable armed force, a country a third of which was already occupied by our ally, the Kurds, a country that had no response to our air power, which was prepared to decimate it. It was always the Occupation that required UN legitimacy as the best shield for the brave men and women left with a responsibility for which so little planning had been done. In its own most basic interest, the United States had to make the enforcement of the 17 UN resolutions violated by Iraq a UN-approved mandate.

There were several occasions during the time when I had the honor of representing the United States in the Security Council that my Soviet counterpart and I would talk very privately of the world that could be achieved if our nations worked together to try to make the UN the effective instrument of international governance that its Founders hoped it to be. As I watched the Iraq debate, I asked myself a variation of that question—What would the UN and our world be like if the American government, now the world's only superpower, truly wanted the UN to succeed? What would a president do who wanted the UN to be effective and successful? Every poll prior to the Iraq confrontation showed more than 70 percent of Americans wanting the UN to be successful and wanting America to be the leader in that effort. Understanding that every such action would have to be defensible as furthering and strengthening our national interests, I wondered what an American government led by someone with the vision and pragmatic discipline of FDR would do today if its purpose was to lead the UN in creating a better world. Here are some thoughts:

1. First of all, we would not begrudge the sum that we pay as our assessed obligation, recognizing that the $300 million annual obligation is probably the most cost effective dollar that we pay in terms of American security. We would never stop reminding our countrymen that the UN is *not* a sovereign body, that it has no power or resources beyond what its members give to it, and that US leadership is indispensable to the UN's success.

2. We would not degrade the character and quality of the international civil servants who serve the United Nations and its specialized agencies. Instead, we would recognize the high standard of their performance and do everything possible to motivate and encourage them to still greater achievements. And we would mourn with them the loss of the brave men and women in the bombing in Baghdad—and the hundreds of UN personnel who have been killed in peacekeeping operations over the years.

3. We would acknowledge the extraordinary good fortune of having a secretary-general of the character, integrity, intelligence, and experience of Kofi Annan. We would take advantage of his tenure to use his diplomatic brilliance and his unparalleled connections to the nations of the world in order to further democratic objectives in the United Nations.

4. We would understand that the world has witnessed immense changes since the founding of the United Nations, that the UN has been the midwife to many of those changes, such as the peaceful end of the colonial era, but that changes in structure and procedure which are never easy in national or in international organizations should be considered. For example, a crucial objective in the years ahead is a capacity to recognize and respond to the needs of nation-building. The summit of world leaders at the UN in September of this year proposed a Nation Building Commission so that the UN, with the assistance of the United States and other member states, could train and have available civil administrators, development experts, teachers, police, firemen, and security experts to assist nations disintegrating because of civil strife in negotiating and enforcing a social contract that would give the possibility of peace and social justice. This should be a priority for us.

5. We would recognize the difficulty in reforming the Security Council as witnessed by the discussions and proposals of the last decade. Instead of being discouraged by political roadblocks that are not easy to resolve, the United States could insist upon close coordination and communication between the Security Council and important member states that under other circumstances will be considered for permanent membership. Close coordination and communication with all member states and regional groups should be the order of the day. In an age of instant communication, such a working procedure is clearly possible.

6. We know that civilization needs a police force just as every one of our communities looks to its local police for security and protection against the lawless. If thugs control the streets, forget the hopes and dreams of civilized society. Adolf Hitler and his Nazi hoodlums brought the

world to the precipice of destruction. The tinhorn dictators who challenge democratic values when they carry out ethnic cleansing and assault innocent people, destroying their lives and their hopes, are in the same gangster tradition. The United States does not want to be nor should it be the Policeman of the World. But for the United Nations to have the ability to enforce its moral authority, the United States must participate and lead. We should encourage the creation of forces that would be available to the Security Council to allow for timely peacekeeping and peacemaking interventions. It is not difficult to organize rapid deployment forces that would be available to the Security Council for specific purposes which its permanent members would have to approve. If the United States wanted such a rapid deployment force, we could make it happen. The Armed Forces of the United States could lend their extraordinary ability and experience to the creation and training of such a force as well as peacekeeping forces. We could invite young American men and women to volunteer for a special unit in our Armed Forces which could be made available for peacekeeping or peacemaking missions. We would show the world how the idealism and courage of our young men and women can serve the purposes of peace and social justice as well as war.

7. Understanding the crucial role of the United Nations in the fight against AIDS and other threatening plagues and epidemics, we would constantly remind Americans that the World Health Organization, one of the specialized agencies of the United Nations, is a major force in protecting our country. We would be proud of the extraordinary achievements of WHO which we have helped bring about, such as the elimination of smallpox and the near eradication of polio—and we would tell Americans that the World Health Organization is indispensable to the international cooperation necessary to fight the plagues and diseases which threaten the world and leave no nation immune.

8. We would use the United Nations as a forum to stand up to tyrants and to lead the world in recognition of the Rule of Law. There is no greater benefit to the national interest of the United States than to have a world which recognizes the Rule of Law. It should be our special mission to encourage the United Nations by every means possible to fulfill this objective. The progress that has been made in the last sixty years is stunning. We have helped make it possible. We should be leaders in extending the concept of the Rule of Law. We should welcome the International Court for Criminal Justice, for example, and if for whatever reason we could not promise ratification

of the treaty that has created it, we certainly should not stand in the way of other nations carrying out its mandate. We would use the United Nations and instruments like the ICCJ to make it clear to tyrants that international legitimacy requires the consent of the governed and that all rational means will be used to end their oppression. We would take pride in the American role in the creation of the Universal Declaration of Human Rights. We would work to make the UN Human Rights Commission more effective—and, in any event, invite the nations of the world to join with us in making human rights a priority consideration on the international agenda. We would recognize the unique possibilities of the UN in mediation, arbitration, and conflict resolution and would move to strengthen those procedures in every possible way.  .

9. We would recognize the indispensable role of the United Nations in achieving a most urgent objective, namely, nuclear nonproliferation. We would strengthen the International Atomic Energy Commission and find the diplomatic means to accomplish the purposes of the nonproliferation agreement while at the same time making it clear that a civilized world cannot tolerate nations threatening the use of nuclear weapons. We would remember the bargain that we made in asking the nations of the world not to pursue the development of nuclear weapons—a bargain that obligated the United States to lead the international effort to reduce armaments and nuclear weapons.

10. We would proudly remind the nations of the world of the obligations that all of us undertook at the Millennium Summit and renewed this past September. We would work to give credibility to our commitment to help the less developed nations of the world in terms of strengthening their civil societies and their economic prospects.

It was clear before the invasion of Iraq and it is abundantly clear now that we would be in a much stronger position in pursuit of our legitimate objectives if the United Nations and through it the nations of the world were with us, strengthening our efforts to bring peace and a representative government to the people of Iraq.

Making the UN a successful part of international governance will serve our country's interests for generations to come. A peaceful and prosperous world cannot be organized without the active engagement and leadership of the United States. Presidential leadership is absolutely vital to our role in the United Nations. The Congress can be hostile, the extremists can continue their rhetorical explosions, but if the president is clear in his purpose and willing to exercise the necessary political will, the United States can inspire the world by making the UN a powerful, effective instrument in the governance of a world that pleads for our leadership. We do not have that leadership.

If history is our guide, we know that the window of opportunity for the beneficent exercise of our power will not remain open forever. Other nations will emerge in this century that will rival us and challenge our dominance. The American dream is not empire; it is constitutional democracy that assures personal freedom and equal opportunity. Our destiny is to create a better world where democratic values are fundamental. In that quest, the United Nations can be a crucial partner.

# 6

# AMERICA AND THE HOLOCAUST

On April 6, 1994, PBS's *American Experience* aired a documentary entitled "America and the Holocaust: Deceit and Indifference." Its premise was that America—its people, its government, and President Roosevelt himself—had turned a blind eye to efforts by European Jews to escape Nazi persecution and eventually the Holocaust. It implied that a combination of anti-Semitism, cold economic calculation, and bureaucratic obstructionism had combined to thwart thousands of Jews seeking asylum in America.

Such accusations were not new. A major conference had been organized in 1993 at the FDR Presidential Library in Hyde Park, chaired by the eminent Yale professor John Morton Blum. A book about the conference, *FDR and the Holocaust*, edited by Verne W. Newton, had been published and widely hailed. Months before the PBS documentary aired, I had been disturbed by a conversation with a dear and close friend and fellow Roosevelt Institute trustee, Fritzi Goodman. She had been at a reception at her synagogue where a number of young people were critical of FDR for not doing more to help the Jews and to stop the Holocaust by bombing extermination camps like Auschwitz. I found it hard to believe, knowing that American Jews idolized Roosevelt and looked to him as their protector and defender—one of the few powerful figures concerned about protecting the Jews from the Nazis. FDR loathed the Nazis and had been the first Western leader to challenge Hitler. He was aware of a significant anti-Semitism in our own country. He had opened the government to the appointment of Jews to the extent that Hitler and Goebbels referred to the Roosevelt administration as the "Jew Deal," rather than the New Deal. I also knew that Rabbi Stephen Wise, the founder and leader of the Zionist movement in America, said that he had never met a man who was less biased than Franklin Roosevelt. Rabbi Wise and FDR and their families were close friends. Rabbi Wise had open access to the White House.

An accusation that a president did not do all that he could to help the Jews in the Holocaust implied a deliberate act of anti-Semitism. I discussed the question with Arthur Schlesinger. We arranged to see a preview of the documentary and were appalled by the superficiality of the presentation. It was certainly not an objective historian's work. I had extensive conversations with several scholars and with the producers of the show. It was clear to me that to leave these charges unanswered was to leave a shadow on Roosevelt's tenure as president that was undeserved and wrong.

I thereupon undertook, as a personal crusade, to make sure that America's record regarding the Holocaust was stated honorably and accurately. I began an odyssey of research and investigation into the subject. Among my teachers, particularly regarding the Hungarian Holocaust, was Professor Randolph Braham, of the Graduate Center of the City University of New York, himself a Holocaust victim, and for more than fifty years an internationally recognized scholar with an impeccable reputation.[1] My efforts resulted in an invitation to lecture at the Holocaust Memorial Museum in Washington, DC, in 1996. In the intervening years, I have participated in public discussions and debates, addressed academic conferences, and written extensively on the subject, including a 1999 article, "America and the Holocaust," in *American Heritage Magazine*. In response to that article, the internationally eminent historian John Lukacs, whom I had never met, called Richard Snow, the editor. "I have just finished William vanden Heuvel's article on the Holocaust," he said, "and I want to say—and I know a good deal about this subject—it is a masterpiece. It is perfect, and utterly true, and I only hope it gets the widest possible distribution." That gave me encouragement and credibility to continue what I regarded as a pursuit of the truth.

The speech "America and the Holocaust" is a distillation of literally scores of speeches I have made on the subject around the country. The following version was given at the Rosenthal Institute for Holocaust Studies at the City University of New York on September 12, 2012. I have never, in the many times I have delivered this speech and its variations, had anyone successfully attack its accuracy.

### America and the Holocaust, by William J. vanden Heuvel

It was Winston Churchill's judgment, which I share, that the Holocaust "was probably the greatest and most terrible crime ever committed in the whole history of the world." The Holocaust was part of a colossal military struggle known as World War II in which 67 million people were killed, where nations were decimated, where democracy's survival was in the balance. In his lunacy to exterminate the Jews of Europe, Hitler and his Nazi followers murdered 6 million innocent men, women, and children for no other reason than that they were Jewish. This crime is of such profound proportions that it can never be fully understood; it must continue to be analyzed from every aspect as to how and why it happened; and its memory must unite all of us so that we can truly say in one voice, "Never again."

We remember also that 9 million non-Jewish civilians were brutally murdered by the Nazis. They were Germans, Poles, Czechs, Serbs, Croats, Ukrainians, Russians, Gypsies. They were political dissidents, labor leaders, Catholic and Protestant clergy, journalists, doctors, lawyers, intellectuals, the mentally and physically disabled, and homosexuals. Most of these victims were killed because of who they were, not for what they did. The Slavs, like the Jews, were a particular target of Hitler's hatred. He described them as *Untermensch* (subhuman). When the Nazis conquered their countries, the Slavs were terrorized and tortured, their property and land expropriated. Eyewitness accounts abound of examples of unspeakable brutality, such as women and children being herded into locked barns that were then set afire. Many shared the fate of the Jews in the extermination camps. Most were hanged, shot, starved, or worked to death. Nine million human beings. *In addition*, the Nazis murdered over 3 million Soviet prisoners of war, approximately 57 percent of those in Nazi custody. (Of the US and British POWs, less than 4 percent lost their lives.)

It was only in the 1960s that the name "Holocaust" came into general use to describe the Nazi genocide of Europe's Jews. Since then, much has been written regarding America's role during those years of persecution and destruction. Accusing the United States not only of abandoning the Jews but of complicity in the Holocaust, David Wyman has written: "The Nazis were the murderers but we"—and here he includes the American government, its president and its people, Christians and Jews indiscriminately—"were the all too passive accomplices." This terrible indictment deserves a response. One response by Peter Novick, the profound and much honored philosopher and historian, in his book *The Holocaust in American Life*, refers to the Wyman arguments as a "comfortable morality tale that has passed for history."[2] He states that most professional historians agree that it is simply bad history. Some commentators are critical of American Jews during that period for being "passive observers," for not wanting to know what was happening in the genocide of Europe's Jews, for being so absorbed in their effort to be accepted or assimilated in American society that they chose silence rather than public outrage at the Nazi crimes. The corollary question to this line of argument is why did American Jews give their overwhelming support to Franklin Delano Roosevelt if, as his critics allege, he was indifferent to the fate of Europe's Jews despite his knowledge of what was happening to them? Perhaps the most frequent question asked is why the Allies did not bomb Auschwitz and the railroad tracks leading to it? Laced through the debate is the generally unspoken allegation that America's leaders and Americans generally were uncaring anti-Semites. After all, if the bombing of Auschwitz was not ordered, then those who did not order the bombing must be—what? Traitors? Anti-Semitic supporters of Hitler's efforts to kill the Jews? Military and civilian leaders without conscience or moral concerns?

As Pieter Geyl, the great Dutch historian, once wrote, "History is indeed an argument without end." My effort is not a definitive answer to those criticisms and questions, but I will try to offer a point of view that tries to frame the discussion in the context of the realities of World War II, putting events, values, and attitudes in their time and place.

### Before the Holocaust, 1933–1941

Five weeks after Adolf Hitler became chancellor of Germany in 1933, Franklin Roosevelt became president of the United States. Roosevelt's loathing of the whole Nazi regime was known the moment he took office. Alone among the leaders of the world, he stood in opposition to Hitler from the very beginning. In a book published in 1937, Winston Churchill—to whom free humanity everywhere must be eternally indebted and without whose courage and strength the defeat of Nazi Germany could never have been achieved—described Hitler's treatment of the Jews, stating that "concentration camps pock-mark the German soil" and concluding his essay by writing that "the world lives on hopes that the worst is over and that we may live to see Hitler a gentler figure in a happier age." Roosevelt had no such hopes. He never wavered in his belief that the malignancy of Hitler and his followers had to be destroyed. Thomas Mann, perhaps the most famous of the non-Jewish refugees from the Nazis, met with FDR at the White House in 1935 and afterwards confided that for the first time he believed the Nazis would be beaten because in Roosevelt he had met someone who truly understood the evil of Adolf Hitler.

To understand those years, we must differentiate between the German Jews who were the immediate and constant subjects of Hitler's persecution and the Jews of central Europe who were the principal victims of the Holocaust. The Jews of Germany numbered about 525,000 in 1933. They were the yeast of Germany's great culture—leaders in literature, music, medicine, science, in its financial and intellectual life. For the most part, they wanted to be thought of as Germans. They had been a proud part of Germany's army in World War I. Anti-Semitism shadowed their lives, but they thought of Germany as *their* country and were deeply rooted in its existence. "We are either Germans, or without a country," said a leading Jewish writer. They witnessed Hitler's coming to power with disbelief and saw Nazi dominance as a temporary phenomenon. In the face of Nazi persecution, those who left Germany did so reluctantly, many seeking refuge in neighboring countries from which they expected to return to Germany when the Hitler madness subsided. In the early years, many—if not most—believed Hitler and his regime could not survive.

In his autobiography, Rabbi Stephen Wise, one of the most powerful and respected leaders of the American Jewish community during that era, and a personal friend and close adviser of President Roosevelt, tells how when he organized a New York rally in March 1933 to protest Nazi treatment of Jews, he received a message from leading German rabbis urging him to cut out such meetings and in a most insulting way indicating that American Jews were doing this for their own purposes and in the process were destroying the Germany that the German Jews loved. Rabbi Wise never wavered in his belief that the only option for the Jews was to leave Germany. As the Nazi persecution intensified, as the Nuremberg Laws degraded the Jews as nothing had before, as Hitler strove to cause their emigration and confiscated Jewish property and wealth, the prospect of escape and exile had to shadow every Jewish family. In 1934, 37,000 Jews fled Germany—but in the relative calm of the next year, 16,000 returned. The good and brave chief rabbi of Berlin, Leo Baeck, opposed mass emigration, setting a personal example of not abandoning his community, surviving even the horror of a wartime concentration camp. Every Jewish group affirmed the right of Jews to be German, to live in and love their country; they affirmed the legal right, the moral necessity, and the religious imperative of not surrendering to the pagan persecutors. As important as any barriers to immigration in Western countries was the attitude of not wanting to leave Germany until absolutely necessary. *It is crucial to our understanding of these years to remember that at the time no one inside or outside of Germany anticipated that the Nazi persecution would lead to the Holocaust.* As Gerhard Weinberg has cogently written, the actions of the German government were generally understood, by both the victims and the bystanders, as a return to the kinds of persecutions and restrictions imposed on Jews in prior centuries, not as steps on the road toward genocide.

The annexation of Austria, the appeasement of the Nazis represented by the Munich pact, and especially Kristallnacht in November 1938 changed the situation dramatically. Especially Kristallnacht. The assassination of a German diplomat in Paris by a seventeen-year-old Jewish youth, whose father had been among the thousands of Polish Jews expelled from Germany and dumped across the Polish border just weeks before, sparked an orgy of arson and looting by Nazi thugs in almost every town and city. Huge, silent crowds looked on. The police did nothing to contain the violence. Many German Jews for the first time understood the hopelessness of their situation.

The America that elected Franklin Delano Roosevelt its president in 1932 was a deeply troubled country. Twenty-five percent of its work force was unemployed—and this at a time when practically every member of that work force was the principal support of a family. The economy was paralyzed; despair hung heavy on the land. Disillusion with Europe after the sacrifices of the First World War encouraged profound isolationist sentiments.

The immigration laws of the United States had been established by legislation in 1921 and 1924 under Presidents Harding and Coolidge and by a Congress that had rejected the League of Nations and defined the new isolationism. Congress controlled the immigration laws and carefully monitored their implementation. A formula assigned a specific quota to countries based on population origins of Americans resident in the United States in 1890. The law was aimed at eastern Europeans, particularly from Russia and Poland, which were seen as seedbeds of Bolshevik revolution. Italians were a target, and Asians were practically excluded. The total number of immigrants that could be admitted annually was set at 153,774.[3] The two countries with the highest quotas were Great Britain (65,721) and Germany (25,957). As the Depression took hold, President Hoover tightened regulations by mandating that no immigrant could be admitted who might become a public charge. The Depression also encouraged an unusual coalition of liberal and conservative forces, labor unions and business leaders, who opposed any enlargement of the immigration quotas, an attitude that Congress adamantly supported. The overwhelming majority of Americans agreed with Congress, opposing the increased admission of immigrants, insisting that refugees be included in the quotas of countries from which they were fleeing. Jewish refugees from Germany, because of the relatively large German quota, had an easier time than anti-Communist refugees from the Soviet Union, not to mention the Chinese who were victims of Japan's aggression, or the Armenians, or the Spanish fleeing a civil war where 500,000 were killed between 1936 and 1939. Spain's annual quota, for example, was 252.

President and Mrs. Roosevelt were leaders in the effort to help those fleeing Nazi persecution. Eleanor Roosevelt was a founder in 1933 of the International Rescue Committee, which brought intellectuals, labor leaders, and political figures escaping Hitler to sanctuary in the United States. President Roosevelt made a public point of inviting many of them to the White House. In 1936, in response to the Nazi confiscation of personal assets as a precondition to Jewish emigration, Roosevelt greatly modified Hoover's ruling regarding financial sponsorship for refugees, thereby allowing a substantially greater number of visas to be issued. *As a result, the United States accepted twice the number of Jewish refugees taken by the rest of the world combined.* As Professor Weinberg has stated, Roosevelt acted in the face of strong and politically damaging criticism for what was generally considered a pro-Jewish attitude by him personally and by his administration.

Hitler's policy never wavered in trying to force the Jews to leave Germany. After the Anschluss in Austria, Roosevelt, on March 25, 1938, called for an international conference on the refugee crisis. Austria's 185,000 Jews were now also in jeopardy. The conference met in Evian, France. There was no political advantage for Roosevelt in calling for a conference "to facilitate the emigration from Germany and Austria of political refugees." No other major political leader in any country matched his concern and involvement. The Evian Conference tried to open new doors in the Western Hemisphere. The Dominican Republic, for example, offered sanctuary to 100,000 refugees. The devastating blow at Evian was the message from the Polish and Romanian governments that they expected the same right as the Germans to expel their Jewish populations. There were fewer than 475,000 Jews left

in Germany and Austria at this point—a number manageable in an emigration plan that the twenty-nine participating nations could prepare; but
with the possibility of 3.5 million more from eastern Europe, the concern
now was that any offer of help would only encourage authoritarian governments to brutalize any unwanted portion of their populations, expecting their criminal acts against their own citizens to force the democracies to
give them haven. The German emigration problem was manageable. Forced
emigration from eastern Europe was not. *The Nazi genocide was in the
future—and unimaginable to the Jews and probably at the time unimagined
by the Nazis.* National attitudes then were not very different than today's.
No country allows any and every refugee to enter without conditions. Quotas are thought even now to deter unscrupulous and impoverished regimes
from forcing their unwanted people on other countries.

The Evian Conference failed except to organize the Inter-Governmental
Committee (IGC), to pressure the Germans to allow Jewish refugees to leave
with enough resources to begin their new lives. It led to direct negotiations
between Hjalmar Schacht, head of the Reichsbank, and George Rublee, a distinguished Washington lawyer personally designated by FDR. Schacht proposed that 150,000 Jews be allowed to emigrate taking 25 percent of their
assets with them, the rest impounded in a trust fund that would serve as col-
lateral on bonds to be issued by the German state. It was an effort by Schacht
to resolve Germany's foreign exchange crisis. Hitler abruptly ordered the end
of the discussions. The negotiations, like all barter negotiations in the years
ahead, failed because Hitler would never allow them to succeed.

By the end of 1938, Kristallnacht had happened. Its impact on the Jews
of Germany and Austria was overwhelming. Munich was a tragic reality.
Truncated Czechoslovakia would last six months before Hitler broke his
promise and occupied the rest of the country. The German Jews at last understood the barbarism of the Nazis—and that Hitler was totally in power.
America's reaction to Kristallnacht was stronger than any of the democracies. Roosevelt recalled his ambassador from Germany. For the first time
since the First World War an American president had summoned home an
ambassador to a major power under such circumstances. At his press conference then, Roosevelt said: "I myself can scarcely believe that such things
could occur in a twentieth-century civilization." He extended the visitors'
visas of 20,000 Germans and Austrians in the United States so they would
not have to return. The reaction of Americans in opinion polls showed overwhelming anger and disgust with the Nazis and sympathy for the Jews.
Roosevelt remained the target of the hardcore anti-Semites in America. He
welcomed them as enemies, and, in brilliant maneuvering, he isolated them

from mainstream America and essentially equated their anti-Semitism with treason and the destruction of both the national interest and the national defense. Recognizing the inertia, frequent hostility, and sometime anti-Semitism in the State Department, he entrusted Sumner Welles, the undersecretary of state and a person totally sympathetic to Jewish needs, to be his instrument of action.

Immigration procedures were complicated and sometimes harshly administered. The immigration laws and quotas were jealously guarded by Congress, supported by a strong, broad cross section of Americans who were against all immigrants, not only Jews. Of course, there were racists and anti-Semites in Congress and in the country—there are today; only now, after eighty years of government based on liberal values, they dare not speak their true attitudes. The State Department, which jealously guarded its administrative authority in the granting of visas, was frequently more concerned with congressional attitudes and criticisms than in reflecting American decency and generosity in helping people in despair and panic. Roosevelt undoubtedly made a mistake in appointing and continuing in office Breckenridge Long as assistant secretary of state. Many allege Long was an anti-Semite. Others argue "that he was in an impossible situation with an insurmountable task." His presence at State was an assurance to Congress that the immigration laws would be strictly enforced. On the other hand, there were countless Foreign Service officers who did everything possible to help persecuted, innocent people—just as they would today. There was an attitude that there were many sanctuaries available in the world besides the United States, so the Department, controlled by a career, conservative elite, in large part anti–New Deal and anti-FDR, was quite prepared to make congressional attitudes, rather than the attitudes of the White House, the guide for their administration of immigration procedures. Congress looked at the turmoil in Germany as a European problem in which it did not want America to be involved. Nevertheless, between 1933 and 1941, 35 percent of all immigrants to America under quota guidelines were Jewish. After Kristallnacht, Jewish immigrants were more than one half of *all* immigrants admitted to the United States. Of course, there were other countries of refuge, many of them preferred by German Jews, who, like everyone else, did not foresee the Nazi madness of conquest and extermination and who wanted to stay in Europe. Public opinion everywhere in the democracies was repelled by the Nazi persecution. Great Britain, for example, after Kristallnacht granted immigration visas essentially without limit. In the first six months of 1939, 91,780 German and Austrian Jews were admitted to England, often as a temporary port en route to the dominions or other parts of the Commonwealth.

Roosevelt from the beginning saw the larger threat of the Nazis. Hitler wanted to present Germany as the champion of a universal struggle against the Jews and Bolshevism. Roosevelt would not let him. The president understood that he had to explain the vital interest that all Americans had in stopping Hitler in terms of their own security. He pressured the Europeans to respond to Hitler. His speech in 1937 calling for the quarantine of the aggressors was met with political hostility at home and abroad. He was constantly seeking havens for the refugees in other countries, knowing that he did not have the power to change the quota system of our own country. His critics refused to acknowledge limitations on presidential power, but clearly the president could not unilaterally command an increase in quotas. In fact, the Democratic congressional leaders, including Representative Dickstein, who chaired the House subcommittee on immigration, warned him that reactionary forces in Congress might well use any attempt to increase the quotas as an opportunity *to reduce them.* The *New York Times* of February 27, 1939, reports a speech by Congressman Emmanuel Celler of Brooklyn, an outspoken defender of Jewish interests, in which he warned that "it would be dangerous at this time because of public opinion in the South and West to press for the passage in Congress of [Celler's] bills to give asylum in the United States to refugees and to re-allot for refugees the unused quotas of various countries." Congressman Celler said he had been warned by representatives from other parts of the country that if he pressed his proposals, other bills "to cut the quotas in half or to stop all immigration would be introduced and probably passed." Nor were the Jews the only refugees Congress was determined to bar. The *New York Times* of March 2, 1939, reports a speech by the Reverend Joseph Ostermann, executive director of the Committee for Catholic Refugees from Germany, saying that there were 500,000 actual or potential Catholic refugees whom "Goebbels and Rosenberg in Germany have attempted to identify with communism."

Seventy-two percent of all German Jews had emigrated before further emigration became impossible with the beginning of the war. Eighty-three percent of all German Jews under twenty-one emigrated. There are many reasons why the others did not get out—some were too old to leave, some believed it their religious duty to stay, some were in concentration camps and prisons, some just did not know what to do. Émigrés were plundered of virtually all of their assets, and not until Jews faced the reality of terrorism and imprisonment were many of them prepared to give up their family's wealth and everything that they had worked for all of their lives.

In his painfully eloquent book, *Bound upon a Wheel of Fire*, John Dipple writes:

> Yes, there *were* tight restrictions on entering into the United States and other countries, but were Germany's Jews really blocked by them before 1938? Most evidence suggests that the Jews could have circumvented these obstacles in greater numbers if they had wanted to escape Germany badly enough, if they had grasped the desperateness of their plight earlier on. But they had not. Despite everything, Germany was still their home. And, despite almost everything they were prepared to stay there.

*It is important to say over and over again, that it was a time and a place when no one foresaw the events that became the Holocaust.* Louis de Jong, an eminent Dutch historian and Holocaust survivor, said in his Erasmus lecture at Harvard University in 1989:

> [There is] an aspect of the Holocaust which is of cardinal importance and which can never be sufficiently underlined: that the Holocaust, when it took place, was beyond the belief and the comprehension of almost all people living at the time, Jews included. Everyone knew that human history had been scarred by endless cruelties. But that thousands, nay millions, of human beings—men, women and children, the old and the young, the healthy and the infirm—would be killed, finished off, mechanically, industrially so to speak, would be exterminated like vermin—that was a notion so alien to the human mind, an event so gruesome, so *new*, that the instinctive, indeed the natural, reaction of most people was: it can't be true.[4]

Given the reality of the Holocaust, all of us in every country—and certainly in America—can only wish that we would have done more, that our immigration barriers had been less, that our Congress had had a broader worldview, that every public servant had reflected the attitudes of Franklin and Eleanor Roosevelt. If anyone had foreseen the Holocaust, perhaps—possibly—maybe—but no one did. Nevertheless, the United States, a nation remote from the world in a way our children can hardly understand—*the United States accepted double the number of Jewish refugees taken by the rest of the world.*

Among the anguishing events we read about is the fate of the ship the *SS St. Louis* of the Hamburg-America Line, which left Germany and arrived in

Cuba on May 27, 1939, with 936 passengers, 930 of them Jewish refugees. This was three months before the outbreak of the war, and three years before the establishment of the death camps. Other ships had made the same journey, and their passengers disembarked successfully, but on May 5 the Cuban government had issued a decree curtailing the power of the corrupt director general of immigration to issue landing certificates. The new regulations requiring $500 bonds from each approved immigrant had been transmitted to the shipping line, but only twenty-two passengers on the *St. Louis* had fulfilled the requirements before leaving Hamburg on May 13. The twenty-two were allowed to land, but intense negotiations with the Cuban government regarding the other passengers—negotiations in which American Jewish agencies participated—broke down despite pressure from our government. It was not an unreported event. Tremendous international attention focused on the *St. Louis*, later made famous in the movie *Voyage of the Damned*. Secretary of State Cordell Hull, Secretary of the Treasury Henry Morgenthau Jr., and others, including Eleanor Roosevelt, worked to avoid the harsh reality of the immigration laws, for example, by attempting to land the passengers as "tourists" in the Virgin Islands. Despite the legal inability of the United States to accept the passengers of the *St. Louis* as immigrants, our diplomats were significantly helpful in resettling them. *None—not one— of the passengers of the SS St. Louis were returned to Nazi Germany*. They were all resettled in democratic countries—288 in the United Kingdom, the rest in France, the Netherlands, Belgium, and Denmark. Some years ago, I interviewed a survivor of the *St. Louis*, a retired professor of human genetics at the University of Washington in Seattle. His father had arrived in Cuba in early 1939. The rest of the family were to join him and were passengers on the *St. Louis*. He described Captain Shroeder of the *St. Louis* as a compassionate man who ordered decent treatment for his Jewish passengers and who told them that he would run his ship aground off of England to assure their sanctuary rather than return them to Germany if Cuba refused admission. The Motulsky family disembarked in Belgium. After an extraordinary saga all of them eventually reached the United States. Their story gives a very different perspective on the voyage of the *St. Louis* than is frequently described or written now.

What were Franklin Roosevelt's own attitudes toward Hitler and the Jews? Did he reflect the social anti-Semitism that was endemic in the America of that era? Contemporary Jews knew that they had never had a better friend, a more sympathetic leader in the White House. Roosevelt opened the offices of government as never before to Jews. Henry Morgenthau Jr., Samuel Rosenman, Felix Frankfurter, Benjamin Cohen, David Niles, Anna

Rosenberg, Sidney Hillman, and David Dubinsky were among his closest advisers in politics and government. Rabbi Stephen Wise, the preeminent spokesman for American Zionism, and his daughter, Justine Polier, were personal friends of Franklin and Eleanor Roosevelt, with as much access to the White House as anyone. Rabbi Wise described FDR by saying, "No one was more genuinely free from religious prejudice and racial bigotry." He recalls in March 1933 how "Roosevelt's soul rebelled at the Nazi doctrine of superior and inferior races," and how in March 1945, days before his death, Roosevelt spoke movingly of his determination to establish "a free and democratic Jewish commonwealth in Palestine."

## The Holocaust, 1941–1945

The persecution of the Jews and their emigration from Germany were the prelude to the Holocaust. Nazi policy changed radically after the outbreak of war. The possibility of emigration ended. Germany's Jews were now prisoners. The Holocaust—the systematic killing of 6 million Jews—took place between 1941 and 1945. The likelihood is that Hitler did not expect Britain and France to go to war over Poland. The Hitler-Stalin pact announced on August 24, 1939, stunned the world. The Soviets had been enemies of Hitler, and this was a rallying point for millions around the world who saw in them the only military force that might confront the Nazis. Suddenly, however, the Soviets and Germany ended their threats toward each other and divided Poland, Hitler gaining *Lebensraum* and Stalin gaining a buffer zone from the Nazi armies he never trusted. Also in the package were more than 3 million Polish Jews, caught between Nazi brutality and Soviet degradation. Seemingly at peace on his eastern flank, occupying Austria, Czechoslovakia, and western Poland, essentially dominant in central Europe through satellite Fascist movements, Hitler moved to the west, occupying Norway, Denmark, Belgium, Luxemburg, and the Netherlands—and again stunning the world by conquering France in a six-week blitzkrieg. France surrendered in June 1940. Mussolini's Italy became Hitler's active ally. Franco, in a Spain prostrated by devastating civil war, owed his victory to Hitler's support. Great Britain stood alone. Its new prime minister, Winston Churchill, expressed the defiance of Britain and its empire, but Britain, facing invasion, desperately in need of arms, shaken by devastating Nazi bombings, looked to America for help and hope. Our debt to the British can never be adequately expressed. It was their "finest hour"—they salvaged the fate of freedom.

In 1939, Roosevelt received a letter from Albert Einstein. FDR understood the message that new scientific discoveries would allow the development of atomic power, threatening a force that could destroy the world—or at least win the war for whichever nation *first* became its master. Roosevelt's decision to launch the Manhattan Project, giving it whatever resources it needed for success, began the nuclear age. It was as fateful a decision as any president has ever made. Hitler had the same option. German scientists were certainly capable of producing atomic weapons. Hitler had all of the necessary resources, but he failed to pursue his option, not comprehending as Roosevelt did that the future of the world was at stake.

As Roosevelt won an unprecedented third term as president, he—better than any American—understood what lay ahead. He had confronted the economic collapse of the United States, but recovery was slow and painful. Now he faced the political collapse of Europe, the military collapse of China, and totalitarian governments in Germany and Japan that threatened America as never before. Nazi Germany, possessed of the most modern, best-trained, best-equipped military force in recorded history, occupied western and central Europe, confident that Hitler's dream of conquest would soon include Great Britain, the Soviet Union—and ultimately the United States itself. Roosevelt's priority was to repeal the Neutrality Act so that he could provide help to Britain. In 1940—with Europe under Hitler's boot—*US military strength ranked as seventeenth in the world, behind Portugal.* We led the world in the production of automobiles but had practically no munitions industry. Whereas Hitler had invaded Belgium and the Netherlands supported by 136 fully equipped divisions, America could barely muster five divisions. Nevertheless, isolationist sentiment remained powerful, fully reflected in Congress. Three months before Pearl Harbor, in September 1941, the continuation of the Selective Service program was sustained by a single vote in the House of Representatives. Roosevelt undid the public image that the isolationists had projected of themselves as peace-loving patriots. His persistent attacks on them turned the tide of public opinion. At great political risk in the midst of a presidential campaign, Roosevelt engineered the deal that sent fifty desperately needed overage destroyers to Britain, an action that helped save its lifeline from the unremitting attacks of German submarines. Hitler called it a belligerent act. It was. Roosevelt proposed Lend Lease—and built a bipartisan coalition to gain its congressional approval. He announced the Four Freedoms as the goal that would justify the terrible sacrifices that lay ahead. He met with Winston Churchill. They announced the Atlantic Charter, the blueprint for the survival of democracy. All this—and America was not yet at war. Nor had the genocide of Europe's Jews yet begun. America's isolationists continued to believe that the United States was protected from harm by the two vast oceans that separated it from Hitler's Europe and Japan's militarism. President Roosevelt believed otherwise. Pearl Harbor would prove Roosevelt's judgment correct—and give him a united country to mobilize for victory.

Hitler's conquest of the European continent let loose the full force of his psychopathic obsession about Jews. With the start of the war on September 1, 1939, emigration from Germany was prohibited. Hundreds, perhaps thousands of German Jews escaped across borders into Holland, Belgium, and Switzerland. But by June 1940, with the fall of France, Europe became a prison for the Jews. Unoccupied France was still an escape route. Despite intense criticism from the political Left, FDR continued to maintain diplomatic relations with Vichy, France—which allowed the escape route to remain open. The International Rescue Committee—a group of which Eleanor Roosevelt remained very supportive—sent a team headed by Varian Fry that helped countless refugees find sanctuary in Spain and Portugal. But the vise was tightening. With the invasion of Russia on June 22, 1941, the lock was put on the most terrible dungeon in history. Special squads of the German SS—the Einsatzgruppen—began the slaughter of 1.5 million Jews behind the German lines in Russia. The Wannsee Conference, which structured the "Final Solution," was held in the suburbs of Berlin in January 1942. The Holocaust was underway.

The Jews of central Europe, the Jews from the occupied nations of western Europe, the Jews of the Soviet Union—the principal victims of the Holocaust—were not refugees either before or after 1939. They were prisoners in a vast prison from which there was no escape and no possible rescue. They were not subject to Nazi rule or persecution prior to the war, and few imagined that they ever would be, let alone that they would be murdered in history's greatest genocide. Just as German Jews imagined that Hitler and Nazi rule would pass quickly, Jews outside of Germany did not imagine themselves in mortal danger. Zionism was not a dominant force in their communities. In 1936, in the Jewish community elections in Poland—the most highly organized Jewish community in Europe—the Social Democratic Bund won a sweeping victory on a pledge of "unyielding hostility to Zionism." Their leaders wanted Polish Jews to remain in Poland. The policies of the Soviet Union forbade emigration. In the Netherlands, a country whose Jewish population suffered a greater percentage loss in the extermination camps than any other in western Europe, not more than 679 individuals, Jews and Gentiles, migrated in any one year before 1940, far less than the Dutch quota would have allowed. The assumption was that Hitler would respect Dutch neutrality just as the Kaiser had in the First World War. Once Hitler's armies marched, the Jews of

Nazi-occupied Europe no longer had the possibility of being refugees. Individuals could and did attempt escape, and through their bravery and the extraordinary courage of those who helped them, they made it to freedom, often at great cost to those left behind. For the overwhelming number, it was now too late. They were prisoners. And only the physical liberation of their prisons—the extermination camps of central Europe—could save their lives.

The doors had been closed, not by the United States or its allies, but by Hitler. Jews were now prisoners of a psychopath who was also the absolute dictator of Europe. On January 30, 1942, Hitler, speaking to the Reichstag, said, "This war can end in two ways—either the extermination of the Aryan peoples or the disappearance of Jewry from Europe." Since the mid-1920s, Hitler had never voluntarily spoken to a Jew. He allowed himself no contact with them. He was the most determined ideologue of racial superiority and racial conflict who ever led a country—and Germany in 1940 was the most powerful country on earth. He was more extreme than anyone around him. His central obsession, the life's mission of this deranged, monomaniacal psychopath, was to kill as many Jews as he could. Nothing diminished this mission—not the defeat of his armies, not the destruction of his country. As Germany lay in ruins, as the demented dictator prepared to end his life in his bunker in Berlin, his Nazi acolytes continued his mission above all else, diverting even urgently needed reinforcements for his retreating armies to complete the assignment of the Final Solution. The extermination camps were the efficient mechanisms of these disciplined lunatics—but 2 million Jews were murdered before Auschwitz was opened, and after it was closed in November 1944, hundreds of thousands more were shot, strangled, or starved to death.

The prisoners of Hitler could be saved only by the total, unconditional surrender of Nazi Germany, and that was a task that required four years and the unprecedented mobilization of all of the resources, human and material, of Great Britain, the Soviet Union, and the United States.

Some critics of America and President Roosevelt say the news of the annihilation of Europe's Jews was deliberately kept secret so that our people would not know about it—and if Americans had been aware of the Final Solution, they would have insisted on doing more than what was done. They suggest that anti-Semitism in the State Department—or elsewhere or everywhere in our government and in our country—determined that news of the extermination process be kept secret. The facts are otherwise. President Roosevelt, Winston Churchill, General Eisenhower, General Marshall, the intelligence services of the Allied nations, every Jewish leader, the Jewish communities in America, Britain, and Palestine, and yes, anyone who had a radio or newspaper in 1942 knew that Jews in colossal numbers were being murdered.[5] They may have received the news with disbelief. There was no precedent for it in human history. But the general information of the genocide was broadly available to anyone who would read or listen. The famous telegram from Gerhart Riegner, a representative of the World Jewish Congress in Switzerland in August 1942, was not even the first knowledge that a death camp *later* to become known as Auschwitz, with its gas chambers and ghastly crematoria, had been built—but Auschwitz, like every extermination camp, was treated as a top-secret project by the Nazis. We publicized what we knew, but the Nazis tried to keep as much information as possible away from everybody. The names, locations, and procedures of the death camps may not have been known—some not until the end of the war—but the fact of the genocide and the Nazi determination to carry it out were not in doubt.

When Sumner Welles confirmed the truth of the Riegner telegram to Rabbi Wise, the rabbi wept—as countless Jews and non-Jews would do in those terrible years when the Nazis were beyond the reach of the armies that would defeat them. Encouraged by Welles to hold a press conference to announce the terrible news, Rabbi Wise did so on November 28, 1942. His announcement of the Nazi plan to annihilate Europe's Jews was widely reported. Rabbi Wise and his colleagues met with the president. They asked the president to warn Hitler and the Germans that they would be held individually responsible for what they were doing to the Jews. Roosevelt agreed immediately. An announcement to that effect in the name of the United Nations was made in Congress and in Britain's Parliament on December 17, 1942. It was repeated many times throughout the war. Parliament for the first time in its history stood in silence to mourn what was happening to the Jews, to pray for the strength needed to destroy the Nazi barbarians. In America, labor unions led the nation in a ten-minute period of mourning for the Jews of Europe. Who can possibly argue that there was a conspiracy of silence regarding the fate of Europe's Jews when America's most popular broadcaster, Edward R. Murrow, listened to by millions, *on December 13, 1942,* reported: "Millions of human beings, most of them Jews, are being gathered up with ruthless efficiency and murdered. . . . It is a picture of mass murder and moral depravity unequaled in the history of the world. It is a horror beyond what imagination can grasp. . . . The Jews are being systematically exterminated throughout all Poland. . . . There are no longer 'concentration camps'—we must speak now only of 'extermination camps.'" Six months earlier, on June 30, 1942, the *New York Times* had already carried a report from the World Jewish Congress that the Germans had by that date already massacred 1 million Jews, that the Nazis had established a "vast slaughterhouse for Jews" in eastern Europe.

American Jewry was not a passive observer of these events, cowering in silence for fear of letting loose waves of anti-Semitism in America. Despite issues that bitterly divided them, primarily relating to Palestine, the Jewish community in America spoke the same words in pleading to do whatever was possible to reach out to Europe's Jews. Plan after plan was produced to rescue the Jews of Europe. Jewish leaders lobbied Congress. Mass rallies were held across the country with overflow crowds throughout those years, praying, pleading for action to stop the genocide we now know as the Holocaust. The unremitting, remorseless massacre of the Jews—carefully concealed by top-secret arrangements of the Nazi murderers—continued because no one, no nation, no alliance of nations, could do anything meaningful to close down the death camps except, as President Roosevelt said over and over again, by winning the war and destroying the Nazis with absolute determination as soon as possible.

President Roosevelt gave frequent audience to Jewish leaders. He sent messages to rallies of Jews across the country. He listened to every plea and proposal for rescue that came to him—but he knew that although the diversion of resources from the unyielding purpose of defeating the Nazi armies might satisfy the desperate anguish felt by so many, no one would be rescued and the rescuers in all likelihood would themselves be killed.

As Richard Lichtheim, a representative of the World Jewish Congress in Switzerland and a hero in informing the world of the genocide, said in December 1942, "You cannot divert a tiger from devouring his prey by adopting resolutions or sending cables. You have to take your gun and shoot him." Franklin Roosevelt understood that, and he mobilized in America an arsenal of such strength that the world would still marvel fifty years later at how the miracle was accomplished.

The only meaningful way to save the intended victims of Hitler's murder machine was to win the war as quickly as possible. Professor Weinberg answers the cynics who question America's policy by suggesting to them that they consider how many more Jews would have survived had the war ended even a week or ten days earlier—and conversely, how many more would have died had the war lasted an additional week or ten days. Given the determination of the Germans to fight on to the bitter end, and knowing what Roosevelt understood then and what all of us should know now—that

Hitler would never let the Jews go, that until his dying day his obsession was their destruction, that the slaughter of the Jews went on into the final moments of the Third Reich, that every day until the final surrender there were thousands of deaths by murder, starvation, and disease—we should know with certainty that the number saved by winning the war as quickly as possible was vastly greater than the total number of Jews who could be saved by any rescue efforts proposed by anyone from 1941 to 1945.

Serious proposals for rescue and response were not disregarded. For example, on September 16, 1944, the Hebrew Committee of National Liberation (HCNL) proposed to the State Department that a warning be issued "stating that unless the practice of using poison gas against the Hebrew people ceases forthwith, retaliation in kind will be immediately ordered against Germany." The State Department forwarded the recommendation to the Joint Chiefs of Staff of the Armed Forces (JCS). A detailed senior JCS staff memorandum responded that such a warning would be disastrous, that the Nazis would continue their genocidal program, and the proposed retaliation would unleash unrestricted gas warfare, resulting in heavy civilian and military losses. The "poison gas" proposal is worth mentioning here if only for the insight that it gives into the profound schism among Jewish organizations as they responded to the genocide in Europe. Attitudes toward Zionism and the future of Palestine were at the core of the conflict. As Rabbi Wise and Rabbi Abba Hillel Silver and Joseph Proskauer spoke for the mainstream Jewish organizations, Peter Bergson emerged as their enemy. When Bergson announced the creation of the HCNL on May 18, 1944, it was immediately denounced in a statement by a coordinated group of major Jewish organizations as a "colossal hoax" promulgated by "half a dozen adventurers from Palestine with no standing, no credentials, no mandate from anyone unless from the Irgun Zevai Leumi in Palestine, an insignificantly small, pistol-packing group of extremists who are claiming credit for the recent terror outrages." The HCNL was seen as supported by the Irgun, the extremist underground army that had declared war on the British Mandate in Palestine and regarded Great Britain and Ben-Gurion as enemies along with Nazi Germany. Chaim Weizmann and David Ben-Gurion were pioneer Zionists who were prepared to negotiate the creation of a Jewish state. They were sensitive to British responsibilities and Arab rights while believing that the Nazi assault on Europe's Jews made the need for a Jewish state ever more urgent. The Bergson/Begin/Irgun movement accepted war on the British and the Arabs even in the context of World War II as a legitimate means to accomplish the creation of a Jewish state.

The proposal to bomb Auschwitz in 1944 has become the symbol for those who argue American indifference and complicity in the Holocaust. Some would have us believe that many American Jewish groups petitioned our government to bomb Auschwitz. In fact, there was considerable Jewish opposition both in the United States and in Palestine. The focal center of the Holocaust Museum's exhibit on bombing Auschwitz is a letter from Leon Kubowitzki, head of the Rescue Department of the World Jewish Congress, in which he forwarded, without endorsement, a request from the Czech State Council (in exile in London) to the War Department in August 1944 to bomb Auschwitz. Much is made of John McCloy's response to Mr. Kubowitzki explaining the War Department's decision not to undertake such a mission. What is not on display and rarely mentioned is a letter dated July 1, 1944, from the same Leon Kubowitzki to the executive director of the War Refugee Board arguing *against* bombing Auschwitz because "the first victims would be the Jews" and the Allied air assault would serve as "a welcome pretext for the Germans to assert that their Jewish victims have been massacred not by their killers, but by Allied bombing."

Mainstream Jewish opinion was against the whole idea of bombing Auschwitz. The very thought of the Allied forces deliberately killing Jews—to open the gates of Auschwitz so the survivors could run where?—was abhorrent then as it is now. The Rescue Committee of the Jewish Agency in Jerusalem voted against even making the bombing request at a meeting with Ben-Gurion presiding. Although only President Roosevelt or General Eisenhower could have ordered the bombing of Auschwitz, there is no record of any kind that indicates that either one was ever asked or even heard of the proposal—even though Jewish leaders of all persuasions had clear access to them both.

We are talking about the summer of 1944. American forces were fully engaged with Japanese aggression across the total expanse of the Pacific Ocean. In Europe, the invasion of Normandy began on June 6. Despite the fact that two-thirds of the Nazi armies were on the Russian front, D-Day and an Allied success were by no means assured. The German armies were holding our forces at bay in Italy, causing heavy casualties, making us fight for every road and hill. The Allies were planning the invasion of southern France for August 15. America and our allies were stretched dangerously across western and southern Europe. The Allied bombing strategy was totally directed toward destroying Nazi fuel supplies, their synthetic oil industries, the oil fields of Romania, and their communication and transport lines wherever possible.

A seemingly more reasonable proposal to bomb the railways to Auschwitz was made to Anthony Eden, the British foreign minister, on July 6, 1944. Eden, with Churchill's immediate support, requested the RAF to examine the feasibility of doing so. The secretary of state for air, Sir Archibald Sinclair, replied several days later: "I entirely agree that it is our duty to consider every possible plan [to stop the murder of the Jews in Hungary] but I am advised that interrupting the railways is out of our power. It is only by an enormous concentration of bomber forces that we have been able to interrupt communications in Normandy; the distance of Silesia from our bases entirely rules out doing anything of the kind." John McCloy had replied to a similar suggestion weeks earlier: "The War Department is of the opinion that the suggested air operation is impracticable for the reason that it could only be executed with the diversion of considerable air support essential to the success of our forces now engaged in decisive operations." Even the severest critics of America's response to the Nazi murder of the Jews acknowledge that successful interruption of railways required close observation of the severed lines and frequent rebombing, since repairs took only a few days. Even bridges, which were costly to hit, were often back in operation in three or four days. Postwar studies of railway bombing totally vindicated the conclusion of the military authorities. Professor Istvan Deak of Columbia University has written: "And if the rail lines had been bombed? The inmates of the cattle cars and those at the departure points would have been allowed to die of thirst, or of the heat, or of the cold, while the lines were being repaired."[6]

It is often noted that American bombers carried out several raids in the summer of 1944 on industrial targets only a few miles away from Auschwitz. America's critics contend that this shows how easy it would have been to bomb the gas chambers. They do not mention that preparation for the D-Day invasion left only 12 percent of the US Army Air Forces available for the destruction of German fuel supplies, the primary mission as defined by General Spaatz. They point to the huge enlargements of reconnaissance photographs at the Holocaust Museum that show not only the Farben synthetic fuel plant—the target of the raids—but the outlines of Auschwitz and columns of prisoners. But they do not tell you that those aerial photographs of Auschwitz on display were not developed until 1978—and their details were only readable then because advanced technology, developed by the CIA more than twenty years after the end of World War II, made it possible. *All* such strategic raids on military-industrial bases proceeded only after months of preparatory intelligence work, entailing the creation of a target folder with specific information about the size, hardness, structure placement, and defenses of the target as well as detailed aerial photography.

These were costly, dangerous raids against heavily protected, frequently remote targets. The losses in men and planes were tragically heavy. The Allied
air forces totally lacked the intelligence base necessary to plan and execute
a bombing raid against the Auschwitz extermination camp. It would have
been a nonmilitary mission. Only Roosevelt or Eisenhower could have ordered it. No one—no one proposed it to them.

The War Refugee Board was created in January 1944 by President Roosevelt immediately upon presentation of the case for doing so by Henry Morgenthau. There were thousands of refugees stranded on the outer peripheries
of Nazi Europe. With the invasion of Italy in 1943, thousands more sought
safety in camps in the south. Tito's success in Yugoslavia enabled many to
escape from Croat Fascism and Serb hatred. *But these were refugees who
were already saved*. These were not escapees from the death camps. Under
pressure from Roosevelt and Churchill, Spain kept open its frontiers, stating
as its policy that "all refugees without exception would be allowed to enter
and remain." Probably more than 40,000 refugees, many of them Jewish,
found safe sanctuary in Spain. Makeshift transit camps in Spain, Portugal,
Italy, and North Africa housed them in abysmal conditions.

The most protected of the Jewish populations in central Europe were those
of Bulgaria, Hungary, and Romania, all nations that were Hitler's allies. Their
governments, although decidedly Fascist, had protected their indigenous populations as long as possible. But on March 19, 1944, the Nazi armies crossed
into Hungary. Adolf Eichmann and his henchmen were in the front rank of
that invasion, moving quickly and with brutal deliberation to organize the deportation of Hungary's Jews to Auschwitz. The Nazis had no greater priority.

What did the world know about Auschwitz in the spring of 1944? The
Nazis treated the location, facilities, and programs of Auschwitz as top secrets to be protected against general awareness by any means. More than
1.5 million people had already been killed in its gas chambers by the time
the Nazis invaded Hungary—and yet those closest to it still referred to Auschwitz as a "resettlement camp." As Martin Gilbert, the foremost British
expert on the Holocaust, has pointed out, the details and even the name
of Auschwitz were not confirmed until the escape of two prisoners in April
1944. The escape by Rudolf Vrba and Alfred Wetzler from Auschwitz and
their written report (known as the Auschwitz Protocols) describing in precise detail what had been and what was happening in the Nazis' principal
extermination camp brought the existence and purpose of Auschwitz to the
attention of those who could do something to save the Jews of Hungary.

Rudolf Vrba was nineteen years old in 1944. He had already spent more
than two years as a prisoner. He and his fellow Slovak, Alfred Wetzler,

understood what was happening when the Auschwitz facilities were ordered to be expanded in early 1944. The crematoria and brutal circumstances of death were being prepared for the hundreds of thousands of Hungarian Jews who had until that time been protected from this terrible fate. Vrba and Wetzler decided to escape to warn the world about what was truly happening in Auschwitz. They knew what their own fate would be if their attempted escape was discovered. They had witnessed the Nazis brutally and publicly murder hundreds who had tried to escape. It was because they knew the operations of Auschwitz so completely that they thought they could escape—and whatever the consequences, they were determined to try. They succeeded beginning on April 7, 1944.

Rudolf Vrba's book, *I Escaped from Auschwitz*, has given us the most extraordinary understanding of what Auschwitz was, how it operated, and its importance to the Nazis. Thanks to Vrba, we know that the Jewish Councils in both Slovakia and Hungary were well informed, on the basis of the detailed and graphic Vrba-Wetzler report, as early as the end of April 1944 about the preparations made in Auschwitz for the impending mass murder of the Hungarian Jews.

Until the Vrba-Wetzler report in April 1944, the real purpose of Auschwitz-Birkenau remained a secret to the outside world. Vrba, who met countless newly arrived prisoners during his two years in Auschwitz, never met one who had known anything about the gas chambers and the mass murders that preceded their arrival. Elie Wiesel has written: "We were taken [made prisoner] just two weeks before D-Day (June 6, 1944) and we did not know that Auschwitz existed. . . . Nobody cared enough to tell us: Don't go." Rudolf Vrba's escape sounded the warning, Tell the Hungarian Jews—Don't go! For six days after safely reaching Slovakia and establishing contact with the Jewish Council in Zilina, Vrba and Wetzler were cross-examined separately to establish the credibility of their story.

In his book, Rudolf Vrba describes his meeting in Slovakia with leaders of the Jewish Council:

> I gave them, in fact, the whole ghastly picture, the information I had been gathering so carefully for so long; and when I had finished, I repeated the very first words I had spoken to them: "One million Hungarians are going to die," I said. "Auschwitz is ready for them. But if you tell them now, they will rebel. They will never go to the ovens. Your turn is coming. But now it is the Hungarians' hour. You must tell them immediately."
>
> "Don't worry," [the Slovak leaders] said soothingly. "We are in daily contact with the Hungarian Jewish leaders. Your report will be in their hands first thing tomorrow."[7]

The date of the meeting was April 25, 1944. The next day, according to Rudolf Vrba, he asked these Slovak leaders whether they had sent his report to the Hungarians. Their reply: "Yes, it is in their hands. At this very minute, it is being examined by Doctor Kastner, the most important man in the whole Hungarian committee."

The final version of the report was completed on April 27. Vrba and Wetzler were identified only as "two young Jews." The mass deportation of Hungary's Jews was beginning. At the same time, the report had been delivered to Rudolf Kastner, a leader of the Jewish Council in Budapest.

As the Nazis invaded Hungary, Eichmann opened negotiations with Rudolf Kastner and several others of the Jewish Council in Budapest, ultimately arranging the transport of 1,682 members of their family and friends to Switzerland. The price for this was "a conspiracy of silence" regarding the true meaning of being sent for "resettlement" in Auschwitz. The testimony of survivors makes clear that the Jewish masses assumed that if something truly horrible was in store for them, these respectable leaders would know about it and would share their knowledge. These leaders—because of Vrba-Wetzler and perhaps before—knew exactly what Auschwitz was about but chose to be silent. It is not insignificant to know that Dr. Kastner intervened in the Nuremberg trials to save the lives (and fortunes) of Eichmann's three top deputies. After being the subject of a trial relating to his wartime activities, a trial that mesmerized Israel, Kastner's story came to an end with his murder in Israel in 1957.

Eminent historians confirm that the subsequent publication of the Vrba-Wetzler report in Switzerland, Great Britain, and the United States, as well as at the Vatican, was decisive in convincing Admiral Miklós Horthy's government to stop the deportation of Hungarian Jews in July 1944—undoubtedly saving the lives of the 500,000 remaining Jews in Hungary.

President Roosevelt's intervention with the government of Hungary, which by then understood that Nazi defeat was inevitable, the actions of the War Refugee Board, including retaining the heroic services of Raoul Wallenberg, and the bombing of the Budapest area—all played a role undoubtedly in the rescue of one half of the Jewish community in Hungary. President Roosevelt was deeply and personally involved in the effort to save the Jews of Hungary. He gave this statement to the nation on March 24, 1944:

In one of the blackest crimes of all history—begun by the Nazis in the days of peace and multiplied by them a hundred times in time of war—the wholesale systematic murder of the Jews of Europe goes on unabated every hour. As a result of the events of the last few days hundreds of thousands of Jews who, while living under persecution, have at least found a haven from death in Hungary and the Balkans, are now threatened with annihilation as Hitler's forces descend more heavily upon these lands. That these innocent people, who have already survived a decade of Hitler's fury, should perish on the very eve of triumph over the barbarism which their persecution symbolizes, would be a major tragedy. It is therefore fitting that we should again proclaim our determination that none who participate in these acts of savagery shall go unpunished. The United Nations have made it clear that they will pursue the guilty and deliver them up in order that justice be done. That warning applies not only to the leaders but also to their functionaries and subordinates in Germany and in the satellite countries. All who knowingly take part in the deportation of Jews to their death in Poland or Norwegians and French to their death in Germany are equally guilty with the executioner. All who share the guilt shall share the punishment.

In the meantime, and until the victory that is now assured is won, the United States will persevere in its efforts to rescue the victims of brutality of the Nazis and the Japanese. In so far as the necessity of military operations permit, this Government will use all means at its command to aid the escape of all intended victims of the Nazi and Japanese executioner—regardless of race or religion or color. We call upon the free peoples of Europe and Asia temporarily to open their frontiers to all victims of oppression. We shall find havens of refuge for them, and we shall find the means for their maintenance and support until the tyrant is driven from their homelands and they may return.

Despite the enormous evidence available to the world, no one understood what really had happened until they saw it for themselves. On the day Franklin Roosevelt died, April 12, 1945, General Eisenhower visited Ohrdruf Nord, the first concentration camp liberated by the American army. "The things I saw beggar description," he wrote General Marshall. According to his biographer Stephen Ambrose, "Eisenhower had heard ominous rumors about the camps, of course, but never in his worst nightmares had he dreamed they could be so bad." He sent immediately for a delegation of congressional leaders and newspaper editors. He wanted to be sure that Americans would never forget the depths of the Nazi horror. Five months later he dismissed his close friend and brilliant army commander General George Patton for using former Nazi officials in his occupation structure and publicly likening "the Nazi thing" to differences between the Republicans and Democrats. Patton had visited the Ohrdruf camp with Eisenhower and had become physically ill from what he had seen. Among the endless crimes of the Holocaust is the fact that so many Nazis escaped accountability for their crimes.

How ironic that our greatest president of the twentieth century—the man Hitler hated most, the leader constantly derided by anti-Semites, vilified by Goebbels as a "mentally ill cripple" and as "that Jew Rosenfeld," violently attacked by the isolationist press—how ironic that he should be faulted for being indifferent to the genocide. For all of us, the shadow of doubt that enough was not done will always remain, even if there was little more that could have been done. But it is the killers who bear the responsibility for their deeds. To say that "we are all guilty" allows the truly guilty to avoid that responsibility. We must remember for all the days of our lives that it was Hitler who imagined the Holocaust and the Nazis who carried it out. *We were not their accomplices. Under Franklin Delano Roosevelt's leadership, we destroyed them.*

We have to be particularly careful of issues that are deeply emotional, and we have to be especially concerned when such issues are used for political purposes. The accusation of American complicity in the Holocaust retains its resonance in part because the false assertions continue to be made, threatening the truth that is vital to our collective memory.

In 1999, the Holocaust survivor, Nobel Prize–winner, and laureate of the Four Freedoms Elie Wiesel published the final volume of his memoirs, *And the Sea Is Never Full*. In it, he described a meeting with President Jimmy Carter at the White House in 1978 in which, he claimed, Carter had given him reconnaissance photographs from CIA archives taken by American bombers flying over Auschwitz in the autumn of 1944 on their way to destroying the nearby IG Farben synthetic fuel plant. The photographs showed in grim detail newly arrived Jewish prisoners standing in line along the railroad tracks. Wiesel wrote that he then asked President Carter if those photos had been available to President Roosevelt at the time they were taken. Carter, Wiesel asserted, had replied, "Yes, they were." Wiesel continued his narrative by asking President Carter: "Then President Roosevelt couldn't help but know what was going on at Auschwitz?" "That is correct," he quoted the president as replying. Wiesel used this anecdote to advance the argument that because Roosevelt had known about the grim details of Auschwitz, he could and should have ordered a bombing attack on the camp.[8]

A retired engineer from Seattle named Richard Levy had also been deeply offended by the PBS documentary, particularly by accusations regarding the failure to bomb Auschwitz. He had done monumental research and analysis and had reached out to me at the Roosevelt Institute to share his work. In light of Wiesel's assertions, Levy suggested that I contact Robert Wolfe, the director of the Captured Records Division of the National Archives from 1963 to 1995.

I called Mr. Wolfe. We had extended conversations. Mr. Wolfe was as outraged as I about the misleading nature of Wiesel's account. He told me that the photographs given to Mr. Wiesel could not have been available to President Roosevelt for the simple reason that they were not even developed until 1978, and even if they had been, the technology of 1944 would not have revealed the details of Auschwitz. The photographs were developed in 1978 by the CIA's National Photographic Interpretation Center, using advanced technology not available during World War II. They were developed at the request of President Carter, who had invited Mr. Wiesel to the White House to encourage him to be chairman of the Holocaust Memorial Commission.

Concerned, I wrote to President Carter in January of 2001 asking if he could recollect the conversation with Elie Wiesel and confirm whether the photographs in question were the ones developed in 1978. After instructing his staff to investigate the matter, and after reviewing his personal diary notes of the time, President Carter assured me that "there is no record, nor do I have any recollection of my having given [Mr. Wiesel] photographs with a statement that President Roosevelt had access to them and must have known in 1944 what was going on at Auschwitz." "In any case," he continued, "this is a moot question because firm evidence seems to exist that the photographs were not developed until long after the president's death."

President Carter wrote to Elie Wiesel and myself explaining his conclusion that the Auschwitz photographs could never have been available to President Roosevelt because they were not developed until 1978. I called Elie to make sure that he had received the president's letter. He had. "We live and learn," he said to me. Such clear evidence made it difficult for me to understand why the libel that President Roosevelt knew about Auschwitz and deliberately did nothing would be repeated, as it was by

Mr. Wiesel on several occasions, as well as by Israeli prime minister Benjamin Netanyahu as recently as April 2017. At that time, two leading Israeli historians, Yehuda Bauer, an Israel Prize laureate and one of Israel's most eminent scholars of the Nazi genocide of European Jewry, and Moshe Zimmerman, the former director of Hebrew University's Richard Koebner Minerva Center for German History, decisively rejected Netanyahu's assertions about any alleged Allied unwillingness to save the Jews.

Why would any responsible person repeat this libel in the face of such clear evidence to the contrary? I do not have a plausible answer.

The FDR Presidential Library in Hyde Park, New York, has created a special archive (The Morgenthau Holocaust Archive) that has received the papers of Rudolf Vrba, the first prisoner to escape from Auschwitz (in April 1944.) I have no illusions that the debate will now be ended, but I also have no doubt that the integrity of Franklin D. Roosevelt will withstand any attack, and that these new contributions to the Holocaust Archive will sustain that point of view.

Franklin Roosevelt now belongs to the ages. He has been researched, written about, studied, examined, torn apart, and celebrated. No president other than Abraham Lincoln has had more written about him than Franklin Roosevelt. Historians today clearly regard him as the greatest president of the twentieth century.

We live in a world where facts and truth and history itself are under assault. My cherished friend Arthur Schlesinger Jr., on the occasion of a ceremony in his honor at the Century Association in December 2006 in New York, spoke the following words:

> It is useful to remember that history is to the nation as memory is to the individual. As persons deprived of memory become disoriented and lost, not knowing where they have been and where they are going, so a nation denied a conception of the past will be disabled in dealing with its present and its future.

Arthur's words give hope that the dangers faced by our democracy today will be challenged by a new generation willing to actively seek Truth, to become informed, to debate with civility, and to embrace the generosity of spirit needed to heal the divisions in our society and our nation.

# THE ROOSEVELT LEGACY

The Roosevelts have had a deep and personal impact on my life. It was Franklin Delano Roosevelt who, with his declaration of a mortgage moratorium, enabled us to refinance rather than lose my childhood home through foreclosure. FDR was the primary force in the creation of the United Nations; I had the privilege of serving as the United States ambassador to the United Nations in both Geneva and New York. As a youth, I took to heart Winston Churchill's description of Franklin Roosevelt as the greatest man he had ever known. President Roosevelt's life, Churchill said, "must be regarded as one of the commanding events in human destiny."[1]

Franklin Roosevelt was a New York patrician, a sophisticated and brilliant political representative of the Empire State, a disciplined and intensely private person. He knew triumph and defeat as he transformed the nation by a social revolution that made hope, opportunity, and justice for all Americans our national commitment. In war, he defined the presidency as our commander in chief and led America to its pinnacle of strength. He brought a united people to understand its responsibilities of international leadership. In August 1921, at the age of thirty-nine, Franklin Roosevelt was stricken with poliomyelitis (infantile paralysis.) It was an ordeal that many believe gave him the courage and character to become a great president, but the path to recovery was a tortured one, with many crises of despair and anguish. The next several years were dominated by his determination to learn to walk again. It became the focus of his life. His forays into public places were carefully planned. Two-thirds of his personal assets went into establishing the Warm Springs Foundation in Georgia. He transformed it into a major treatment center for polio victims. He created an enterprise that is today one of the most successful rehabilitation centers in the country. But he would never walk or stand again without help. With infinite patience, he learned to move again, to rely on the physical support of others, never giving in to despair, to self-pity, to discouragement. He was once asked if he had the patience to see a certain piece of legislation through to its conclusion. He replied, "You acquire patience after you've spent two years learning how to wiggle your big toe again."[2]

In 1924, Governor Alfred E. Smith chose FDR to nominate him for president at the Democratic National Convention in New York City. On the arm of his son, with his legs firm in locked braces, a crutch under his right arm, holding a cane in his other hand, FDR advanced slowly to the podium in Madison Square Garden. It was a moment that no one who saw it would ever forget. His palpable courage, his eloquence, his magnificent voice, brought the delegates to their feet—and at that moment Franklin Roosevelt resumed a national political career. Seven years after his polio attack, Roosevelt was elected governor of New York. Roosevelt had perfected so effective an illusion of his strength and well-being that most Americans never realized until after his death that he was, in fact, a paraplegic. He founded the March of Dimes, which financed the research of Dr. Jonas Salk and Dr. Albert Sabin, resulting in the vaccine that vanquished polio. FDR would have been deeply satisfied by the conquest of that cruel enemy.

The achievements of the New Deal and the international role and responsibility that Franklin Roosevelt bequeathed to us, representing as they do a fundamental restructuring of our nation and the world, are under constant attack in contemporary politics. Of course, Roosevelt himself insisted that change was the order of the day—that programs and experiments had to be tried; if they worked, then let them go forward, but if they needed to be reorganized, reformed, or abolished, then be not afraid to do so. He was a pragmatic idealist, and both of those words have bold meaning as biographers and historians search the archives continually seeking new evidence to reconstruct the complicated and extraordinary years of the Roosevelt legacy.

He was a master of the American political system, an intuitive genius regarding public opinion, a communicator who used the media of his time—the radio—to amplify his magnificent voice into millions of households through his fireside chats, becoming the neighbor and friend of most who heard him. Four times he was elected president of the United States; he led his party to seven consecutive congressional election victories. By temperament and talent, by energy and instinct, Franklin Roosevelt came to the presidency ready for the challenges that confronted him. He was a breath of fresh air in our political life—so vital, so confident and optimistic, so warm and good-humored. He gave courage to his country at a time of its greatest need. He replaced fear with faith, transforming our government into an active instrument of social justice.

It was a time when heroes were possible, when idealism was admired, when public service was the highest calling. It was also a time when Adolf Hitler laid claim to the future. President Roosevelt's response was to make America the arsenal of democracy. He was commander in chief of the greatest military force in history. He crafted the victorious alliance that won the war. He was the father of the nuclear age. He guided the blueprint for the world that was to follow. The vision of the United Nations, the commitment to collective security, the determination to end colonialism, the economic plan for a prosperous world: this is the legacy of Franklin Roosevelt that we memorialize.

Roosevelt was not a man who sought any kind of self-glorification. He rejected very specifically the notion of any grand monuments or statues dedicated to him after his death. Years before, in a relaxed conversation with Supreme Court Justice Felix Frankfurter, he mentioned that he only wanted one monument: a five-by-five-foot block of stone with just his name inscribed on it, placed on a triangular plot on Pennsylvania Avenue near the National Archives building. A small group of New Dealers ensured that this transpired, and the modest memorial was dedicated on April 12, 1965, twenty years to the day after FDR's death.

Nonetheless, the country wanted to memorialize what Franklin Roosevelt had done. In 1956, Congress voted that a national monument be constructed to honor FDR. After several significant plans were rejected, a design was finally accepted in 1978; the designer was Lawrence Halprin of San Francisco, a renowned landscape architect. The 7.5-acre memorial is built around four rooms, each reflecting one of Roosevelt's four terms, sited on the Tidal Basin, midway between the Washington Monument and the Jefferson Memorial.

When Ronald Reagan became president, I met with Claude Pepper, a congressman from Florida and an early New Dealer who had served fourteen years in the US Senate before being defeated in the Democratic primary by George Smathers in 1950. He had been elected to the House in 1962. Pepper had considerable influence in Washington and managed to get a personal appointment for us with President Reagan. Congressman Pepper led off with a brief history of the project. The President asked the cost. I replied that it would be approximately $50 million. When Congressman Pepper suggested that private donors could be asked for $10 million, President Reagan turned to the two of us and said, "Franklin Roosevelt was the greatest president of this century. I voted for him four times. Of course, the monument should be built. I'll support it." He did. More than $40 million was allocated by the federal government to the project; $10 million was raised from private donations. The monument was built and dedicated in 1997, and it immediately became, next to the Lincoln Memorial, one of the most visited sites in Washington. In 2005, for example, it recorded more than 2.85 million visitors.

After the memorial was opened, there was a strong sentiment among the communities of the disabled in America to include a statue of Roosevelt in his wheelchair. This was accomplished in 2001 and dedicated by President Clinton. Alan Reich, who was president of the National Organization on Disabilities and a close colleague, was the moving force in this project, as he was in the United Nations, where he played a major role in the writing and adoption of the Convention on the Rights of Persons with Disabilities. Together, we established the Franklin Delano Roosevelt International Disability Award, given annually to the representative of the nation that has made significant progress in improving the lives of its disabled citizens. The award was the only privately organized award given at the United Nations, with the secretary-general always in attendance. It inspired many significant accomplishments. Canada, for example, added a minister for the disabled to the cabinet. The award kept disability on the international agenda in an important way.

Roosevelt was an inspiration to disabled people around the world. The grandson of a very prominent New Dealer was injured in the 1980s in a severe automobile accident, leaving him disabled and despairing. His father took the young man to Hyde Park. They made their way through the exhibit, which showed how Roosevelt had responded to and conquered the disability of polio. Roosevelt's advocacy of independent living for the disabled gave the young man hope and comfort.

In January 1989, the Franklin and Eleanor Roosevelt Institute organized a luncheon at the National Archives to honor FDR. I asked President Reagan, who had only ten days left in the White House, to speak at the occasion. He agreed. Among the sixty special guests was Steve Ross, the founder of Time Warner, which owned Warner Brothers Studio. As the three of us sat in a private room, awaiting the time to begin, the president and Steve regaled each other with stories of Hollywood. Warner Brothers had been President Reagan's studio during his acting career. Steve, more serious than not, asked the president to come back to Warner Brothers when he left the presidency. Ronald Reagan made it clear he would love to do that, but he had other plans for the moment.

After President Reagan died, there was a movement among Republicans to practically rename the country for him. Among the proposals was the suggestion that the dime be engraved with President Reagan's portrait rather than FDR's. I called Nancy Reagan to discuss this with her. "Ronnie would never want that," she said. "He greatly admired Franklin Roosevelt and the dime belongs to the Roosevelt identity, if only because of the March of Dimes, which played such a major role in controlling polio." Without any hesitation or pressure, she issued a statement saying that although she appreciated the various proposals honoring President Reagan, anything that would affect the identity of the dime with FDR would be totally contrary to his wishes.

Eleanor Roosevelt also played a significant role in my life, but in a completely different, more personal way. It was she who shook my hand and kindly allowed me to introduce my mother to her at an "I am an American" rally in 1939 in Rochester, New York. It was she who intervened and allowed me to stay for the ceremonies on April 12, 1946, when the president's home and archives were made a gift to the nation, and

Harry Truman led Americans in prayerful remembrance at the site of FDR's burial. As a young lawyer in New York, I worked with Eleanor Roosevelt in the reform of the Democratic Party and in causes relating to public housing and human rights. I had the privilege of traveling with her to Chicago to speak at a rally for fair housing. She and I flew to Chicago together. At the dinner, I was introduced first. The chairman of the dinner, having briefly stated my credentials, stumbled over the difficult pronunciation of my name and avoided the problem by concluding, "I give you the next speaker." When Mrs. Roosevelt's turn came to speak, she began by saying, "Mr. vanden Heuvel, I have no doubt that when my husband's ancestors came to America, those who greeted them had difficulty pronouncing their name. But they did learn how to pronounce it, and I have no doubt that they will learn how to pronounce yours, too."

Eleanor Roosevelt supported me in my race for Congress in 1960. During that campaign, I escorted the Democratic nominee for president, John F. Kennedy, to Mrs. Roosevelt's apartment on East Seventy-Fourth Street, where they breakfasted. Mrs. Roosevelt had supported Adlai Stevenson for the nomination, and she had her misgivings about the Kennedys and their commitment to liberal ideas. She wrote a particularly harsh article in her column "My Day" in which she noted that the problem with Mr. Kennedy was that he was showing too much profile and not enough courage. After he was nominated, JFK traveled to Hyde Park and lunched with Eleanor Roosevelt, after which she endorsed him and campaigned for him extensively.

Gore Vidal was also a candidate for Congress in 1960, running in the Hudson Valley district in which Mrs. Roosevelt was the leading constituent. He told me that he went to call on Mrs. Roosevelt. The discussion turned to the reform politics of the Democratic Party. Mrs. Roosevelt, along with former governor Herbert Lehman, had led a movement against the "bosses." The discussion came around to Carmine De Sapio, the head of Tammany Hall. Mrs. Roosevelt's son, FDR Jr., had aspired to run for governor of New York in 1954. Carmine De Sapio had blocked FDR Jr.'s effort and had instead supported Averell Harriman for the nomination. Hoping to embarrass the Tammany Hall leaders, FDR Jr. accepted the nomination for attorney general, expecting to lead the ticket by a substantial margin. He hoped to show that the leaders had made a mistake not to back him. Instead, Harriman was elected by a very narrow margin, and FDR Jr. lost to Jack Javits. The reform efforts that Mrs. Roosevelt spearheaded effectively destroyed De Sapio's political career; he lost the district leadership in the primary election of 1961, and as a result lost his leadership of Tammany Hall. Mrs. Roosevelt, in discussing the course of her efforts to reform the party, said to Gore, "I told Mr. de Sapio that I would get him for what he did to my son, Franklin . . . and I got him." Gore so enjoyed telling this story that one has to question its total accuracy.

In 1961, after the Bay of Pigs debacle, Cuban leader Fidel Castro offered to repatriate the hundreds of prisoners of the CIA invasion force captured on the beaches of Cuba in exchange for tractors and pharmaceutical supplies. Shortly thereafter, in a taxi on my way to a meeting at the home of Mary Lasker, I spied Mrs. Roosevelt, standing on the corner, hailing a cab. I stopped and offered her a ride. She happened to be going to the same meeting. Castro had just given the speech making the offer, and I said that I. thought the needed funds could be raised if a national committee was formed with the endorsement of the president. I asked her if she might be willing to join such a committee. She agreed. When we arrived at the meeting, I called the attorney general (RFK) to tell him of her willingness to participate. The result was the formation of a national committee that gathered the resources that allowed the prisoners of that ill-fated mission to be freed. Mrs. Roosevelt was an honorary officer of the group.

Eleanor Roosevelt regarded the adoption of the Universal Declaration of Human Rights as her most important public legacy. President Truman appointed her as a member of the first delegation to the United Nations General Assembly, which convened in London in January 1946. She was the only woman to be a participant. She was reluctant to accept, feeling inadequate to the task. President Truman wisely insisted. Her male colleagues scoffed at her appointment and prepared to discount her role and influence by having her appointed to Committee 3, which dealt with humanitarian and human rights issues. She quickly showed how mistaken they were. In the course of the debate in the General Assembly on forced repatriation of prisoners of war, she confronted Andrei Vishinsky, the Soviet representative and former prosecutor of the "show trials" of the 1930s. The Soviet position was that repatriation should be mandatory. Eleanor Roosevelt understood the political and humane issues involved and insisted that repatriation should be decided by the individual, through a voluntary, not a mandated procedure. Her debates with Vishinsky and his Soviet colleagues were presented with grace, intelligence, and respect, but there was no question of who prevailed. Even John Foster Dulles, who had opposed her appointment, ended the session by complimenting Mrs. Roosevelt's extraordinary effectiveness. The General Assembly, as it ended its first session, designated Eleanor Roosevelt as chairman of the Human Rights Commission, whose mandate was to create an International Bill of Rights, an unprecedented assignment. It required monumental effort. She would chair more than 3,000 hours of contentious debate, showing her political skill, her extraordinary stamina, and her incomparable capacity to find principled compromise among the nations of the world. When she presented the Universal Declaration of Human Rights to the General Assembly meeting in Paris on December 10, 1948, she declared:

> We stand today at the threshold of a great event both in the life of the United Nations and in the life of mankind. This Universal Declaration of Human Rights may well become the international Magna Carta of all men everywhere.[3]

The declaration was adopted without a negative vote—and the representatives of the world stood and gave her a prolonged ovation.

Eleanor Roosevelt understood that the United Nations could be truly effective only if American leadership and ideas rallied to support it. She was aware that the UN reflected the ambitions, goals, and imperfections of its member states (today 193 members.) She argued that the world needed an international structure to maintain peace, to help resist aggression, and to seek social justice. She believed the United Nations could be an invaluable part of that governance effort to achieve that purpose, and she believed that our nation, with its strength and wealth and history, would look upon the UN as a challenge worthy of our effort. Each summer, she would invite representatives of the UN and their families to come to Val-Kill, her home in Hyde Park, for picnics, luncheons, and dinners, which she often cooked herself (culinary excellence was not one of Mrs. Roosevelt's talents.) Her personal impact was overwhelming.

Her message was a definition of human rights. In a speech at the United Nations in 1958, she made clear what she meant:

> Where, after all, do universal human rights begin? In small places, close to home—so close and so small that they cannot be seen on any maps of the world. Yet they are the world of the individual person; the neighborhood he lives in; the school or college he attends; the factory, farm, or office where

he works. Such are the places where every man, woman, and child seeks equal justice, equal opportunity, equal dignity without discrimination. Unless these rights have meaning there, they have little meaning anywhere. Without concerted citizen action to uphold them close to home, we shall look in vain for progress in the larger world.[4]

In the last ten years of her life, no longer in government, no longer with an official title, Eleanor Roosevelt worked full-time as a volunteer at the United Nations Association to bring the message of international cooperation to the peoples of the world.

Eleanor Roosevelt was certainly the First Lady of the world, as Adlai Stevenson referred to her in his eulogy after her death on November 7, 1962. She touched so many lives with the magic wand of her humanity. Countless young people had their lives' ambitions enabled by her personal interest in their efforts. She was kind and endlessly generous. She was courageous and fearless. She was the most effective champion of social justice in our time. Eleanor Roosevelt survived the president by seventeen years and added a brilliant luster to the name that was always her own.

Over the years, I have spoken many times of the courage and legacy of Franklin and Eleanor Roosevelt. It is also important to remember that all three Roosevelts—Theodore, Franklin, and Eleanor—were a combined force in shaping the United States in the twentieth century, as James MacGregor Burns and Susan Dunn showed in their important book, *The Three Roosevelts*. In September of 2002, on the 101st anniversary of the beginning of TR's presidency, I spoke in Buffalo, New York, the place of President McKinley's assassination, of the battles and triumphs of Theodore, Franklin, and Eleanor Roosevelt. (The speech, originally planned for September 15, 2001, was postponed due to the 9/11 attacks.)

Theodore and Franklin and Eleanor Roosevelt: A 20th-Century
Triumvirate That Transformed America
Address by William J. vanden Heuvel on the Occasion of the
100th Anniversary of Theodore Roosevelt's Becoming President
of the United States, Buffalo, New York, September 15, 2001

We have come to Buffalo, New York, to recall the events of a century ago, the assassination of William McKinley, a much-admired, kind, conservative, principled man, who had but six months before been inaugurated for his second term as America's twenty-fifth President; and the accession to that office of Theodore Roosevelt, who, though the youngest man ever to become president, was already a national hero, an experienced leader in local, state, and federal governments, and a fearsome terror to the political bosses who had created and administered the McKinley era, particularly Mark Hanna, a senator from Ohio, and an industrialist of great wealth who was the shield and protector of the corporate and business interests which dominated both the economic and the political scene as the twentieth century began.

The shock of McKinley's death was enormous. In certain powerful quarters, the shock of who was to succeed him was even more shattering. On the McKinley funeral train, Mark Hanna was in an intensely bitter state of mind. He damned Roosevelt and said to a friend: "I told William McKinley it was a mistake to nominate that wild man. I asked him if he realized what would happen if he should die. Now look, that damned cowboy is President of the United States."[5]

And so he was. Theodore Roosevelt was a fearless man of iron discipline, brilliant, a person of unquestioned moral principle, an author of thirty-eight books, an admired journalist and a prolific correspondent, a naturalist and ornithologist, profoundly devoted to his family and forever loyal to his friends, a man of kinetic energy and temper, a soldier who won the nation's highest medal for bravery and the first American to win the Nobel prize for peace, a magnetic personality whose memory continues to inspire young men and women in the cause of progressive government, a patrician who believed the highest duty of every citizen was service to his country. The name Roosevelt would dominate the twentieth century. Together, Theodore, Franklin, and Eleanor Roosevelt transformed America, making our government into a creative instrument of social justice and our nation into the most powerful military and economic force the world has ever seen—and all this while enhancing democracy and preserving democratic values.

The endlessly dramatic story of Theodore Roosevelt is the cornerstone of the century. We are greatly indebted to James MacGregor Burns and Susan Dunn for their magisterial work, *The Three Roosevelts,* which illuminates these days of our meeting and will be the sourcebook of this story for generations to come.[6]

The Roosevelts were directly descended from Claes Martenson van Rosevelt who came to New Amsterdam in 1648 from the Province of Zeeland, the Netherlands, and his son Nicholas who was born in the New World a decade later. Two principal branches emerged from this immigrant beginning, identified to us by the names of the New York villages which became their homesteads, Oyster Bay and Hyde Park. The saga of these two preeminent families hardly needs retelling. For our purposes today, let us remind ourselves that Eleanor was the niece of TR, the daughter of his younger brother, Elliott, whose early death and tragic life made TR her special guardian. Eleanor's father had been godfather at the christening of Franklin, his distant cousin, at Hyde Park in 1882. When Franklin married Eleanor in 1905, the president of the United States—TR—gave the bride away and dominated the event by his presence. There was probably no one whom FDR admired more than Theodore Roosevelt. He often said that TR was the greatest man he had ever known.[7] The extraordinary parallel of their careers was undoubtedly influenced greatly by that admiration. Those parallels include the following: both TR and FDR, separated by a generation in time, were elected to the New York state legislature (TR at twenty-three, FDR at twenty-eight); both were appointed assistant secretary of the Navy (TR at thirty-eight, FDR at thirty-one); both were vice presidential candidates (TR at forty-one, FDR at thirty-eight); both knew political defeat, TR as a candidate for mayor of New York (1886) and in his Bull Moose campaign for president (1912), FDR in the Democratic primary campaign for the United States Senate (1914) and as the running mate of James Cox in the 1920 presidential election; both married at a young age, TR at twenty-two, FDR at twenty-three, and both had four sons as brave participants in the two world wars. And, of course, both were Harvard graduates and recognized ornithologists.

And both loved Eleanor Roosevelt. Eleanor, orphaned and vulnerable at age ten, enjoyed her visits to Sagamore Hill where TR gave her special attention as his godchild and favorite niece. He taught her not to be afraid. "When you are afraid to do a thing, that was the time to go and do it," her cherished uncle told her.[8] It was not politics and government that she learned from him but rather character and the energetic pursuit of life and public purpose. On her childhood visits to Oyster Bay, TR's influence "was primarily exerted in outdoor life and in character building. He would," Eleanor wrote later, "never permit any child to shirk or be afraid of anything. [His children] learned that courage was a cardinal virtue and the lack of it intolerable."[9] In her book *The Roosevelt Cousins*, Linda Donn describes the complex relationship between TR's children and Eleanor and Franklin.[10] After TR's death, political rivalry, frustrated ambitions, and undoubtedly a sense among his children that the greatness of his name and accomplishments had been misappropriated by the Hudson Valley cousins caused some writers to declare that a family feud was the order of the day. It is not difficult to understand. TR's oldest son and namesake, a soldier in World War I, then elected to the New York legislature and appointed assistant secretary of the Navy by President Harding, aspired to follow in his father's foot-steps, the next move being election as governor of New York. TR had died in 1919. The Oyster Bay Roosevelts despised Warren Harding, but anxious to deny the benefit of TR's legacy to the Democratic ticket, which carried FDR as its vice presidential candidate in 1920, they campaigned for Harding to assure his obligation to TR Jr. and to block Franklin's progress. The Republican National Committee sent TR Jr. to the western states to follow FDR's campaign trail and assert himself as the proper spokesman for his father's legacy. In Wyoming, young Ted said: "He [FDR] is a maverick. He does not have the brand of our family."[11] The words were long remembered in Hyde Park.

FDR, disabled by polio three years earlier, had nominated Al Smith for president at the 1924 Democratic convention in Madison Square Garden in a memorable speech which brought him national attention and admiration. The Happy Warrior, Al Smith, lost out in the bitter nomination fight that year but he was renominated for governor. Eleanor gave the seconding speech. Her cousin, TR Jr., was nominated by the Republicans to run against him. She had described TR Jr. as a "personally nice young man whose public service record shows him willing to do the bidding of his friends."[12] The Teapot Dome scandal had destroyed the reputations of Harding and "the Ohio gang" and left a shadow on the Navy Department where TR Jr. held office. A Senate investigation had declared him innocent of any complicity, but Teapot Dome was the best issue the Democrats had in their hope to win the presidency. Eleanor, and Louis Howe, who had dedicated his life to the political career of FDR, had an enormous teapot built on the chassis of a car which followed TR Jr.'s campaign around New York State.[13] Eleanor later said the teapot affair was a "rough stunt."[14] Eleanor's cousins never forgave her, and their families talked about it still, sixty years later. Alice Longworth's clever but painful mimicking of Eleanor for her dinner party guests in later years silenced the joyful, supporting relationship they had had in their many days together as young girls in Oyster Bay.

"The Lion is dead," son Archibald wired his brothers on January 6, 1919. Theodore Roosevelt, only sixty years old, had died in his sleep after months of illness that certainly reflected the strains of the strenuous life he had lived and advocated for others.

Many thought that he would definitely have been the Republican candidate for president again in 1920, but TR had told a close friend that though he was pleased to have the antiWilson sentiment rally around him, he would absolutely never make another campaign tour nor be a candidate again. He intended to make a public announcement to that effect long enough before 1920 "to get out of the way of anyone who wants the nomination."[15] But it is hard to believe that he could have accepted the nomination of Warren Harding as his family did—a nomination engineered in a smoke-filled room by the very political bosses TR had spent his lifetime fighting.

The legacy of Theodore Roosevelt as represented by his character, moral values, integrity, patriotism, exemplary citizenship, passed to his children as their rightful inheritance, but his political legacy—his vision of the presidency, his progressive definition of issues, the flag of the Square Deal, the commitment to social reform, the determination that the sovereign power of the United States had to be exercised for all of its people and their general welfare—this legacy was inherited by Franklin and Eleanor Roosevelt and made the presidencies of the two Roosevelts the most influential administrations of the twentieth century, leaving behind a foundation of liberal values and programs that no successor administration has been able to diminish.

In fulfilling their political destinies, each of the Roosevelts established their independence by doing battle with bosses who dominated both the Republican and the Democratic parties. In his autobiography, Theodore Roosevelt describes the opposition of Senator Thomas Platt, the Republican boss of New York State, to TR's proposal as governor to tax the franchises given by the state to private corporations. In a letter, Platt urged reconsideration, telling TR that he had not objected to his being independent in politics but pointed out that he had been warned before allowing TR's gubernatorial nomination in 1898 that TR "was a dangerous man" because he was "altruistic"—or as Senator Platt went on to explain: "You were a little loose on the relations of capital and labor, on trusts and combinations . . . and the right of a man to run his own business in his own way."[16] TR was told that if he continued to press for the franchise tax, he would never be nominated for another public office. The red flag was down. TR convened a special session of the legislature and submitted his bill. The legislature tried to adjourn without the required reading of the proposal by the Speaker. TR appeared directly at the Assembly door, threatening to read it to the legislature himself. The opposition collapsed.[17] This struggle had an extraordinary result. Platt now wanted TR out of the governorship and out of New York politics. What better place than the vice presidency, a powerless sinecure where the hero of San Juan Hill could do no harm. TR thereupon announced that he would not accept the vice presidency, challenging Platt to fight him for the gubernatorial nomination. Mark Hanna's appraisal of TR was the same as Platt's, but the last thing he wanted was to have TR on the McKinley ticket. He urged McKinley to name his choice, whom the convention would then nominate by acclamation. McKinley refused, instead authorizing Charles G. Dawes to tell the delegates that he had no personal choice. He would not allow Mark Hanna to tell the delegates that he was speaking for the president in rejecting Roosevelt. As one journalist expressed it, "That Convention was distinguished by the fact that more men refused to be nominated for Vice President than in any other convention of either party. Even TR tried to dodge it."[18] TR refused to allow the New York delegation to nominate him, but his admirers were at work—and in a direct challenge to Hanna and Platt, the steamroller was set in motion by the other states. The ironic ending came a century ago here in Buffalo as Theodore Roosevelt took the oath as president, and Mark Hanna took his bitter ride back to Ohio.

FDR's first battle in a lifelong struggle with the bosses came shortly after his astonishing victory in 1910 for the State Senate seat in Dutchess County, an election that had been won by the Democrats only once since the Civil War. Having cast his first vote for TR for president, and greatly influenced by TR's ideals and principles, FDR's decision to be a Democrat could not be taken for granted, but, as Boss Plunkitt said, "he seen his opportunity and he took it."[19] The party elders thought the nomination was worthless. FDR, exuding self-confidence, seized the opportunity, campaigned night and day, organized a brilliant campaign, listened to the voters, improved his speaking ability—and riding a national Democratic tide with a name—Roosevelt— more popular than any other in the nation, FDR won by 1,140 votes. "Big Tim" Sullivan, the Tammany boss of the Bowery, spotting FDR's name among the Democratic winners is supposed to have said: "Well, if we've caught a Roosevelt, we'd better take him down and drop him off the dock. The Roosevelts run true to form."[20] Tammany did not have to wait long. FDR led the reformers against the bosses' candidate for the US Senate, then still chosen by the legislature. FDR called the final compromise "a victory." It wasn't, in the sense that Tammany ended up with its own acceptable candidate, but to his constituents, to journalists, to politicians throughout the country, another Roosevelt had emerged who was tough, independent, willing to fight for democratic principles, and who enjoyed the battle.

Eleanor, too, took on the bosses. She led the effort in the 1950s that destroyed the last vestiges of Tammany's strength. She was nearing the end of her life. She was the most admired woman in the world, certainly not needing an alley fight with the politicians who fought to control the streets of New York. Joined by Herbert Lehman and Thomas Finletter, they campaigned from bus stop to dingy clubhouse. The reformers won—with ER proving to be a campaigner and strategist of Rooseveltian dimensions.

Comparing the political skills of Theodore and Franklin, let it be said that both were masters of the art who left behind a scattered field of precedents, of broken traditions, of errors, heroic victories, and extraordinary battles. In perhaps the most significant political issue that confronted them both—the decision to seek a third term—a telling of the story puts their skills in focus. On election night in 1904, TR, having scored an overwhelming victory, stunned his family, his followers, and the nation by stating: "Under no circumstances will I be a candidate for or accept another term."[21] No one had asked him that question. He had not consulted with anyone, including his wife, whose love was his dearest treasure and whose judgment he valued greatly. It was a deliberate, carefully worded statement. He had not been *elected* to two terms, so even the precedent of two terms that he was trying to honor was ambiguous. He knew that the nomination in 1908, the next presidential election, was his just by *not* refusing to accept it. He knew he needed more time to consolidate a progressive foundation in the Republican Party. He knew that his announcement made him a "lame duck" incumbent with his power diminishing with every day of his new term. He later explained that he believed in the limitation on two consecutive terms because "the power of the President can be effectively used to secure a nomination, especially if the President has the support of certain great political and financial interests."[22] The statement can be rationalized, but given the nature of politics, TR's youth (he was forty-six when he issued the statement) and his understanding and commitment to presidential power, there are many who believe it to be the most significant misjudgment of his life. Justifying his attempt to regain the presidency in 1912, TR wrote that he was opposed to a third term for presidents but only if it was a consecutive third term. He rejected out of hand a constitutional amendment limiting the presidency to two terms because "the American people are fit to take care of themselves and have no need of an irrevocable self-denying ordinance."[23]

At the same time, TR laid out the argument that FDR used in justifying his decision to accept a third term. If, TR wrote later, a tremendous crisis should occur at the end of a second term, it would be calamitous if the American people were precluded from continuing to use the services of the one man they knew and trusted, a leader who had their confidence to carry them through the crisis. FDR certainly understood TR's admonition regarding a third term. But he had also watched TR's distress as his progressive programs and principles were pushed aside by the political forces that he himself had chosen to succeed him. Like TR, FDR did not share his thought processes with anyone on whether to seek a third term. He proceeded as though the two-term limitation was a constraint that was unbreakable. As his second term came to a close, he built a retirement cottage at Hyde Park, established the first presidential library to receive the papers of his administration (establishing thereby that such papers were the property of the people of the United States) and created an office where he could work and write after his presidency.

The 1938 elections had reduced the Democratic majorities in Congress. FDR in his famous "purge" had tried to defeat several of the key Democratic lawmakers who represented the vested interests and conservative viewpoints that threatened the reforms of the New Deal. He was not successful, and the nation's press, like later historians, regarded the election as a turning point for the reform era that FDR had so successfully led for the country. FDR, better than anyone, understood that no electorate can sustain on a continuing basis the energy, focus, and high resolve needed to advance a reform movement. It also seemed clear that no leading Democrat was available for the nomination who could win the election and protect the legacy of the New Deal.

On the horizon, events in Europe and the Far East threatened devastating war and destruction for much of the world. Japan, dominated by an inflexible militarism, had invaded China and had sought to establish its domination of Asia. The dictators were on the march in Europe. Germany, rearmed under Hitler, began its conquest of Europe, occupying Austria, Czechoslovakia, and on September 1, 1939, invading Poland, beginning the Second World War. As the American political parties were preparing their conventions in 1940, France surrendered to the Nazis. The world was stunned. Was this the "tremendous crisis" that TR had written of that would justify a sitting president seeking a third consecutive term? FDR was silent, like a sphinx, as reporters and politicians asked constantly whether he would run. Undoubtedly, he did not make a final decision until the world-shattering events played out around him. He had encouraged those who had presidential ambitions to announce themselves and to seek support. As long as the possibility existed that FDR might be available, however, no candidate could build a base that could independently win the nomination. As Arthur Schlesinger has described in his brilliant memoir, the nation was more bitterly divided over the issue of the war in Europe and America's role and responsibility than by any other crisis of the twentieth century.[24] FDR's handling of the third-term decision was brilliant, not deceptive or manipulative as some writers describe it. He kept all of his options open. He accepted the nomination in the only way that the anti-third-term tradition could have been broken—that is, by a Democratic convention that drafted him. For those who thought that FDR had lost control in the purge of 1938, his nomination for a third term showed that he still dominated the Democratic Party, and his victory over Wendell Willkie, a man of charm, culture, and conviction, showed FDR's command of the nation.

In comparing the political leadership of TR and FDR, it is also significant to consider how each managed the succession to their presidency. As 1908 began, there was no front-runner for the Republican nomination to succeed TR. The conservative leaders in Congress suspected and were fearful that TR would create "a crisis" to justify his renomination, setting aside his written pledge not to run. In January 1908 William Loeb, TR's private secretary, interrupted the president's breakfast on an early January morning to discuss the upcoming convention. Loeb argued that TR could only sustain the credibility of his promise not to run by endorsing a candidate. Loeb told TR that any nominee could win—naming William Howard Taft, Elihu Root, Charles Evans Hughes, and George Cortelyou (the secretary of the treasury)—if only TR would back him. In response, TR said that he would favor Elihu Root and authorized Loeb at that moment to go to see Root and make the offer of his endorsement. Root, then secretary of state, was astonished by Loeb's message but without hesitation asked him to assure the president of his gratitude but also of his inability to accept because he judged himself to be unelectable. Loeb interrupted the president's schedule that same day to report on his meeting. TR accepted Root's decision. He then told Loeb that his choice was William Howard Taft, saying that he had the experience to run the government. Taft could hardly believe his good fortune. Meeting immediately with the president, he expressed his profound appreciation. TR told him that he would announce immediately that Taft would be his choice, but that he would not interfere with the convention processes in any other way. Taft, however, could not be nominated without TR's active involvement. In order to force every possible delegate to select Taft, TR followed two courses in his many private discussions. To the conservatives he would declare "It's Taft or me" which sent them running to Taft. To the progressives he would declare "It's Taft—I'm out!" whereupon most of them reluctantly accepted Taft. Taft had never been elected to anything except a municipal judgeship in Ohio. TR had known him as an administrator and as an intelligent, loyal member of his cabinet. TR's choice seems careless in the context of consolidating the progressive leadership he had worked so hard to put in place. Ironically, fearful that he would seem subservient to TR, Taft did not talk to or see TR again after the nominating convention until December of that year. Outside of his inaugural address, Taft had no kind words for TR, nor for his policies.[25] Because he was a man of moral righteousness and principle, because he was so profoundly committed to a progressive direction for the nation and his party, TR must have reflected often and sadly on the fateful judgments he had made that brought Taft to the presidency.

FDR was equally anxious to preserve the liberal accomplishments of this administration. The problem was temporarily solved by his acceptance of the nomination for a third term. But he was not going to trust to chance or to southern domination at the convention in a choice of his vice president. He made it very clear to the Democratic convention in 1940—an event to which he sent Eleanor to be his spokesman—that he would not accept the nomination unless Henry Wallace was his running mate. Wallace had been secretary of agriculture for eight years, a quintessential New Dealer, a former Republican from Iowa, a spokesman for the "common man," and a proven liberal in every one of the battles FDR had faced.[26] By 1944, when FDR again agreed to be renominated, he no longer had the political or physical strength to compel the convention to accept his sole choice, but he insisted upon choosing from three candidates—Henry Wallace, Harry Truman, William O. Douglas—any one of whom was a liberal guarantor of the New Deal and of the progressive principles for which FDR had lived.[27] FDR's shadow, as William Leuchtenberg has written, remained a dominating force in all of the administrations that succeeded his presidency in the twentieth century.[28]

For those who like to play history's game of "what might have been," the political fate of Theodore Roosevelt is certainly fascinating. What if TR had won in 1912, had wrested the Republican nomination from Taft and stood alone against Wilson, and been elected again as president? Vernon Bogdahor, a professor at Oxford University, has discussed this possibility.[29] He suggests that TR as president would have brought the United States into World War I much sooner than Woodrow Wilson did, possibly after the sinking of the *Lusitania* in 1915. With the United States as an active belligerent at this early stage of the struggle, World War I would have ended much sooner, preventing the Bolshevik Revolution and the disintegration of Europe and the rise of Hitler that the Versailles Treaty encouraged. Given the tragic consequences of the two world wars, this is a remarkable scenario to contemplate.

Winston Churchill imagined a different role for Theodore Roosevelt. Writing in *Scribner's* magazine in 1930 on the assumption that the South had triumphed in the Civil War, he supposes that General Robert E. Lee, in a masterstroke, abolishes slavery, thereby eliminating the moral issue of the war.[30] Churchill then sees two Republics emerging, both of them gaining Great Britain's friendship in due course. He sees Theodore Roosevelt elected as president of the Northern Republic, entering into negotiations with Prime Minister Balfour regarding an alliance with Great Britain, a true precursor of the Atlantic Alliance we know today. The Roosevelt/Balfour discussions are then joined by the new president of the Southern Republic, Woodrow Wilson. The idea of a United States of Europe emerges, and allied with the glittering spectacle of the English-speaking alliance of Great Britain and the two American republics, these forces would assure by their boundless power and enormous wealth the peace and prosperity of the twentieth century. Of course, more than ending slavery was at issue in the Civil War, and Abraham Lincoln's commitment to our constitutional union prevailed. Time and reality otherwise altered this vision, but ultimately, ironically, it was a Churchill/Roosevelt—Franklin Delano Roosevelt—partnership that did make a United States of Europe possible and which created an Atlantic Alliance that remains the best hope for peace in a fractious, often brutal world.

Although Winston Churchill and Theodore Roosevelt were not well known to each other, they should have been. Both were patricians turned politician in the heroic mold. Like TR, Churchill combined books and journalism, expeditions and splendid little wars, into brilliant public careers. When TR said in a masterful address at the Naval War College in 1897, "No triumph of peace is quite so great as the supreme triumph of war," he could have been echoing Churchill. In fact, Churchill's famous wartime speech about "blood, sweat, and tears" was a direct quote from TR's Naval War College speech.[31] They shared a magnificent rhetorical style.

During their presidencies, Theodore and Franklin Delano Roosevelt advocated reforms and new directions that made TR's Square Deal and FDR's New Deal the most dramatic periods of the twentieth century in furtherance of social justice and in the establishment of an international role for America's power. It is in these commitments that the three Roosevelts come together and give their achievements a unifying bond.

In one of her last "My Day" columns, Eleanor Roosevelt denounced reactionary politicians—"those evil men who combine together to scratch each other's backs."[32] The particular target of her concern was the effort to block legislation on government testing and regulation of pharmaceutical drugs. We can hear the echo of her uncle, TR, as she denounced "those who consider free enterprise more sacred than human lives." The Roosevelts, each of them, fought a continuing struggle against the corporate and economic interests that they believed constantly sought domination of the American government for their own selfish purposes. Theodore Roosevelt

was forever urging men of great wealth to repudiate lives of leisure and re-
finement. Like a missionary, he traveled the land arguing that only work,
public service, and contact with the working class could save the rich from
themselves. He struck out against the "mean and sordid commercial ideal"
which he believed the reactionary business community had tried to advance
in superseding national honor, courage, loyalty, and unselfishness. As a
young assemblyman in Albany, TR denounced "the wealthy criminal class,"
identifying Jay Gould, one of the country's richest and most powerful men,
as its representative.[33] As governors and as presidents, both TR and FDR
called for comprehensive reform of the tax structure so that "the man of
means and the great corporations shall pay their full share of taxes and bear
their full share of the public burdens."[34] The Roosevelts—Theodore, Franklin, and Eleanor—were determined to create democratic forces that could
contend with the entrenched power of wealth and corporate domination.
Again, TR sounded the trumpet: "The reactionaries of the business world
and their allies and instruments among politicians and newspaper editors
demand for themselves an immunity from government control. . . . Many of
them are evil men, unable to understand what the public interest really is. Of
all forms of tyranny, the least attractive and the most vulgar is the tyranny
of mere wealth, the tyranny of plutocracy."[35]

The burning issue was who was going to run the United States—the
elected representatives of the people or those whose control and power depended upon their wealth and corporate position. The Roosevelts were not
against business and corporations. They understood the indispensable, creative role that business had in creating wealth and jobs and economic opportunity, but they were determined that this immense power be regulated
and restrained in the context of the national interest, a national interest that
the president was elected to define and that Congress was elected to advance. Taxation then, as it is now, was the issue that defined the battle. His
Bull Moose campaign in 1912 gave TR the platform to continue his advocacy of the income tax and the inheritance tax, both of which were adopted
in the next four years. TR was one of the most powerful advocates of the
inheritance tax, writing in 1914: "I would not apply the inheritance tax to
small inheritances, but I would apply it progressively and with such heavi-
ness to big inheritances as to completely block the transmission of enormous
fortunes to the young Rockefellers, Vanderbilts, Astors or Morgans."[36] He
was not talking economics. He was talking about morality, community, a
just society. He understood that wealth could be the foundation on which
to build a real life, but the life that he advocated—the strenuous existence,

the life of spiritual and moral effort and achievement—did not need "vast fortunes." In fact, he believed the accumulation of such wealth could only be harmful to the generations which inherited it. Giving away money was not an alternative to participating in democracy. Great fortunes caused the disintegration of character, and frequently brought about lives without purpose, passion, or achievement.

TR's rhetorical missiles against the "malefactors of great wealth" set the stage for FDR's battle against the "economic royalists." When Franklin Roosevelt proposed the 1935 Wealth Tax Act, he echoed TR's denunciations of "the swollen fortunes" of the plutocrats. "Our revenue laws have operated in many ways to the unfair advantage of the few and they have done little to prevent an unjust concentration of wealth and economic power."[37] Income taxes on small corporations were lowered; on larger corporations they were raised. Significant graduated income taxes were imposed on individual incomes above $1 million, reaching a maximum tax of 75 percent on incomes over $5 million—but it must be remembered that those numbers translated into today's figures represent annual incomes of at least $10 million, with the maximum tax imposed on annual incomes only over $50 million.

TR's attitudes undoubtedly emerged during the time when he was seeking his life's direction as a young man, the era of the robber barons. The selfishness, corruption, the plundering of public assets, the derogatory attitudes toward government and public servants—all these were characteristics of the age which TR ended in the years of his presidency.

As he saw his accomplishments endangered by the Taft administration, TR traveled the country preaching the New Nationalism. His words, in countless speeches, articles, and letters, were the vanguard of political revolution, not the adjustment of the rules by which the Republican Party intended to govern the country. TR was against "violent and foolish radicalism," but it was radical change that he preached. Like a Jack Russell terrier, he had the "sordid money interests," as he described them, in his teeth, and he was not about to let go, even in the face of bitter repudiation by his own social class and old political friends and supporters.[38] He recognized that large corporations were here to stay, but they were not elected to run the country, and he was determined that government regulation remind them of their proper relationship to the nation and to the people's interests. TR's explosive rhetoric against his political opponents and the forces of "entrenched privilege" make today's political debating and sound-bite prose dull and painfully boring by comparison. He spared no words in making the fight.

Nor did FDR, who enjoyed his enemies as much as TR did. Having promised "this generation of Americans a rendezvous with destiny" in his acceptance speech at the Democratic convention in 1936, having warned "the royalists of the economic order that he would not allow them to prevent a New Deal for the American people," he concluded his campaign for reelection at Madison Square Garden. It was one of the memorable moments of political campaigns. FDR, in that voice that had no peer, confronted the powerful forces that were determined to defeat him. "Never before in all our history have these forces been so united against the candidate as they stand today," he declared. "They are unanimous in their hate for me—and I welcome their hatred. I should like to have it said of my first administration that in it the forces of selfishness and lust for power met their match. I should like to have it said of my second administration that in it these forces met their master!"

It was as though FDR and TR were standing there together, speaking in one voice to the ancient enemies of the sovereignty of the people, telescoping the years of the progressive struggle and now, with the power of government in their hands, sensing a victory that history rarely records, declaring, "For all these things we have only just begun to fight."[39]

Franklin and Eleanor Roosevelt brought a response of invective and hatred rarely if ever seen in American history. Having become president in the midst of the greatest economic crisis in the nation's history, FDR had responded with an extraordinary program of leadership that resulted in the TVA, the WPA, the Social Security Act, rural electrification, the SEC, the AAA, the CCC, unprecedented programs of conservation, a bank moratorium and regulation, public and subsidized housing, and new rights for labor, for farmers, for the poor and the working man, the middle class, for a new society of decency and equality of opportunity for all Americans. FDR and ER received the special venom of the demagogues and anti-Semites who found the despair of the Depression to be a fertile ground for their hatred. There was a classic struggle between federal power and states' rights—and all the Roosevelts knew that the states' rights banner gave cover to forces of selfishness, racism, and civil injustice and, in turn, that the Supreme Court had time and again given a constitutional sanctuary to the enemies of social reform. The struggle as TR, FDR, and ER defined it was whether property rights were paramount over human values and whether the Constitution was so inflexible that the reforms that were needed to save democracy as determined by the elected representatives of the people could be thwarted by courts which saw themselves as the ultimate defender of the propertied interests.

Which Roosevelt denounced the Supreme Court for upholding "property rights against human rights?"[40] Which Roosevelt proposed public referenda on judicial decisions? Which Roosevelt was convinced that American judges were "absolutely reactionary" and that their decisions virtually barred the "path to industrial, economic, and social reform?" Which Roosevelt ran on a platform describing as essential objectives of American democracy a free market in a free society where workers could earn enough to provide their basic needs, where farmers could assure themselves and their families of a decent living, where every businessman could participate without unfair competition and monopolistic domination, where every family had a decent income and adequate medical care, and where government would assure protection from the economic fears of old age and sickness, and where every child had the opportunity of a good education? Those are the words and pledges of Theodore Roosevelt in the 1912 campaign and the Progressive Party platform on which he ran.[41] "We stand at Armageddon, and we battle for the Lord," TR declared. In 1912, liberated from the domination of political bosses and the endless commitments demanded by the conservative essence of the Republican party, TR was able to speak as he truly felt. The full passion of his bursting vision for the country he loved so much found expression. One cannot read the platform of the National Convention of the Progressive Party or the speeches that TR made in the course of that extraordinary year without understanding how closely the three Roosevelts agreed about the nature of government.[42] TR believed, as FDR expressed it in his 1944 speech, that all citizens had economic rights, that it was the obligation of government to help in the fulfillment of those rights.[43] The political party does not exist today that has the leadership and courage to adopt the platform on which Theodore Roosevelt ran in 1912. Franklin and Eleanor later presided over an era where FDR's pragmatic idealism and political skills engineered a profound social and economic transformation of the nation. Eleanor, acting with courage, idealism, and commitment became the conscience of the nation, becoming a most powerful advocate for a better world. But the words and magnificent obsession of Theodore Roosevelt with justice and opportunity offered a powerful springboard for their great efforts.

No one can talk of the Roosevelt legacy without mentioning the extraordinary contribution of Theodore and Franklin in the fields of conservation and environmental concern. Some, like Robert Lafollette of Wisconsin, one of the great progressive leaders of the twentieth century, regarded TR's commitment to the conservation movement as the most significant accomplishment of his presidency.[44] Both TR and FDR literally changed the landscape of our country. They regarded the majestic beauty of America, its resources, its soil, its water, its forests, to be the common heritage of all of our people. They brought a new sense of responsibility to land management, and a new partner—the federal government. After the nineteenth-century plunder and reckless handling of the national heritage of natural resources, they regarded the remaining wilderness and wildlife as national treasures. They added hundreds of millions of acres to the national parks and the public lands. TR created the National Park System. Naturalists like John Burroughs were no longer eccentric scientists pleading for conservation—Burroughs was the president's camping companion, and Gifford Pinchot was in TR's "inner circle."

The enemies of the countryside—catastrophic floods and droughts, de-forested lands eroding, turning valleys and fertile plains into dust bowls—these destructive forces were met by the Roosevelts and their administrations with top priority programs to prevent their damage. FDR invited our unem-ployed youth to join the Civilian Conservation Corps. It helped save their lives and remade the natural infrastructure of our nation. Both TR and FDR understood that the quality of life of our citizens directly reflected our pro-tection and preservation of our natural resources and of nature's bounty. When FDR dedicated a wing of the American Museum of Natural History in 1936 to the memory of Theodore Roosevelt, the occasion bore witness to what both of them had done to conserve the natural wealth of America for all of its citizens.[45]

A word remains to be said about the world as the three Roosevelts saw it, as they influenced it, and as they left it. One of the many paradoxes re-garding TR is that he spoke of the glories of battle and the constant need for a national test of combat, but he was the first American to win the Nobel Peace Prize. One of his proudest boasts was that he had kept our country out of war. Nevertheless, his greatest disappointment came when Wood-row Wilson denied his request to lead a division of American soldiers after the United States had entered World War I.[46] He took enormous pride in the gallantry of his sons, and the loss of his youngest son in combat, a pro-foundly sorrowful event for him and his family, he regarded as the price of citizenship.

TR's bitterness toward Wilson was so intense that one has to differenti-ate his opposition to the League of Nations from his determination to inflict an overpowering defeat on "that old gray skunk in the White House," who had denied him an opportunity to serve in the war.[47] If TR had lived, he un-doubtedly would have been the leader of the fight that Senator Henry Cabot Lodge won against the League of Nations. Woodrow Wilson's failure to build a basic coalition with the Republican Senate in negotiating the Treaty of Versailles and his intransigent misunderstanding of the American public's demand for protection of the national sovereignty against involvement in future European conflicts doomed ratification of the treaty. In observing the defeat in the Senate, FDR learned the lessons of limitation regarding America's international involvement. In creating the United Nations, FDR carefully avoided the mistakes Wilson had made. He involved the Senate, both Republicans and Democrats, in the political process of its creation. He educated the American people as to the opportunities and responsibilities of international leadership. He organized an instrument through the Security Council veto so that American interests could never be damaged. He drafted a charter creating the United Nations that enabled American ideals to have a dramatic possibility of fulfillment. It was left to Eleanor Roosevelt to show what could be done in a world where the United States was prepared to lead.

Anticipating the devastation of the war, Franklin Delano Roosevelt addressed Congress on January 6, 1941, and spoke of his vision for the world made possible and necessary by the terrible sacrifices that the war would demand. He called for a world where every person and every nation would be assured of Four Freedoms—the fundamental requirement of a civilized and just social order—freedom of speech and expression, freedom of worship, freedom from want, and freedom from fear. These words were made part of the Charter of the United Nations, and they became the essence of what Eleanor Roosevelt regarded as her most important public accomplishment, the Universal Declaration of Human Rights. The declaration was a monumental achievement. It became possible only because of Eleanor's leadership, her extraordinary political skills, her idealism, her sympathetic understanding of both power and despair, her toughness, flexibility, resilience, and imagination. Eleanor's quiet nobility both charmed and inspired her colleagues. Eleanor Roosevelt was the American spokesman in the most memorable debate of the first meeting of the UN General Assembly in London in January 1946. Without a note, she replied in a powerful, brilliant speech to the demand by the Soviet Union for the forceful repatriation of displaced persons to their homeland. Her opponents vanquished, Eleanor Roosevelt emerged as the world's most effective advocate for human rights, unafraid of the totalitarian states and equally unafraid of standing up to her own government.

The example of her uncle was part of who she was. Together with her husband she coauthored an era that left her the most powerful, influential, and respected woman in the world. History will recognize the Universal Declaration, as many countries and people now do, as one of the basic charters of human freedom.[48] It challenged the view that a sovereign state's treatment of its own citizens was not subject to international control and intervention, certainly one of the lessons of the Holocaust that Eleanor Roosevelt taught us never to forget. Just as the Declaration helped bring an end to the colonial era, so has it provided a rallying point for freedom movements that brought about the collapse of Communism and the totalitarian regimes of Eastern Europe and the demise of apartheid. It is a pillar of the international system that holds the possibility of enhancing peace and social justice in our world. Eleanor Roosevelt was much more than the heir or the helpmate of the two great Roosevelt presidents. She was their partner, and in a time of unprecedented change in America and the world, she, as well as Franklin and Theodore Roosevelt, represented hope, determination, commitment, and decency. What is it that binds these three extraordinary individuals together—Theodore, Franklin, and Eleanor Roosevelt? Clearly, they were optimists—optimists about human nature and human possibilities. They were individuals of courage, tested both spiritually and physically, each surmounting every obstacle to achieve a new level of possibility. They were confident of their objectives and of themselves, so their enemies held no fear for them. They brought a sense of purpose, challenge, and inspiration to the political struggles of their time. It must have been exciting to be with them, to share a sense of public adventure with each of them. They inspired and continue to inspire generations of Americans. They believed deeply in democracy and democratic principles. A grateful nation remembers them for their historic achievements and for the noble purposes of their lives.

The passion and promise of the 1960s found expression in the New Frontier of John Kennedy and the Great Society programs of Lyndon Johnson. The years of Kennedy and Johnson promised and delivered the historic extension of what Roosevelt had begun. In the darkest years of the Great Depression, Franklin Roosevelt understood that America must be transformed in order to achieve its promise. He created the government structures necessary to mold the mind-set of a nation, creating an American self-image of a fair and tolerant land, even if the reality sometimes did not live up to the dream. After the tragedy of Dallas, LBJ continued to work to make the dream into a reality. He was a true disciple of FDR, and President Roosevelt had prophesied that the young congressman from Texas would one day become the first president from the South since the Civil War. Their relationship had a pivotal influence upon the shaping of America, even decades after FDR's death.

Franklin Delano Roosevelt and Lyndon Baines Johnson: Architects of a Nation
Address by William J. vanden Heuvel, LBJ Presidential Library, Austin, Texas, March 14, 2000

The twentieth century, that tumultuous, insane, brilliant, brutal, creative, awe-inspiring moment in the history of the world, is over. If democracy's victory over the Great Depression at home and totalitarianism abroad is the defining challenge of the twentieth century, then surely the historians are correct in judging Franklin Delano Roosevelt to be its greatest president. Here in the shadow of his magnificent library, here in his home country amidst the wild flowers of his beloved Pedernales River, we can hear Lyndon Johnson's shout of affirmation for that judgment. If ever two presidents were united in spirit and vision, bound as teacher and student, as master and disciple, as founder and heir, they were Franklin Roosevelt and Lyndon Johnson.

FDR's influence was profound, on the world, on his country, on countless individuals who shaped the postwar world, and most certainly on the thirty-sixth president of the United States, Lyndon Baines Johnson. The similarities and differences between FDR and LBJ make the story of their relationship one of the most interesting in our political history. New York patrician and Texas country boy; one sophisticated, the other rough-hewn and determined to remain so; Empire State and Lone Star State conquerors; master politicians; one significantly disabled but strengthened by his disability, the other physically overpowering in both size and energy; one disciplined and intensely private, the other gargantuan in his appetites and attitudes; both knew triumph and defeat; one has survived as history's hero, the other awaits its verdict; both transformed the nation by social revolution that made hope, opportunity, and justice for all Americans our national commitment; both led the nation in war, and the consequences of those struggles have defined their place in our memory.

It is fascinating to see each of these titans through the eyes of observers who served their presidencies. Joseph Califano, LBJ's assistant for domestic affairs, gave a brilliant speech here last May entitled "The Legacy of Lyndon Johnson." Secretary Califano described President Johnson in the following terms: brave and brutal, compassionate and cruel, incredibly intelligent and infuriatingly insensitive, altruistic and petty, generous and petulant, bluntly honest and calculatingly devious with a determination to succeed that ran over or around whoever and whatever got in his way. Doris Kearns Goodwin, the brilliant historian who was a White House Fellow and worked with LBJ on his memoirs, has written: "The price Johnson exacted for the gifts he bestowed upon his aides—personal intimacy, access to the presidential office, power for themselves—was often nothing less than their dignity."[49] In his memoirs, James Reston, the *New York Times* correspondent who dominated the journalistic scene in Washington during the Johnson era, wrote that Lyndon Johnson "saw conspiracies everywhere. He doubted everything, including members of his own staff."[50] Others describe LBJ's almost manic moods of exhilaration and depression, and friend and foe alike describe classic strength undermined by painful insecurity.

Practically none of those descriptions apply to Franklin Delano Roosevelt. James Rowe, one of six anonymous administrative assistants to the president who constituted the White House staff—and later a cherished friend of Lyndon Johnson—has written about FDR that "all the staff adored him, and that's not true of any other President I know of. That complete charm was always there."[51] He was as tough and demanding as any leader we have ever had, but his personal dominance was leavened by good humor, wit, and a respect for others built on self-respect and his sense of office. He knew who he was, comfortable in his own skin as the expression goes, confident and self-assured, so that the paranoia of power never was his problem. Isaiah Berlin, the incomparable British intellectual and philosopher, in an essay cataloging President Roosevelt's qualities of mind and spirit, wrote: "Above all, he was absolutely fearless. He was one of the few statesmen in the 20th or any other century who seemed to have no fear at all of the future. He believed in the capacity and loyalty of his lieutenants."[52] Confident of his own strength and ability to manage, FDR looked upon the future with a calm eye, his confidence inspiring confidence, his personal and public courage creating a moral authority that carried through the unprecedented years of his presidency.

Franklin Roosevelt died on April 12, 1945, less than three months into his fourth term as president. His loss was a profoundly sad event for the nation and for much of the world. For Lyndon Johnson, it was devastating. In a *New York Times* story the next day, Congressman Johnson was quoted as saying: "He was just like a daddy to me always; he always talked to me just that way. I don't know that I'd ever have come to Congress if it hadn't been for him. But I do know I got my first great desire for public office because of him."

Lyndon Johnson's first campaign for Congress is where the extraordinary relationship between a powerful president from upstate New York and an ambitious young politician from rural Texas begins.

Every echo in this place carries the legend of LBJ—growing up in circumstances in rural Texas that both taught him hardship and hardened him for the struggle, given discipline and inspiration by parents for whom he was always a devoted son, recognizing that education was the door of opportunity and seizing its possibilities as both a student and a teacher, and then in 1931 accepting appointment in the Washington office of Congressman Richard Kleberg, the mandarin of the fabled King Ranch—and so arriving in the city on the hill where his presence was a factor in the nation's destiny for forty years. Kleberg, a conservative Democrat elected as the turmoil of the Great Depression was taking hold, had one quality that suited the twenty-three-year-old LBJ very well: Kleberg was not interested in being a congressman. Young Lyndon filled the vacuum, setting a pattern for establishing contacts, learning the levers of power, understanding both need and possibility in confronting issues, and organizing a foundation of political power based on listening to constituent needs and to the problems of his fellow congressional staffers. A young person can only exercise such power by being extraordinarily sensitive to the personality and purposes of his mentor, the person who holds the position which creates the power base. It is a skill that is a basic platform for progress in every world, be it politics, business, academia, or the world of cultural achievement. LBJ was the master of that skill.

The 1932 election changed Washington and America forever. Faced with a revolution in its streets, the country chose a revolution in its leadership. For only the third time since the Civil War, the Democrats gained power, their leader and new president the governor of New York, who had claimed the nomination of his party by pledging a New Deal for the American people. "The only thing we have to fear is fear itself," spoke Franklin Delano Roosevelt to his fellow citizens as the banking system collapsed, as 25 percent of the workforce was unemployed, as hunger, deprivation, and loss devastated the country as never before. Thus began the most innovative reform period of our history, led by a man who, disabled by infantile paralysis, could not stand up alone but had the strength to lift a crippled nation to its feet. With a commanding majority in Congress and with the New Deal a magnet for thousands of the most talented, idealistic young Americans, FDR began his fabled 100 days of legislative accomplishment. Lyndon Johnson was one of those young Americans, and none had greater commitment, energy, and determination to be part of this new world than he.

By executive act, on June 26, 1935, FDR created the National Youth Administration to help young people between the ages of sixteen and twenty-five stay in school and get job training. The NYA needed a Texas state director. The appointment process became vintage LBJ. FDR saw the formidable political capacity of this twenty-seven-year-old who could get Maury

Maverick and Martin Dies, congressmen representing the extremes of Texas democracy, to plead his case, as well as Senators Connally and Sheppard to endorse it. Probably no word of support meant more than Sam Rayburn's, already a mentor to LBJ, reflecting another of the father-son relationships that perhaps, as only those in the lonely, often superficial world of political friendships can understand, gave Lyndon Johnson emotional and vital support and stability. FDR gave LBJ the job.

As the results subsequently showed, no one could have been a better choice. In establishing the NYA, FDR was determined to save a young generation already alienated by despair and lack of opportunity. LBJ showed how to do it. He understood FDR's vision and brought passion to its purpose. The state directors met in Washington with Aubrey Williams, the NYA administrator, who took them to the White House to meet the president. It was August 20, 1935—the first time LBJ had a face-to-face meeting with Franklin Roosevelt. The political offensive that had landed LBJ the appointment clearly amused and intrigued the president. He asked Lyndon to stay behind. The master and the student talked about what was happening in Texas.

Like a whirling dervish, LBJ returned to his appointed task, working endless days and nights, enlisting the governor and every mayor he could reach, building necessary public support through a statewide advisory board and press conferences and editorial meetings and radio interviews and speaking to any audience that would hear him. Thousands of young people stayed in high school and college because of his work. His idea for "roadside parks" brought employment—and the flattery of repetition in other states. He broke through racial barriers that were not even challenged in other states. Eleanor Roosevelt, wanting "to find out why the Texas NYA director was doing such an effective job," came to his office and went with him to a vocational training center for girls in Austin. When FDR came to Texas in June 1936, he threw back his head and laughed as his motorcade passed a roadside park project where Lyndon Johnson had his NYA boys saluting the president with shovels at "present arms." In the process of his ferocious work, LBJ had laid the groundwork for a political organization that would be ready if an electoral opportunity presented itself.

And it did on February 22, 1937, with the death of Texas congressman James P. Buchanan of the Tenth District. The special election was set for April 10. The leading vote-getter would be the winner—no runoff. On February 28, LBJ announced he would run, heading off the possible candidacy of Buchanan's widow. Eight other candidates entered the race, at least half of them seemingly in a position to overwhelm the ambition of the young upstart from Blanco, the smallest county in the district. LBJ's campaign can be described in three words: Franklin Delano Roosevelt. The president had just won the district by a 9–1 margin. The other candidates had experience, status, money, and even New Deal respectability, but none of them understood what Alvin Wirtz and his protégé, Lyndon Johnson, understood: that in a multicandidate race, the candidate who embraced Roosevelt, the one who stood out as his unqualified supporter, would win.

One of the most dramatic events in the history of the New Deal intervened. On February 5, just days before Congressman Buchanan's death, President Roosevelt proposed that when a federal judge, including those on the Supreme Court, reached the age of seventy and chose not to retire, the president could add a new justice to the bench. As William Leuchtenberg has written, "FDR's message generated an intensity of response unmatched by any legislative controversy in this century."

A contextual word about Roosevelt's court reorganization plan is necessary. Herbert Hoover and the Republican leadership had rejoiced at the choice of FDR by the Democratic convention in 1932 as its candidate for president, telling each other that FDR was "the weakest available candidate." FDR, however, because of both the crisis and the strength of his personality and character, quickly emerged as the most powerful president in US peacetime history. He made liberalism the dominant note in national politics. He talked directly to the people. He educated them on the issues as he saw them and shared his concerns with them. He convinced Congress that the federal government had responsibility for the general welfare as well as the public safety. By the winter of 1935, the Supreme Court had become the last hope of reactionary forces that were committed to blocking the New Deal. FDR's concept of the constitutional powers of the president and Congress to cope with the Great Depression was very different from that of William Howard Taft, Warren Harding, Calvin Coolidge, and Herbert Hoover, who had appointed the clear majority of the Supreme Court. The anti–New Deal forces started literally thousands of legal actions to stop the fulfillment of programs which the president had initiated, Congress had legislated, and the people in landslide elections had approved.

The first significant confrontation came in the Gold Clause Cases, which challenged the right of Congress to regulate the currency. A ruling of unconstitutionality could have added $70 billion to the national debt, creating financial chaos. Awaiting the court's decision, Roosevelt took comfort in reading these words from Abraham Lincoln's first inaugural address:

The candid citizen must confess that if the policy of the government upon vital questions affecting the whole people is to be irrevocably fixed by decisions of the Supreme Court, the people will have ceased to be their own rulers, having to that extent practically resigned their government into the hands of that eminent tribunal.

On February 18, 1935, the Supreme Court, in a 5–4 decision, upheld the constitutionality of the Gold Clause legislation, but three months later, in another 5–4 decision, the court invalidated the Railroad Retirement Act. The implication was clear that the pending social security bill would also be ruled unconstitutional. Within weeks, the court unanimously invalidated the National Recovery Act, the keystone of FDR's industrial recovery program, and the mortgage moratorium legislation as well. "We have been relegated to the horse and buggy definition of interstate commerce," said FDR, whose words were greeted with an editorial explosion of criticism— but then, more than 80 percent of the editorial writers had opposed his election and would oppose his reelection. In 1936, the Supreme Court ruled the Agricultural Adjustment Act unconstitutional. Harlan Fiske Stone, appointed by Calvin Coolidge, wrote a dissent accusing his majority of colleagues of deciding on the basis of their own economic theories rather than fair constitutional interpretation. Harold Ickes, a Bull Moose Republican who served as FDR's secretary of the interior, wrote that "we are not prepared to submit to the arbitrary and final dictates of a group of men who are not elected by the people and who are not responsible to the people—a judicial tyranny imposed by men appointed for life who cannot be reached except by impeachment."

In the spring of 1936, the court, in 5–4 decisions, overturned administration legislation designed to bring order and safety to the desperate coal-mining industry; then it overturned the Municipal Bankruptcy Act created to save local governments across the country in financial distress; and then it ruled unconstitutional the New York State law establishing minimum wages, outlawing child labor, and regulating the hours and labor conditions affecting women. Even the opponents of the New Deal were embarrassed. Roosevelt commented that the court had now established a "no-man's land" where no government—state or federal—could function. With the polls indicating a close battle for reelection, the president chose to fight on what the New Deal had accomplished, waiting for the election results before deciding if and how to press for judicial reform. FDR was reelected in 1936 in the greatest landslide in history, receiving 60.8 percent of the popular vote and capturing the electoral votes of every state except Maine and Vermont. The court was about to decide the constitutionality of the Social Security Act, the Wagner Act, establishing collective bargaining and protecting the right of labor to organize, and the minimum wage and unemployment laws. It was a dramatic moment in our history. Would the economic and social revolution enacted by the elected representatives of the people be defeated—not at the polls but by a court whose majority philosophy the people had decisively repudiated? In its *Dred Scott* decision in 1857, the Supreme Court had invited and hastened the Civil War. Would it now return the demand for change to the anarchy and violence of the streets? The conservative/radical justices who dominated the court, though aged and in declining health, were determined to stay in office as long as Roosevelt was president in order to frustrate his programs.

Having carefully reviewed his options, FDR determined his course. Sensing certainly the outcry his action would bring, he presented his reorganization proposal to Congress. The date was February 5, 1937. Seventeen days later, Congressman Buchanan of the Tenth Congressional District of Texas died.

Alone of the nine candidates in the special election to fill the vacancy on April 10, Lyndon Johnson embraced President Roosevelt completely, including enthusiastic support for the court reform bill, creating the impression that he alone did so without reservation. Several of the other candidates in fact took the same position, but they chose to speak softly in Texas, where the legislature had voted its opposition to the Roosevelt proposal within days of its presentation. Not Lyndon Johnson. "I didn't have to hang back like a steer on the way to the dipping vat," he said. "I'm for the President. When he calls on me for help I'll be where I can give him a quick lift, not out in the woodshed practicing a quick way to duck." If you want to help the president, he told voters, then vote for me. That "will show the President's enemies that the people are behind him," Lyndon orated. "Mr. Roosevelt is in trouble now. When we needed help, he helped us. Now *he* needs help. Are we going to give it to him? Are *you* going to give it to him? Are you going to help Mr. Roosevelt? That's what this election is all about." Living in Texas, Elliott Roosevelt, the president's son, endorsed Johnson. James Farley, chairman of the Democratic National Committee and postmaster general, called Johnson "FDR's champion." The strategy worked. Campaigning every day and every night, never giving a speech without mentioning Roosevelt, Lyndon Johnson won a stunning victory which was widely hailed as a vote of confidence for the president and his court plan. The people in my district are "as strong as horse radish for Roosevelt," Lyndon told an interviewer.

The national press played the Johnson election as a victory for FDR and his court reorganization plan. A beleaguered White House welcomed the news. The president was planning a fishing vacation in the Gulf of Mexico, disembarking in Galveston and then traveling through Texas by train on his return trip to Washington. Of course, LBJ wanted a meeting, but so did the White House advance men. Johnson, who had been stricken with appendicitis on election eve and was only slowly recovering from his medical emergency, asked his friend and fellow New Dealer Governor Allred to assure the meeting and photographs of it. The meeting was everything LBJ could have wished—a treasured photograph with the president, traveling with the presidential cavalcade through thunderously cheering crowds in Galveston, an invitation to ride with the president in his private car to College Station and then to Fort Worth. They had a full day to talk and FDR's impression of the congressman-elect was enthusiastic. He advised LBJ to seek a seat on the House Naval Affairs Committee and promised to help him get it. Scribbling a telephone number on a piece of paper, the president told LBJ that if he needed any help to "call Tommy"—Tommy the Cork—Thomas Corcoran, one of FDR's key aides. When he returned to the White House, the president himself telephoned Corcoran to say, "I've just met the most remarkable young man. Now I like this boy. Help him with anything you can." And so began the extraordinary odyssey, fatefully predicted by FDR in a conversation with Harold Ickes: "In the next generation," Roosevelt told him, "the balance of power will shift south and west and this boy could well be the first southern president since the Civil War."

In 1964, having won an even greater majority than did FDR in his landslide 1936 victory, President Johnson reflected on the Supreme Court fight and concluded that FDR had moved too quickly. "Here was a man," LBJ told a meeting of government lobbyists, "who had just been elected by the biggest landslide in history and had the Congress slap him down. That poor man sat there in his wheelchair in the White House and just couldn't get around to all the Congressional offices." That recollection misjudged both the outcome and the meaning of the Court Reform fight.

Roosevelt fought to reform the Supreme Court to save the revolution of the New Deal. Because of Roosevelt, Johnson did not have to worry about the constitutionality of the Great Society programs which he brought about. Roosevelt won his fight. Within weeks of FDR's challenge, under pressure from Chief Justice Hughes, the court reversed its course, upholding the Wagner Act and the Social Security legislation and even the state minimum-wage laws it had ruled unconstitutional just months before. Unexpectedly, one of the anti–New Deal justices retired to give FDR the opportunity of making his first appointment—and creating a new majority. Hugo

Black, a senator from Alabama who became one of the great judicial influences of the century, was appointed to the vacancy. Roosevelt's opponent in the 1940 presidential election, Wendell Willkie, wrote: "Mr. Roosevelt has won. The Court is now his. . . . Mr. Roosevelt has accomplished exactly what he would have accomplished if Congress had approved his proposal." Willkie was right. The revolution which had taken place, a transformation mightily approved by the American people, was not to be undone. These changes are happily accepted today as the core structure of our society. Roosevelt had enormous respect for the constitutional framework of the balance of power and for the integrity of the Supreme Court as an independent branch of our government. But he stood with Lincoln in rejecting the concept that the Constitution was a rigid, inflexible instrument that could prevent the government from responding to crises that threatened to destroy the nation. FDR's proposal of February 1937 elected Lyndon Johnson to Congress. Both men as presidents risked their enormous popularity in what they perceived to be great causes. Roosevelt had saved the New Deal—and twice afterward the people of the United States reelected him as their president.

Roosevelt was true to his word. The White House door was open to Lyndon Johnson as to no other young congressman. The official diaries record twenty-three meetings between 1937 and 1945. There were probably twice as many never recorded because every presidential assistant and secretary became a friend to LBJ, always taking his calls, giving his messages to FDR, enlisting his support in every vital battle, and slipping him into the Oval Office because they knew "the Boss" would be delighted to see him. Shortly after LBJ had been sworn in, Fred Vinson, a central figure on the House Ways and Means Committee, which made committee assignments (and later Chief Justice of the Supreme Court), thanked Lyndon "for a good dinner" and "an excellent conversation," explaining that at a White House dinner "I kept wondering just what it was that the President wanted from me. I knew it was something. Finally, he said casually—oh so casually—'Fred, there's a fine young man just come to the Congress. Fred, you know that young fellow, Lyndon Johnson? I think he would be a great help on Naval Affairs.'" Need it be said? LBJ was appointed to the committee and its iron-fisted, very powerful chairman, Carl Vinson of Georgia, became another of LBJ's mentors. But no one in the House was more important to Lyndon Johnson than his fellow Texan and majority leader, Sam Rayburn, a man for whom the Johnsons had the deepest personal affection; but when "Daddy" Roosevelt and "Daddy" Rayburn collided—which was not often—LBJ was loyal to FDR. Johnson came to the House not as a career but as a waystation to the Senate and beyond. In that journey, the personal support of the president (and through him the White House staff that could facilitate the needs of his electoral base) was more important than any leader of the Congress.

A case in point: in 1940 FDR maintained a sphinx-like silence about running for a third term. John Nance Garner, a conservative Texan and Roosevelt's vice president for two terms, announced his candidacy for the presidential nomination. John L. Lewis, the eloquent and very powerful leader of the United Mine Workers—and by then, no friend of FDR—denounced Garner as "a poker playing, whiskey drinking, evil old man who was trying to drive a knife into the heart of labor." Sam Rayburn promptly summoned a meeting of the entire Texas delegation in the House. Each member was asked to sign a resolution which declared that Garner was not a drinker of whiskey nor unfriendly to labor. The entire delegation agreed, except for Lyndon Johnson, who startled the delegation—and Mr. Rayburn—by saying the proposed statement would make everyone look foolish. Everybody in Washington, LBJ said, knew that Garner was a two-fisted drinker and that he always opposed what labor wanted. "I will not sign the resolution," said young congressman Johnson. For two hours the delegation and Mr. Rayburn argued for him to change his mind. Mr. Rayburn then took him aside for a private meeting. LBJ would not budge. Finally, an amended resolution was adopted which LBJ himself had written. When the president heard the story of what had happened—and LBJ made sure that he did hear it—he was greatly amused. When the third-term strategy regarding Texas was discussed, LBJ was in the inner circle, treated as a confidant by President Roosevelt.

Having been accused of being a water boy for the president, Johnson once wrote FDR that he would "be glad to carry a bucket of water to the Commander in Chief any time his thirsty throat or his thirsty soul needed support." He meant those words, and his voting record reflected that commitment. Lyndon's name was always on the short list of House members whom the White House regarded as loyal and dependable. Only twenty-two southerners, including Johnson, Rayburn, and Maury Maverick, voted as FDR requested to force a vote on the Fair Labor Standards Act. Both Roosevelt and Johnson were, however, pragmatic political leaders. LBJ followed the axiom that the first responsibility is to get elected, and the second obligation is to get reelected. The story of Maury Maverick was a constant reminder of essential priorities. Maverick was elected from the San Antonio congressional district in 1934 with Lyndon's invaluable help. Maverick was a fiery radical, an outspoken advocate of every progressive cause, an organizer of a rebel caucus in the House. The conservative political establishment of Texas, quietly led by Vice President Garner, targeted Maverick for defeat. Despite FDR's personal support, Maverick lost his seat in the 1938 election. When the White House staff pushed LBJ to a point where he thought his political base was endangered, he would say: "Don't forget our friend Maury. . . . There's nothing more useless than a dead liberal."

LBJ used his favored status with the president and the White House to the great advantage of his congressional district. The WPA and PWA awarded millions of dollars of construction projects to his district, as did the Federal Housing Authority, as did the Rural Electrification Administration. "He got more projects, and more money for his district, than anybody else," Tom Corcoran told an interviewer. "He was the best Congressman for a district that ever was." President Roosevelt wanted to bring electricity to rural America, understanding that the poverty and hard labor of the farmers could not be alleviated without it. Lyndon Johnson was such an effective instrument for this mission that FDR offered to appoint him as REA administrator in 1939. LBJ did not take the offer, not for lack of commitment but because he was determined on an elective career.

Both FDR and Lyndon Johnson were excellent storytellers, and stories were a constant part of how they operated. Probably no one was better at it than President Johnson, but he had some early lessons from the master. The first fifteen-minute meeting LBJ had with President Roosevelt was arranged to get FDR's support for an REA grant which was being denied because the population density in Johnson's Hill Country did not meet REA specifications. Johnson never had a chance. FDR talked about the impact of heavy work on the physique of Russian women and then lectured on the design and utility of multiarch dams—and then the door of the Oval Office opened, and Missy Le Hand reported that the next appointment had arrived. Another meeting was quickly arranged. This time, LBJ was determined not to be filibustered. He came armed with charts, maps, and statistics, and before the president could speak, LBJ cried out, "Water, water everywhere and not a drop to drink; public power everywhere and not a drop for my poor people." For the next ten minutes, Johnson never stopped talking. Roosevelt loved histrionic talent—he had just seen a masterful performance—and LBJ got the REA funding. Like Roosevelt, and perhaps learning from him, Johnson was a master at sensing what a person wanted. Telling stories was part of the strategy for controlling a meeting and reaching the result the president wanted.

By 1939, the great reform momentum of the New Deal was over. The challenge was to hold the achievements in place. The president had been unsuccessful in the 1938 elections in seeking the defeat of the anti–New Deal ultraconservative congressional barons, primarily from the South, who had enormous power through their seniority. Lyndon Johnson was a liberal from a conservative state, a loyalist whom the president admired as an extraordinary operator in the political arena. The added dividend was that the president liked him and enjoyed his company and was prepared to assist his future career.

In the 1940 election, the Democrats faced the prospect of losing control of the House of Representatives. Sam Rayburn had just been elected Speaker. Lyndon wrote FDR that the Democrats could lose fifty seats—"The present margin gives me the night-sweats at 3 am." The party hierarchy would not give him a title, but the president told him to go out and "assist the Congressional Campaign Committee." LBJ ran it, raised funds for the marginal districts—$5000 brought victory in most races—he never stopped, all the time building obligations that could become due bills among candidates who owed their election to him. Assured of his own victory, President Roosevelt telephoned Johnson on election night to see how many seats would be lost. Astonishingly, the Democrats had gained six seats. Drew Pearson wrote in his column that "the hero of the hair-raising campaign was no big shot party figure but . . . a rangy 32-year-old Texan . . . who has political magic at his fingertips." LBJ became so involved in drawing a blueprint for FDR to improve the president's relations with the House Democrats, and thought of the assignment as so urgent, that he stayed in Washington rather than return to Texas for the wedding of John and Nellie Connally.

When Senator Morris Sheppard died in April 1941, there was no doubt Lyndon would run to fill the vacancy. Once again, the polls showed Johnson to be the least known of the four probable candidates, who included Governor Lee "Pass the Biscuits Pappy" O'Daniel, Texas attorney general Gerald Mann, and Martin Dies, the congressional inquisitor. Roosevelt knew LBJ was the long shot, but he called him to a meeting and advised him to announce his candidacy from the White House portico. And that is what LBJ did.

FDR had been reelected to a third term in large part because of the threat of war in Europe and Asia. Against this difficult backdrop, Lyndon's Senate campaign once more was Roosevelt, Roosevelt—Roosevelt and Unity—Roosevelt and elect LBJ. On May 31, FDR declared a national emergency. Candidate Johnson wired him: "If my Commander-in-Chief needs me . . . I will come at once." Roosevelt sent a public message telling him to stay in the campaign, essentially saying come back to Washington as a senator. Other prearranged messages extolled LBJ's support of the farm program and the

Social Security legislation. Despite his having told LBJ that he would not be a candidate, Governor O'Daniel entered the race, announcing his platform as "100% approval of the Lord God Jehovah, widows, orphans, low taxes, the Ten Commandments, and the Golden Rule." (As Yogi Berra said, it seemed like déjà vu all over again.)

On June 28, 1941, election day, they counted the votes. Lyndon was ahead by 5,150. Before another day passed, the results from East Texas came in, and Lyndon had lost by 1,095 votes. The election had been stolen, and with one of those ironic twists that make politics a blood sport, the gambling, horse-racing, and liquor interests had supplied the necessary money and "votes" to elect Governor O'Daniel because they wanted him out of the state. They could do business with his successor, Coke Stevenson, the lieutenant governor. Lyndon returned to Washington terribly depressed—even FDR could not cheer him up. The president told him: "I thought you had learned, Lyndon, to sit on the ballot boxes until the final vote is counted. I learned that long ago in New York." To lift his spirits, FDR asked Lyndon to keynote the August convention of the Young Democrats in Louisville, Kentucky. FDR was there too, telling the young people of his party that war and the possibility of making peace would be transcendent events in their lives. In September 1941, with LBJ as an indispensable whip and strategist, the Selective Service Act was extended by a single-vote margin in the House of Representatives. LBJ undoubtedly expected to run again in the Senate race in 1942. He scheduled a meeting at the White House with FDR on December 6 to discuss his future. The meeting was postponed. The next day, Pearl Harbor was attacked, and Lyndon Johnson's political fortunes became the fortunes of war.

He immediately asked for active service, being a lieutenant commander in the Naval Reserve. He went to the South Pacific on a special mission at the behest of FDR, visited with General McArthur in Australia, and flew on a mission that gave him a taste of war's danger. FDR asked all congressmen on active duty to return to Congress or resign to allow special elections. The White House wanted Lyndon to return to Congress, which he did. Although the Democrats retained control of both the House and the Senate in the 1942 elections, the conservative Democrat-Republican coalition now dominated the scene. The war commanded FDR's total time and attention. He rallied the country to stupendous efforts on both the war and the home fronts. In September 1940, the United States ranked seventeenth in military strength—behind Portugal! By 1944, we were the colossus of the world. At this point, a brief comment is in order about FDR and LBJ in the context of the Vietnam War, where President Johnson was commander in chief.

It is difficult for me to this day to understand why President Johnson put his enormous domestic achievements at risk to wage war in Vietnam. I was the executive assistant to General "Wild Bill" Donovan, the US ambassador to Thailand in 1953–54 when the General, one of America's greatest war heroes and founder of the OSS, the intelligence agency of the United States during World War II, served as President Eisenhower's ambassador to Thailand and special representative in Southeast Asia. As the climactic battle of Dien Bien Phu raged in May 1954, President Eisenhower, rejecting the advice of Nixon, Dulles, and Admiral Radford, the chairman of the Joint Chiefs of Staff, to intervene with American forces, had the strong, powerful support of Lyndon Johnson, then minority leader of the Senate. In faraway Southeast Asia on that day, we hailed Lyndon Johnson's wisdom and courage. Vietnam was engaged in a war of liberation from colonial oppression. France could not prevail. It was certainly appropriate for the United States to support anti-Communist, anticolonial nationalists in the hope that they could contend with the Communist Viet Cong. We had seen—and can see today—what US/UN intervention had meant in 1950, when North Korea's Communist armies invaded the South—South Korea, today a leading industrial democracy; the North, a totalitarian lunatic asylum. But what we should also have learned in Korea were the limits of intervention. China would not allow a Communist ally bordering its frontiers to be destroyed. The risk of war between nuclear powers was unacceptable. Korea was a war fought in the context of our treaty obligations under the UN Charter to resist aggression as defined by the Security Council, which our veto controlled. Vietnam never had that larger purpose. Nevertheless, Presidents Eisenhower, Kennedy, and Johnson were justified in doing everything possible to help the antiCommunist forces prevail—except making the struggle an American war, because no government could do what was necessary to win such a war. Clark Clifford and George Ball so advised LBJ that in 1965. In the months following becoming president, Lyndon Johnson repeatedly made the case himself with Senator Fulbright, Senator Russell, and others that the United States must not make the struggle in Vietnam its war.

Franklin Roosevelt and Lyndon Johnson shared a great vision of America, but they saw the world differently. FDR in the years before World War II foresaw the end of colonialism and the wave of nationalism that would follow it. He had long advocated that the states of Indochina should be freed from colonial rule. In the world he foresaw, the age of empire was over.

President Johnson had supreme confidence that the United States could do anything it set its mind to. He believed that the country's resources, human and material, could answer any challenge to our power. He feared a right-wing backlash if he did not fight the war. It is at this point that consensus politics becomes self-defeating. Roosevelt never made the mistake of adopting the policies of his opponents in order to avoid their attacks. In later years, Johnson disparaged the speech by FDR in which he confronted and identified the enemies of the New Deal and said, "They have met their match—in this election, they will meet their master." But those leaders who accept their opponents' position in order to avoid confrontation have already lost the battle. In 1964, the people gave Lyndon Johnson an overwhelming landslide victory because, in large part, they thought he would block the pressures from the Right for greater and direct American intervention in Vietnam. That was his explicit promise in the campaign. LBJ often quoted President Roosevelt, saying, "It is fine to be a leader, but you better make sure that when you turn around, somebody is following you." By 1967, in the front rank of those following President Johnson were the same forces who had opposed the liberal essence of his public life.

The Vietnam War left a painfully divided America, a disenchanted generation, a Nixon victory, a diminution of the presidency's power and credibility, an empowerment of the forces that would never accept Lyndon Johnson's dream, his vision, his hope for the country he loved so much. History, therefore, is left to resolve the ambiguities in deciding his place in its ultimate book.

With the nation in 1944 confident that the Allies would prevail against the Axis powers, FDR went before Congress to give one of his most extraordinary speeches—a blueprint for winning a lasting peace and the establishment of an American standard of living higher than ever known before, an economic bill of rights for all Americans. Eight days before, LBJ had addressed the Texas legislature. Deeply moved by a visit to wounded veterans in a Texas hospital, he told the legislature that he would assure these valiant men—and all Americans—equal opportunity. He hoped the local and state governments would assume that responsibility, but if they didn't, he would work for federal legislation to make sure it was done. These two radical speeches, intertwined by fate, became the clarion call that brought the next great social revolution in America, the Great Society of Lyndon Johnson.

Both Franklin Roosevelt and Lyndon Johnson were committed to the liberation of the South, and the nation, from poverty and the bondage of racism. The mandate of President Roosevelt's message in 1944 was left to Presidents Truman, Kennedy, and, most of all, Johnson to fulfill. Of all of LBJ's accomplishments, none was more significant and enduring than his breakthroughs on civil rights, voting rights, and racial justice. How proud FDR would have been—how proud all of us were—to witness Lyndon Johnson's address to Congress on March 15, 1965, when he ended with words that only a president from the South could have delivered and made truly meaningful. Reflecting on the race riots in Selma, Alabama, President Johnson called upon his countrymen—black and white together—to overcome the crippling legacy of bigotry and injustice that marred the American dream. And then, after a dramatic pause, he lifted his arms as a conductor would to begin the Hallelujah Chorus and said the words of the crusade he would now lead: "We Shall Overcome." It was an unforgettable moment.

Lyndon Johnson did more for equal opportunity and racial justice in America than any president since Abraham Lincoln. He carried the New Deal into the next era of possible reform, and using his great intelligence, energy, and political skill, he solidified the foundation and raised the edifice of the New Deal to great new heights. Lyndon Johnson's genius created the Great Society. It is an extraordinary legacy.

Lyndon Johnson's first words to the nation in the tragic days of November 1963 were to invoke the name of FDR in asserting America's confidence and capacity to survive any crisis. Lyndon Johnson's final action as president on the last morning of his presidency was to sign a proclamation establishing the Franklin Delano Roosevelt Memorial Park, a final gesture of respect and devotion to the man who had so deeply influenced his life. As Arthur Schlesinger Jr. has written, "Our world today is the world of the Four Freedoms, Franklin Roosevelt's world, constructed on his terms, propelled by his hope and his vision." I believe Lyndon Johnson would agree. And Franklin Roosevelt would have said that America's greatness today owes much to the extraordinary contribution of Lyndon Johnson.

Adolf Berle, an eminent New Dealer, once said that "great men have two lives; one which occurs while they work on the earth; a second which begins at the day of their death and continues as long as their ideas and conceptions remain powerful."

The "ideas and conceptions" of Franklin Delano Roosevelt and Lyndon Johnson remain and will remain powerful and inspiring as America's young men and women lead us into a new millennium, remembering the historic alliance for social justice of these two presidents and their role as architects of our nation.

In the oratory of the twentieth century, no speech is more significant than that given to Congress on January 6, 1941, by Franklin Delano Roosevelt as the thirty-second president of the United States. History knows it as the Four Freedoms speech. In it, the president asked not only his countrymen but also the people of the world to understand that the terrible scourge of war that was upon us could be justified to our children's children only if we, in faith and honor, determined to create a different world to assure the peace. The world at that time—beset by war, oppressed by Nazi domination, brutalized by racist thugs—was a world where every tenet of democracy was threatened and ridiculed.

President Roosevelt's power as a speaker was to present profound ideas in simple language. Those who were with him as he worked on the draft of the Four Freedoms speech describe how he sat quietly in a swivel chair in his small private study on the second floor of the White House on New Year's Day, 1941, for a long time saying nothing. Then the president began dictating, slowly, decisively, as though the words were part of his memory. With hardly a word changed, those thoughts became his address to Congress. And so he gave us a vision of the world that would be worthy of our civilization. Simply, eloquently, he spoke of a nation dedicated to the Four Freedoms—everywhere in the world:

Freedom of Speech and Expression: the best defense against the corruption of democracy.

Freedom of Worship: our shield against the forces of bigotry, intolerance, and fanaticism.

Freedom from Want: a commitment to erase hunger, poverty, and pestilence from the earth.

Freedom from Fear: a freedom dependent on collective security, governments dedicated to peaceful solution of conflict, a concept to be carried forward through our leadership in the United Nations.

The Four Freedoms brought the past and present together and defined the challenge for future generations. These were the freedoms for which the most terrible war in human history had been fought. They were fundamental values of the world we would leave to our children. Upon hearing the Four Freedoms speech, the Kansas newspaper editor William Allen White, one of the nation's most prominent Republicans, declared, "The Four Freedoms mark the opening of a new era for the world."[53]

President Roosevelt made clear that the Four Freedoms were no vision of a distant millennium. "They are," he said, "a definite basis for a kind of world attainable in our own time and generation." His concluding words on that epic day in 1941 were "Freedom means supremacy of human rights everywhere."[54] Each succeeding generation must take hold of this dream, understand it, believe in it, work for it, and go forth with new strength and purpose in our commitment to democracy and freedom.

Beginning in 1956, the Four Freedoms Medal was awarded annually to Americans whose lives and principles reflected the message of Roosevelt's words. Past recipients have included Eleanor Roosevelt, Harry Truman, John Kennedy, Katherine Graham, and Thurgood Marshall. In 1982, to mark the 100th anniversary of FDR's birth and the bicentennial of the Netherlands' diplomatic recognition of the original thirteen colonies, the Franklin and Eleanor Roosevelt Institute hosted a dinner with New York governor Hugh Carey at his residence in Albany on the occasion of the state visit of Queen Beatrix of the Netherlands. A bust of Roosevelt by the sculptor Jo Davison was presented to the queen. In further celebration of FDR's centennial, it was decided to expand the Four Freedoms Award program to include international laureates every other year. To mark the importance of the relationship with the Netherlands, we chose Princess Juliana as the first of the international laureates. She had known the Roosevelts personally and had frequently stayed at the White House during the war. President Roosevelt was the godfather of one of her daughters. And her mother, the doughty Queen Wilhelmina, was a favorite of Americans, as was Juliana herself. When Princess Juliana died in March 2004, she was buried in Delft, the traditional resting place of the Dutch royal family. The only medal to accompany her on her coffin was the medal of the Four Freedoms awarded in that 1982 ceremony.

The international ceremonies were sited in Middelburg, in the province of Zeeland, from where the Roosevelts emigrated in 1648. They continue to be held in the magnificent twelfth-century abbey, a proud monument to freedom of worship. A Roosevelt study center was created in Middelburg; it now holds the largest collection of materials on the American presidency outside of the United States. Han Polen, the king's commissioner in Zeeland, is chairman of the Four Freedoms Foundation in the Netherlands. The programming related to the awards ceremonies is creative and widely admired. For the Dutch, Franklin Roosevelt, a man of the sea, brings Zeeland and Hyde Park together.

International laureates over the years have included Nelson Mandela, Angela Merkel, Mikhail Gorbachev, and Shimon Peres, among others, and the ceremonies are widely broadcast and deeply respected in the Netherlands.

In all of these Roosevelt enterprises, Anna Eleanor Roosevelt, the granddaughter of Franklin and Eleanor, has been a significant leader. She has the ideals and determination of her namesake. She has the strength and the purpose of her grandfather. She continues to serve as chairman of the Roosevelt Institute and is an inspiration for all who work with her.

On September 24, 1973, at the invitation of Nelson A. Rockefeller, governor of New York, and John V. Lindsay, mayor of New York City, 500 guests gathered to mark the renaming of Welfare Island as Franklin D. Roosevelt Island, the future home of the Four Freedoms Park, a monument to Roosevelt. I attended that windblown ceremony. Louis Kahn, considered at the time to be America's foremost living architect, had created a monumental design of granite, an open room, lined with trees, covering the southern tip of the island and facing the United Nations building. Then, tragedy. Louis Kahn died suddenly—victim of a heart attack in Penn Station in March 1974, in his briefcase a sketchbook containing drawings of the memorial. Meanwhile, Nelson Rockefeller, a powerful patron of the project, moved to Washington, having been selected as vice president of the United States. Further endangering the project, New York City verged on bankruptcy.

The question remained: Would FDR be memorialized properly in his native state? Could the last work of this great architect be built? In 2005, newly emeritus in my relationship to the Franklin and Eleanor Roosevelt Institute, I suggested that we explore the situation to see if this monument to Franklin Roosevelt could at last become a reality.

It was a momentous project, requiring the strength and energy and goodwill of so many. Yet the optimism of FDR, and the generosity he represented, lightened our task. The lead donor was the Alphawood Foundation, founded by Fred Eychaner, a Chicago philanthropist who was a great partisan of Louis Kahn and Franklin Roosevelt. Over the course of five years, we were able, publicly and privately, to raise over $54 million to make Four Freedoms Park a reality.

Construction began on March 29, 2010. As the magnificence of the Kahn design emerged, it became clear that this stunningly beautiful work of art would be an enduring gift to New York and to the nation. By the

**Figure 21.** The Franklin D. Roosevelt Four Freedoms Park. (Photo: Paul Warchol)

autumn of 2012, the park was complete. Michael Kimmelman, the eminent architectural critic, described the glorious new space in a front-page review in the *New York Times* on September 12. "It gives New York nothing less than a new spiritual heart," he wrote. "It is as solemn as the Roosevelt wartime speech it honors, a call to safeguard the freedoms of speech and worship and the freedoms from want and fear. From inside the great, open granite enclosure that Kahn called the 'room' at the tip of the island, a long fly ball away from the United Nations, a visitor looks out over the city and the churning waters of the East River in the direction of the Statue of Liberty, the ocean and Europe. It is the long view that Roosevelt had for America."[55]

Now in its sixth year, the park has hosted over a million visitors. It remains as a place of contemplation and beauty, a place to reflect on the courage and legacy of FDR, and to gain new strength and hope in the challenges that face us today, challenges that can find answers in FDR's own struggles.

We gathered together—President Clinton, Governor Cuomo, Mayor Bloomberg, Tom Brokaw, Anna Eleanor Roosevelt, Mrs. Franklin D. Roosevelt Jr., and myself—surrounded by freshly cut granite and newly planted linden trees, on a crisp October morning in 2012. As I spoke that day, our sense of dedication and thanksgiving was complete:

> It is not worldly power and grandeur that cause us to remember Franklin Roosevelt this day. It is the cause of human freedom and social justice to which he gave so much of his life.

The Four Freedoms Park will be an eternal reminder for all of us and those who inherit our places of what America's dream truly means.

Let children everywhere hear the bells of freedom.

Let our leaders be unafraid in the quest for peace and social justice.

Come my friends, come all of us, come to this place and find again inspiration, courage, strength. It is not too late to seek a better world.

# 8

# REFLECTIONS ON YEARS TO COME

Americans are confronted today with the most fundamental clash of values that we have seen in my lifetime. As I reflect on the challenges, I believe that the greatest threats to our democracy are endless war, racism, corruption and the abuse of money, and the determined assault on the integrity of our democratic institutions.

The election of 2016 put our country in the hands of a cabal of fortune hunters who think that history began with their election to office. They have no respect for the struggles of the last eighty years that have made the United States the greatest country in the world, worthy of the respect it has earned. They have mastered the art of insult and threat. They are bullies, with the character and integrity of bullies. They have humiliated good and decent people. They have demeaned our allies and given comfort to enemies of peace and social justice. They have given us an authoritarian government without respect for democracy. They have fanned the fires of racism. They have pretended to patriotism while insulting an authentic hero, Senator John McCain, whose service to his country is legendary—while their own is nonexistent.

## Endless War

I believe that a mission of our country should be to use its great power to support and achieve a goal that has eluded mankind for all of the days of human history—namely, to stop war and preserve the peace. Peace is not just the absence of war. It involves the creation of a civil society based on the rule of law and the respect for the dignity of every individual.

There is so little talk of peace in our society today. Even at the United Nations, where the prevention of war is a primary mission, there is a sense of fatalism as valiant efforts are reduced to failure. The Syrian civil war is an example. The Great Powers could stop it, but they do not. Ancient countries are destroyed. Any pretense of civilization is ravaged. Five hundred thousand people have been killed—500,000 people have been killed, and there is hardly anyone who can tell us what the war is about. It has produced refugees and displaced populations that are numbered in the millions, and whose attempted migration to Western Europe undermines the governments of nations that have been our principal allies.

Those individuals and organizations that have carried the flag of peace are often disdained as feckless idealists. As we witnessed in the American invasion of Iraq in 2003, deliberate deceit dominated the decision-making structure. Our constitutional restraints giving only Congress the right to declare war were pushed aside. Patriotism became the edge of the samurai sword. Our sons and daughters were killed. Hundreds of thousands of Iraqis, whose only crime was being in our way, were the principal casualties. Our national treasure was devoured, never to be seen again. For me, the Iraq war and its aftermath represent the most grotesque error in presidential judgment that I have witnessed.

We must listen to those forces and individuals who have spoken against war with decency and common sense. The longest war in our history is continuing in Afghanistan. The threat of war engages practically every continent. The most formidable challenge is to determine whether we can do anything about what seems to be the innate disposition of humankind to war in all of its destructive aspects. Our best minds should be directed to this task.

Resources should be available to encourage massive efforts to accept the responsibility of peace. The Security Council of the United Nations should be reorganized so that its members are given the mandate to end war. Franklin Roosevelt understood that being "policemen of the world" required the full commitment of the nations that had the power to stop war. Such a responsibility would require an understanding of negotiation, diplomacy, and compromise. But is there an alternative, when the world in which we live and the nuclear age make clear that wars can no longer be won? That our purposes require a different approach to prevent the annihilation of hope? The Defense Department should be made a complete partner in the search for peace. The secretary of defense should have a leadership role in this basic search for a different way to run the world. And the people of all nations, who have access to social media, should become participants in the dialogue that will force change. That dialogue should begin with the basic assumption that war is not an alternative for the resolution of human conflicts. Those who have the power to end the calamity and for whatever reason do not do so risk becoming the new definition of war criminals.

A great constituency awaits the leadership that this fundamental change requires. We should remember that the first words of the United Nations Charter are "We the *peoples* of the United Nations, determined to save succeeding generations from the scourge of war . . ." It is time to bring the "peoples" into the effort that is required. It is time to begin listening to their hopes and their ideas, and at the same time prove that our national interest can be better defended by peace than by war. It is time to humanize the United Nations to allow the "peoples" who have created it to participate in building the peace that was promised at its creation. All of us might be surprised by the constructive and positive response that would come from an invitation to join this effort.

I do not underestimate either the gravity or the difficulty of a challenge that has eluded humankind's abilities for all of its recorded history. But we might be surprised by what American leadership can do to make peace possible—American leadership in every form of endeavor. Those who have led the technological revolution, which has created some incredible fortunes, could have deeper satisfaction if a moral dimension of peace were added to their labors.

## Racism

Our Founding Fathers gave us their courage. These extraordinary men wrote the greatest documents of liberal democracy—the Declaration of Independence and the Constitution of the United States—and yet this work was done by men who tolerated slavery, the most brutal and vicious of all human relationships. It took a civil war to end its legality, a war in which over 600,000 Americans were killed, under circumstances that are generally described as heroic, but were in fact horrific. The constitutional haven of states' rights became the weapon by which apartheid, lynching, and the denial of due process continued. The defenders of human rights have won great victories, but at appalling cost. If not for the intervention of a unanimous Supreme Court in *Brown v. Board of Education* in 1954, one wonders how the southern states would have allowed us to give meaning to the constitutional guarantee of equality. A "Southern Manifesto" was drafted against the Supreme Court decision, which included among the signatories some of the finest representatives and senators in our country. They were not only against desegregation; they were willing to declare political war on it, despite the Supreme Court ruling. The "Manifesto" was, strangely, an echo of what had confronted Lincoln 100 years earlier.

The denial of educational opportunity is a profound cost of racism. It continues in new and differing forms in many states of the Union. Progress is recorded in our great cities as segregation is outlawed, but then we turn around within a decade and find that public schools have been abandoned by the white leadership of the community.

The assurance of the right to vote—certainly the most basic of laws in a democracy—is under constant pressure. In a decade of greatest progress, the 1960s, three champions of human rights were assassinated. John Fitzgerald Kennedy, Robert Francis Kennedy, Martin Luther King Jr: The political system of but few nations could have survived the loss of such leaders. They were victims of a violence that truly threatened the Republic. In remembering them, we renew the commitment of their lives. They were leaders without fear. They liberated freedom to give us hope.

The continual clash between the criminal justice system and black Americans is further evidence of a racism that is still deeply rooted in our society. A nation that has over 2 million citizens in prison should understand how sham justice can be an oppressor. The eradication of racism is our continuing challenge. We had extraordinary success in coping with anti-Semitism. *Brown v. Board of Education* represents a proud and enduring milestone in the struggle against racism. History gives us hope.

## Corruption and the Abuse of Money

Corruption is a universal scourge, and it is becoming an ever-greater threat to democracy. We read constantly about the Russian oligarchs, who are accused of robbing their nation of its patrimony. We have watched their translation of wealth into the domination of their country. Russia is not unique. The international army of oligarchs is the fastest-growing source of power in the world today. There are nearly 600 billionaires in the United States alone. Fortunately for America, most of those who have great wealth are generous and honorable, with a sense of responsibility for the preservation of democratic values. But money is power, and the vast accumulation of wealth is a threat to governance.

In a sense, corruption has been legalized in many of its forms. We witness the veto of major legislation, not by the president, but by a Congress in which key votes are controlled by lobbyists. Congressmen and staff alike, concerned about their next jobs, develop useful relations with those who are employed by private interests to influence their work. The problem of this concealed corruption in the process of lawmaking cannot be easily solved. The impact of money on our political processes is a daily story in our media. The Supreme Court decision in *Citizens United v. Federal Election Commission* practically destroyed honorable attempts by representatives of both parties to control the flood of anonymous money.

It is a form of corruption to allow our fiscal integrity, in both private and public life, to be compromised. My instinct tells me that our enormous budget deficits are a mortgage on our future that are a threat to our growth, our stability, and our national security. My concern is amplified by the fact that the capital needs of our country, of which our infrastructure is a critically important part, are being ignored. The beauty of our buildings, of our parks, of our roads, is part of the definition of the greatness of a nation. Oliver Goldsmith, in his despairing poem "The Deserted Village," wrote, "Ill fares the land, to hastening ills a prey, where wealth accumulates, and men decay." It is an admonition worth remembering.

## Assault on Democratic Institutions

We are blessed in America that the overwhelming percentage of our public servants are men and women of integrity, intelligence, and purposeful commitment. The bureaucracies at every level have served us well. But now, in the name of conservatism, we witness an unending attack on men and women in the political process, as well as those who carry appointed responsibilities. No one expects perfection or the total absence of chicanery, or even bribery, but the democratic structure of the nation itself is weakened by the relentless attacks by people and organizations that have little or no responsibility for telling the truth. The high standards that we must demand must be established by our leaders and the agencies they control—the presidency, Congress, the judiciary.

And of course, the press, the media, have a special responsibility. The First Amendment is certainly one of the most significant guarantors of our democracy. The extraordinary power and outreach of the media demand the highest integrity.

Two years ago, the Four Freedoms Award was given to Canada and Mexico to mark the anniversary of the Good Neighbor policy established by President Roosevelt, assuring the countries of the Western Hemisphere that a new era of cooperation, dignity, and respect had begun. Franklin Roosevelt ended decades of heavy-handed intervention, pledging a mutual commitment to peace and social justice. We must affirm the respect and profound friendship of the United States with Canada and Mexico. As the *New York Times* columnist David Brooks has written, those who have the power of our government have taken "every relationship that has been historically based on affection, loyalty, trust and reciprocity" and turned it into "a relationship based on competition, self-interest, suspicion and efforts to establish dominance."[1] Let us, as a unified nation, fight to keep the spirit and success of the Good Neighbor policy—grateful for the friendship that has fortified our borders.

General Donovan once said to me, "Bill, live life at as many points as you can. Touch it at every corner, and never be afraid to embrace something new." I have had the pleasure and challenge of doing that.

The development of political attitudes and values is somewhat mysterious. Mine was not a political family. My parents, immigrant and working-class, were almost illiterate in the sense of understanding and speaking English. There was something inside me that was drawn to liberal values and to political action, something I don't think you can inculcate in another. It has to be a part of you, and for me, Franklin D. Roosevelt was the cornerstone of that.

Seamus Heaney, the great Irish poet and Nobel laureate, drew from his own perspective on the conflict in Northern Ireland when he wrote "The Cure at Troy" as a tribute to the South African freedom fighter Nelson Mandela. "Once in a lifetime," he wrote, "the longed-for tidal wave of justice can rise up, and hope and history rhyme."

My life has been lived with hope and with history. It has been an extraordinary time. I have had great good fortune with my family, my friends, my colleagues. I have had my share of disappointment and defeat. The privilege of public service has been an important part of my career. I have the pride of knowing that my financial independence was earned, in careers as a lawyer and an investment banker.

Melinda and I have tried to instruct our children that to love nature and to have the beauty of literature and the magnificence of music as part of one's being is to have wealth that no one can ever take away. Bertrand Russell, the English philosopher, advised friends that if they wanted to avoid growing old, they should identify themselves with a cause that has no end. The unhappiest people that he had known were the suffragettes, who were totally dedicated to their movement. Suddenly, women got the vote, and the suffrage movement came to an end. Roger Baldwin instructed me by saying, "Bill, stay involved with the fight for liberty and justice. These are causes that never end, and the reward of your effort will be a long and fruitful life." In our lifetime, we have witnessed the greatest barbarism in human history—the Nazis and what they did in the Holocaust—and the terrible human cost of the Second World War. We have been constantly reminded that the veneer of civilization is very thin. But that is the struggle, to make the roots of civilization deeper and stronger, and to accept and discharge our responsibilities as citizens of our great country.

Our message to our children: take each day as it comes, seize that day, make it your own. Fill it with love and adventure; fill it with friendship and laughter; fill it with purpose. Choose your own path. Understand that failure can be a part of success. Take pride in who you are.

In 1933, the longed-for tidal wave of justice arose, and hope and history found expression in Franklin Delano Roosevelt. Let hope and history rhyme again. Let us seek renewal in this great country. Let the echoes of the Four Freedoms be heard. The wind and the rain—the sun and its shadows—will carry the message. We will not be afraid. Hope and history will be affirmed. And happy days will come again.

# Notes

1. **Growing Up in the Age of Roosevelt**

   1. James A. Hard died in 1953, at the age of 111.

2. **Heroes and Mentors: Roger Baldwin and William J. "Wild Bill" Donovan**

   1. Roger Nash Baldwin, excerpts from "The Faith of a Heretic," *The Nation*, November 9, 1918, 549.
   2. Brig. Gen. Christian de la Croix de Castries, the French cavalry officer who defended Dien Bien Phu.
   3. Ambassador Louis Dauge, chargé d'affaires for France in Thailand.
   4. That same year, I was elected to the IRC board, thereby providing a link to enable the General to participate in the work without having to attend most of the committee meetings. I have now (2018) served sixty-three years as a director/overseer.
   5. Claiborne Pell, elected in 1960 to the US Senate, where he served for forty years as senator from Rhode Island; Herman Steinkraus, CEO of the Bridgeport Brass Company; John Whitehead, investment banker, later cochair of Goldman Sachs and deputy secretary of state under President Reagan.

4. **Prisons and Prisoners**

   1. Peter Wagner and Bernadette Rabuym, "Mass Incarceration: The Whole Pie 2017," press release, Prison Policy Initiative, March 14, 2017, https://www.prisonpolicy.org/reports/pie2017.html; Danielle Kaeble and Thomas P. Bonczar, "Probation and Parole in the United

States, 2015," US Department of Justice, Office of Justice Programs, Bureau of Justice Statistics, https://www.bjs.gov/content/pub/pdf/ppus15.pdf.

2. Over $334,000 in 2018.

3. Joseph Morgenstern, "Death of a Citizen," *Newsweek*, December 7, 1970.

4. "Excerpts from Correction Board's Report on the 'Death of a Citizen, Julio Roldan,'" *New York Times*, November 18, 1970, 52.

### 5. The Carter Presidency and the United Nations

1. George H. W. Bush and Brent Scowcroft, *A World Transformed* (New York: Alfred A. Knopf, 1998), 489.

### 6. America and the Holocaust

1. Together, we would go on to plan a special program at the institute in April 2011 focusing on the Hungarian Holocaust, about which no one was more expert than he. Professor Braham died on November 25, 2018, in his ninety-sixth year. In 2014, he returned the top Hungarian honors that he had received and demanded that the Holocaust Memorial Center in Budapest strip his name from the library that had been dedicated in his honor. He did this to protest the move of Victor Orban's government to erect a memorial to the German occupation of Hungary and to downplay the Hungarian fascists' role in the murder of thousands of Hungarian Jews. His commitment was to truth, not politics.

2. See Henry L. Feingold, review of *American Refugee Policy and European Jewry, 1933–1945*, by Richard Breitman and Alan M. Kraut, *Moment* 17 (April 1992): 61–62. See Peter Novick, *The Holocaust in American Life* (Boston: Houghton Mifflin, 1999), 47ff.

3. For the purposes of comparison, it may be helpful to note that United States law in fiscal year 1998 allowed 75,000 refugee admissions. President Clinton proposed raising this ceiling to 80,000.

4. Louis de Jong, *The Netherlands and Nazi Germany*, Erasmus Lectures (Cambridge, MA: Harvard University Press, 1990), 6.

5. John Keegan, the famed military historian, wrote in his book *The Second World War* (New York: Penguin Books, 1989), 282: "The removal and transportation of Europe's Jews was a fact known to every inhabitant of the continent between 1942 and 1945."

6. Istvan Deak, "Horror and Hindsight," *New Republic*, February 15, 1999.

7. Rudolf Vrba, *I Escaped from Auschwitz* (Fort Lee, NJ: Barricade Books, 2002), 263.

8. Elie Wiesel, *And the Sea Is Never Full* (New York: Alfred A. Knopf, 1999), 183.

### 7. The Roosevelt Legacy

1. Winston Churchill, "Address to Pilgrim's Society for Eleanor Roosevelt at the Savoy Hotel, London, April 12, 1948," in *Winston S. Churchill: His Complete Speeches, 1897–1963*, ed. Robert Rhodes James (London: Chelsea House Publications, 1974), 7:7624–25.

2. Ed Weiner, *Let's Go to Press: A Biography of Walter Winchell* (New York: G.P. Putnam's Sons, 1955), 182.

3. Eleanor Roosevelt, Statement to the United Nations' General Assembly on the Universal Declaration of Human Rights, December 9, 1948, https://erpapers.columbian.gwu.edu/eleanor-roosevelt-and-universal-declaration-human-rights.

4. Eleanor Roosevelt, "The Great Question," Remarks at Presentation of Booklet on Declaration of Human Rights, *In Your Hands*, to the United Nations Commission on Human Rights, United Nations, New York, March 27, 1958.

5. H. H. Kohlsaat, *From McKinley to Harding: Personal Recollections of Our Presidents* (New York: Charles Scribner's Sons, 1923), 101.

6. James MacGregor Burns and Susan Dunn, *The Three Roosevelts: Patrician Leaders Who Transformed America* (New York: Atlantic Monthly Press, 2001).

7. John M. Blum, "The Presidential Leadership of Theodore Roosevelt," *Michigan Alumnus Quarterly Review* 65 (December 6, 1958), 9.

8. Eleanor Roosevelt, "Keepers of Democracy," *Virginia Quarterly Review* (Winter 1939): 1–5. And with great appreciation to Dr. Allida Black, editor in chief of the Eleanor Roosevelt Papers project.

9. Eleanor Roosevelt, "Wives of Great Men," *Liberty Magazine*, October 1932, 12–16.

10. Linda Donn, *The Roosevelt Cousins* (New York: Alfred A. Knopf, 2001).

11. Donn, *The Roosevelt Cousins*, 171–73.

12. *New York Herald Tribune*, June 7, 1924.

13. Eleanor Roosevelt, *This Is My Story* (New York: Garden City Publishing, 1939), 32.

14. Eleanor Roosevelt, *This I Remember* (1949; repr., Santa Barbara, CA: Praeger, 1975), 31–32. The Roosevelt Institute for American Studies (formerly the Roosevelt Study Center) in Middelburg, the Netherlands, is dedicated to the memory of Franklin and Eleanor and Theodore Roosevelt. On biennial occasions, the institute is the site for the awarding of the Franklin Delano Roosevelt International Four Freedoms Medals. In 1986, the delegation attending these ceremonies was made up of representatives of both families, headed by Franklin Delano Roosevelt Jr. and P. J. Roosevelt, a kinsman of TR and then-chairman of the Theodore Roosevelt Association. While they visited in Utrecht, the family history was broadly discussed, and FDR Jr. and P. J. Roosevelt stood to make appropriate toasts and speeches that are now known within the family as "the Treaty of Utrecht," hopefully and formally ending whatever ill feelings survived from the years of their parents.

15. Henry L. Stoddard, *As I Knew Them: Presidents and Politics from Grant to Coolidge* (New York: Harper & Row, 1927), 320.

16. Theodore Roosevelt, *Autobiography* (New York: Macmillan, 1913), 300.

17. Roosevelt, *Autobiography*, 301–4.

18. Stoddard, *As I Knew Them*, 248.

19. Burns and Dunn, *The Three Roosevelts*, 115.

20. Geoffrey Ward, *A First-Class Temperament* (New York: Harper & Row, 1989), 131.

21. Burns and Dunn, *The Three Roosevelts*, 115. See also Roosevelt, *Autobiography*, 301–4.

22. Roosevelt, *Autobiography*, 388.

23. Roosevelt, *Autobiography*, 389.

24. Arthur Schlesinger Jr., *A Life in the 20th Century* (Boston: Houghton Mifflin, 2000).

25. Stoddard, *As I Knew Them*, 322ff.

26. Doris Kearns Goodwin, *No Ordinary Time* (New York: Simon and Schuster, 1994), 129.

27. Goodwin, *No Ordinary Time*, 527–28.

28. William Leuchtenburg, *In the Shadow of FDR: From Harry Truman to Barack Obama*, 4th ed. (Ithaca, NY: Cornell University Press, 2009).

29. Professor Bogdahor discussed this possibility with Professor Arthur M. Schlesinger Jr. at a conference held in El Escorial, Spain, August 2001.

30. Winston Churchill, "If Lee Had Not Won the Battle of Gettysburg," *Scribner's Magazine*, December 1930, 587.

31. Theodore Roosevelt, Address of Hon. Theodore Roosevelt . . . : Before the Naval War College, Newport, R.I., Wednesday, June 2, 1897 (Washington, DC: Navy Branch, G.P.O., 1897); see also Martin Walker, *Makers of the American Century* (London: Chatto & Windus, 2000), 6.

32. Eleanor Roosevelt, "My Day," August 6, 1962, United Feature Syndicate, Inc.

33. Burns and Dunn, *The Three Roosevelts*, 36.

34. Burns and Dunn, *The Three Roosevelts*, 53.

35. Walker, *Makers of the American Century*, 12.

36. Theodore Roosevelt to Raymond Robins, August 12, 1914, in *The Letters of Theodore Roosevelt*, ed. Elting E. Morison (Cambridge, MA: Harvard University Press, 1954), 7:801.

37. Franklin D. Roosevelt, Annual Message to Congress—State of the Union, January 11, 1944, Master Speech File no. 1501, Franklin D. Roosevelt Presidential Library.

38. See Theodore Roosevelt to Joseph Dixon, March 8, 1912; Theodore Roosevelt to John Strachey, March 26, 1912, in Morison, *Letters*, 7:522–23, 532.

39. Franklin D. Roosevelt, campaign address, Madison Square Garden, New York City, October 31, 1936. See Arthur M. Schlesinger Jr.'s magnificent volumes in the series *The Age of Roosevelt* (Boston: Houghton Mifflin): vol. 1, *The Crisis of the Old Order* (1957); vol. 2, *The Coming of the New Deal* (1959); vol. 3, *The Politics of Upheaval* (1960). See also Arthur M. Schlesinger Jr., *The Vital Center* (Boston: Houghton Mifflin, 1949), 23–24; Burns and Dunn, *The Three Roosevelts*, 123–36; George E. Mowry, *Theodore Roosevelt and the Progressive Movement* (New York: Hill & Wang, 1960), 140ff.; Frank Freidel, *Franklin D. Roosevelt: A Rendezvous with Destiny* (Boston: Little, Brown, 1990); John Allen Gable, *The Bull Moose Years: Theodore Roosevelt and the Progressive Party* (Port Washington, NY: Kennikat Press, 1978). John Gable, the executive director of the Theodore Roosevelt Association, has done as much as any contemporary to make the life and times of Theodore Roosevelt a continuing force in American political thought and action.

40. Roosevelt, *Autobiography*, 463.

41. See William Henry Harbaugh, *Power and Responsibility: The Life and Times of Theodore Roosevelt* (New York: Farrar, Straus & Coudahy, 1961), 399; Roosevelt to Governor Hiram Johnson of California, October 27, 1911, in Morison, *Letters*, 7:418–22.

42. See generally the excellent work of Harbaugh, *Power and Responsibility*; see also Samuel Eliot Morison, Henry Steele Commager, and William E. Leuchtenburg, *The Growth of the American Republic* (Oxford: Oxford University Press, 1969).

43. Franklin D. Roosevelt, "State of the Union Message to Congress," January 11, 1944, www.fdrlibrary.marist.edu/archives/pdfs/state_union.pdf.

44. Walker, *Makers of the American Century*, 11.

45. Franklin D. Roosevelt, Speech at Dedication of the New York State Roosevelt Memorial to the Trustees of the American Museum of Natural History, New York, January 19, 1936, Master Speech File no. 839, Franklin D. Roosevelt Presidential Library.

46. Stoddard, *As I Knew Them*, 318.

47. Louis Auchincloss, *Theodore Roosevelt* (New York: Times Books, 2001), 136.

48. See generally Mary Ann Glendon's excellent book, *A World Made New: Eleanor Roosevelt and the Universal Declaration of Human Rights* (New York: Random House, 2001).

49. Doris Kearns Goodwin, *Lyndon Johnson and the American Dream* (New York: St. Martin's Griffin, 1977), 252.

50. James Reston, *Deadline: A Memoir* (New York: Random House, 1991), 300–301.

51. Personal conversation with the author.

52. Isaiah Berlin, *Personal Impressions* (London: The Hogarth Press, 1980), 26.

53. Townsend Hoopes and Douglas Brinkley, *FDR and the Creation of the U.N.* (New Haven: Yale University Press, 1997), 27.

54. Franklin D. Roosevelt, "Annual Message to Congress on the State of the Union, January 6, 1941," in *The Public Papers and Addresses of Franklin D. Roosevelt*, 1940 vol., *War and Aid to Democracies*, with a special introduction and explanatory notes by President Roosevelt (New York: Macmillan, 1941), 663–78.

55. Michael Kimmelman, "Decades Later, a Vision Survives," *New York Times*, September 12, 2012.

### 8. Reflections on Years to Come

1. David Brooks, "Donald Trump Is Not Playing by Your Rules," *New York Times*, June 11, 2018.

# BIBLIOGRAPHY

## Archival Sources

Eleanor Roosevelt Papers, Franklin D. Roosevelt Presidential Library, Hyde Park, NY.
Franklin D. Roosevelt Papers, Franklin D. Roosevelt Presidential Library, Hyde Park, NY.
Theodore Roosevelt Collection, Harvard University, Cambridge, MA.
William vanden Heuvel Papers, Franklin D. Roosevelt Presidential Library, Hyde Park, NY.
William vanden Heuvel Papers, Jimmy Carter Presidential Library, Atlanta, GA.
William vanden Heuvel Papers, John F. Kennedy Presidential Library, Boston, MA.

## Secondary Sources

Alsop, Joseph, and Turner Catledge. *The 168 Days*. New York: Doubleday, Doran, 1938.
Auchincloss, Louis. *Theodore Roosevelt*. New York: Times Books, 2001.
Baldwin, Roger Nash. "The Faith of a Heretic." *The Nation*, November 9, 1918.

Barber, Benjamin R. *A Passion for Democracy*. Princeton: Princeton University Press, 1998.

Berlin, Isaiah. *Personal Impressions*. London: The Hogarth Press, 1980.

Beschloss, Michael R., ed. *Taking Charge: The Johnson White House Tapes, 1963–64*. New York: Simon & Schuster, 1998.

Blum, John M. "The Presidential Leadership of Theodore Roosevelt." *Michigan Alumnus Quarterly Review* 65 (December 6, 1958).

Boller, Paul F., Jr. *Presidential Campaigns: From George Washington to George W. Bush*. Oxford: Oxford University Press, 2004.

Brinkley, Alan. *The End of Reform*. New York: Alfred A. Knopf, 1995.

Brinkley, Alan, and David Dyer, eds. *The Reader's Companion to the American Presidency*. Boston: Houghton Mifflin, 2000.

Brooks, David. "Donald Trump Is Not Playing by Your Rules," *New York Times*, June 11, 2018.

Burns, James MacGregor. *Roosevelt: The Lion and the Fox, 1882–1940*. New York: Harcourt, 1963.

———. *Roosevelt: Soldier of Freedom*. New York: Harcourt, 1970.

Burns, James MacGregor, and Susan Dunn. *The Three Roosevelts: Patrician Leaders Who Transformed America*. New York: Atlantic Monthly Press, 2001.

Bush, George H. W., and Brent Scowcroft. *A World Transformed*. New York: Alfred A. Knopf, 1998.

Califano, Joseph A., Jr. *The Triumph and Tragedy of Lyndon Johnson: The White House Years*. New York: Touchstone, 1991.

Caro, Robert A. *The Path to Power: The Years of Lyndon Johnson*. New York: Alfred A. Knopf, 1982.

———. *The Means of Ascent: The Years of Lyndon Johnson*. New York: Alfred A. Knopf, 1990.

Churchill, Winston. "If Lee Had Not Won the Battle of Gettysburg." *Scribner's Magazine*, December 1930.

———. *Winston S. Churchill: His Complete Speeches, 1897–1963*. Edited by Robert Rhodes James. London: Chelsea House Publications, 1974.

Clifford, Clark, and Richard Holbrooke. *Counsel to the President: A Memoir*. New York: Random House, 1991.

Dallek, Robert. *Franklin D. Roosevelt and American Foreign Policy, 1932–1945*. Oxford: Oxford University Press, 1979.

———. *Lone Star Rising: Lyndon Johnson and His Times, 1908–1960*. Oxford: Oxford University Press, 1991.

———. *Flawed Giant: Lyndon Johnson and His Times, 1961–1973*. Oxford: Oxford University Press, 1999.

Deak, Istvan. "Horror and Hindsight." *New Republic*, February 15, 1999.

de Jong, Louis. *The Netherlands and Nazi Germany*. Erasmus Lectures. Cambridge, MA: Harvard University Press, 1990.

Donn, Linda. *The Roosevelt Cousins*. New York: Alfred A. Knopf, 2001.

Edsforth, Ronald. *The New Deal: America's Response to the Great Depression*. Problems in American History. Oxford: Blackwell, 2000.

Evans, Rowley, and Robert Novak. *Lyndon B. Johnson: The Exercise of Power*. New York: Signet, 1968.

"Excerpts from Correction Board's Report on the 'Death of a Citizen, Julio Roldan.'" *New York Times*, November 18, 1970, 52.

Feingold, Henry L. Review of *American Refugee Policy and European Jewry, 1933–1945*, by Richard Breitman and Alan M. Kraut. *Moment* 17. April 1992.

Freidel, Frank. *Franklin D. Roosevelt: A Rendezvous with Destiny*. New York: Little Brown, 1990.

Gable, John Allen. *The Bull Moose Years: Theodore Roosevelt and the Progressive Party*. Port Washington, NY: Kennikat Press, 1978.

Galbraith, John Kenneth. *The Great Crash, 1929*. Boston: Houghton Mifflin, 1954.

Gentry, Curt. *J. Edgar Hoover: The Man and the Secrets*. New York: W.W. Norton, 1991.

Glendon, Mary Ann. *A World Made New: Eleanor Roosevelt and the Universal Declaration of Human Rights*. New York: Random House, 2001.

Goldman, Eric. *The Tragedy of Lyndon Johnson*. New York: Alfred A. Knopf, 1969.

Goodwin, Doris Kearns. *Lyndon Johnson and the American Dream*. New York: Harper & Row, 1976.

——. *No Ordinary Time*. New York: Simon and Schuster, 1994.

Goodwin, Richard. *Remembering America: A Voice from the Sixties*. New York: Harper, 1988.

Harbaugh, William Henry. *Power and Responsibility: The Life and Times of Theodore Roosevelt*. New York: Farrar, Straus & Coudahy, 1961.

Hoopes, Townsend. *The Limits of Intervention: An Inside Account of How the Johnson Policy of Escalation in Vietnam Was Reversed*. Philadelphia: David McKay, 1973.

Hoopes, Townsend, and Douglas Brinkley. *FDR and the Creation of the U.N.* New Haven: Yale University Press, 1997.

Ickes, Harold L. *The Secret Diaries of Harold L. Ickes: The Inside Struggle, 1936–1939*. New York: Simon & Schuster, 1954.

Kaeble, Danielle, and Thomas P. Bonczar. "Probation and Parole in the United States, 2015." US Department of Justice, Office of Justice Programs, Bureau of Justice Statistics. https://www.bjs.gov/content/pub/pdf/ppus15.pdf.

Keegan, John. *The Second World War*. New York: Penguin Books, 1989.

Kempton, Murray. *Rebellions, Perversities, and Main Events*. New York: Three Rivers Press, 1995.

Kennedy, David. *Freedom from Fear: The American People in Depression and War, 1929–1945*. Oxford: Oxford University Press, 1999.

Kimmelman, Michael. "Decades Later, a Vision Survives." *New York Times*, September 12, 2012.

Kohlsaat, H. H. *From McKinley to Harding: Personal Recollections of Our Presidents*. New York: Charles Scribner's Sons, 1923.

Larrabee, Eric. *FDR: Commander-in-Chief*. New York: Harper & Row, 1987.

Lash, Joseph P. *Eleanor and Franklin*. New York: W.W. Norton, 1969.

——. *Eleanor: The Years Alone*. New York: W.W. Norton, 1972.

——. *Dealers and Dreamers: A New Look at the New Deal.* New York: Doubleday, 1988.

Leuchtenberg, William. *In the Shadow of FDR.* Ithaca, NY: Cornell University Press, 1983.

——. *The Perils of Prosperity.* Chicago: University of Chicago Press, 1993.

——. *The FDR Years: On Roosevelt and His Legacy.* New York: Columbia University Press, 1995.

——. *The Supreme Court Reborn.* Oxford: Oxford University Press, 1995.

——. *In the Shadow of FDR: From Harry Truman to Barack Obama.* 4th ed. Ithaca, NY: Cornell University Press, 2009.

Louchheim, Katie. *The Making of the New Deal: The Insiders Speak.* Cambridge, MA: Harvard University Press, 1983.

Morgenstern, Joseph. "Death of a Citizen." *Newsweek*, December 7, 1970.

Morison, Samuel Eliot, Henry Steele Commager, and William E. Leuchtenburg. *The Growth of the American Republic.* Oxford: Oxford University Press, 1969.

Mowry, George E. *Theodore Roosevelt and the Progressive Movement.* New York: Hill & Wang, 1960.

Neal, Steve. *Dark Horse: A Biography of Wendell Willkie.* New York: Doubleday, 1984.

Novick, Peter. *The Holocaust in American Life.* Boston: Houghton Mifflin, 1999.

Reich, Cary. *The Life of Nelson Rockefeller.* New York: Doubleday, 1996.

Reston, James. *Deadline: A Memoir.* New York: Random House, 1991.

Roosevelt, Eleanor. "Wives of Great Men." *Liberty Magazine*, October 1932.

——. "Keepers of Democracy." *Virginia Quarterly Review*, Winter 1939.

——. *This Is My Story.* New York: Garden City Publishing, 1939.

——. *This I Remember.* 1949. Reprint, Santa Barbara, CA: Praeger, 1975.

Roosevelt, Theodore. *Autobiography.* New York: Macmillan, 1913.

——. *The Letters of Theodore Roosevelt.* Edited by Elting Elmore Morison. Cambridge, MA: Harvard University Press, 1954.

Schlesinger, Arthur M., Jr. *The Vital Center.* Boston: Houghton Mifflin, 1949.

——. *The Crisis of the Old Order, 1919–1933.* The Age of Roosevelt 1. Boston: Houghton Mifflin, 1957.

——. *The Coming of the New Deal.* The Age of Roosevelt 2. Boston: Houghton Mifflin, 1959.

——. *The Politics of Upheaval.* The Age of Roosevelt 3. Boston: Houghton Mifflin, 1960.

——. *A Life in the 20th Century.* Boston: Houghton Mifflin, 2000.

Schwarz, Jordan A. *The New Dealers: Power Politics in the Age of Roosevelt.* New York: Alfred A. Knopf, 1993.

Shapley, Deborah. *Promise and Power: The Life and Times of Robert McNamara.* New York: Little, Brown, 1993.

Shesol, Jeff. *Mutual Contempt: Lyndon Johnson, Robert Kennedy, and the Feud That Defined a Decade.* New York: W.W. Norton, 1998.

Sidey, Hugh. *A Very Personal Presidency: Lyndon Johnson in the White House.* New York: Harper Collins, 1968.

Steinberg, Alfred. *Sam Johnson's Boy: A Close-Up of the President from Texas.* New York: Macmillan, 1968.

——. *Sam Rayburn: A Biography*. New York: Hawthorn Books, 1975.

Stoddard, Henry L. *As I Knew Them: Presidents and Politics from Grant to Coolidge*. New York: Harper & Row, 1927.

Tully, Grace. *FDR, My Boss*. New York: Scribner, 1949.

Vrba, Rudolph. *I Escaped from Auschwitz*. Fort Lee, NJ: Barricade Books, 2002.

Wagner, Peter, and Bernadette Rabuym. "Mass Incarceration: The Whole Pie 2017." Press release, Prison Policy Initiative, March 14, 2017. https://www.prisonpolicy.org/reports/pie2017.html.

Walker, Martin. *Makers of the American Century*. London: Chatto & Windus, 2000.

Ward, Geoffrey. *A First-Class Temperament*. New York: Harper & Row, 1989.

Watkins, T. H. *The Hungry Years*. New York: Henry Holt, 1999.

Weiner, Ed. *Let's Go to Press: A Biography of Walter Winchell*. New York: G.P. Putnam's Sons, 1955.

White, Theodore H. *The Making of the President, 1964*. New York: Cape, 1965.

Wiesel, Elie. *And the Sea Is Never Full*. New York: Alfred A. Knopf, 1999.

Zevin, Benjamin D., ed. *Nothing to Fear: The Selected Addresses of Franklin Delano Roosevelt*. Boston: Houghton Mifflin, 1946.

# INDEX

Page numbers followed by letter *f* refer to figures.

Adams, Samuel, 19
Afghanistan, 143, 238
AFL-CIO, 134
African Americans: and civil rights revolution, 60–62; and criminal justice system, 20, 97, 113; JFK and, 73; in leadership positions, 61, 69, 83–84; in Prince Edward County, Virginia, 64, 70–74; RFK and, 62, 87, 94; in Rochester, New York, 7; during World War II, 61. *See also* desegregation; racism
Alabama: civil rights protests in, 60; race riots in, 61, 231. *See also* Birmingham
Algeria, independence of, 38
Alliance for Progress, 88
Allred, James, 223
Alphawood Foundation, 234

Al Qaeda, 156
Ambrose, Stephen, 186
American Civil Liberties Union (ACLU): Baldwin and, 15, 17, 20; on media regulations, 118
Ames, Oliver, 27–28, 29–30, 32
Annan, Kofi, 158
Anthony, Susan B., 14
anti-Semitism: in America, coping with, 240; in America, FDR's awareness of, 163, 169–70, 187, 211; and America's response to Holocaust, accusations of, 162, 163, 165, 170, 173, 177; in Germany, 166
Apablaza, Robert, 104–5
Arab nations: in Gulf War, 155; and UN politics, 138, 144

Atlantic Alliance, 208
Atlantic Charter, 153, 175
Attica Correctional Facility: press coverage of, 116, 117; riots at, 105–6, 108, 110–14, 118
Auschwitz: Allied bombing of, failure to order, 163, 165, 181–83, 187–88; deportation of Hungarian Jews to, 183–85; genocide prior to opening of, 177; knowledge about, 178, 183, 184; reconnaissance photographs of, 182, 187, 188; Vrba-Wetzler report on, 183–85
Austria: Hungarian refugees in, 47, 48, 53, 54–56, 96; Nazi occupation of, 167, 174; Soviet departure from, 47; in World War I, 24–25
authoritarian governments, 237, 240–41

Baeck, Leo, 167
Bagdikian, Ben H., 119
Bailey, Etta Rose, 77
bail system, 103–4, 108, 109–10, 120
Baldwin, Evelyn, 15
Baldwin, Roger, 15–23; and American Civil Liberties Union, 15, 17, 20; background of, 16; as conscientious objector, 16–17; as hero and mentor, 14, 132, 243; and Presidential Medal of Freedom Award, 17, 18*f*, 19; at Telluride House, 12
Balfour, Arthur, 208
Ball, George, 229
Bass, Stanley, 118
Bauer, Yehuda, 189
Bay of Pigs debacle, 196
Beame, Abe, 130–31, 132
Beatrix (Queen of the Netherlands), 233
Belafonte, Harry, 103
Belgium: Jewish refugees in, 173, 176; mother's emigration from, 4, 7; during World War I, 4, 25; during World War II, 8, 174, 175
Ben-Gurion, David, 180, 181
Bergson, Peter, 180
Berle, Adolf, 231

Berlin, Isaiah, 217
Bernstein, Leonard, 81
Berra, Yogi, 228
Bethe, Hans, 12
Biddle, Francis, 64
Bin Laden, Osama, 152
Bird, Bill, 41
Birmingham, Alabama: church bombing in, 79, 84; civil rights protests in, 60; riots in, 61
Black, Allida, 246n8
Black, Hugo, 82, 223–24
Blix, Hans, 149
Bloomberg, Michael, 235
Blum, John Morton, 162
Blum, Yehuda, 138
Blumenthal, Ralph, 121
Blyden, Herbert X., 121
Bogdahor, Vernon, 207, 247n29
Böhm, Karl, 47
Braham, Randolph, 163
Branch, John, 83
Brandeis, Louis, 15, 19
Brezhnev, Leonid, 143–44
Brickman, John, 98
Brill, Steve, 127
Britain. *See* Great Britain
Brokaw, Tom, 235
Bromwell, Herbert, Jr., 96
Brooke, Rupert, 30
Brooklyn House of Detention, New York City, 101
Brooks, David, 242
Brown, James, 103
Brown, Jerry, 130, 131
Brown, Richard, 56
*Brown v. Board of Education*, 60, 61, 71, 240
Brzezinski, Zbigniew, 131
Buchanan, James P., 219, 220, 222
budget deficits, 241
Bulgaria, Jewish population in, 183
Bull, Bartle, 127
Bunche, Ralph, 81
Burke, David, 131

Burma, independence of, 37
Burns, James MacGregor, 198, 199
Burroughs, John, 213
Bush, George H. W., 149, 155–56
Bush, George W.: extremist ideological
  advisers of, 150, 156; and invasion of
  Iraq, 148, 149

Califano, Joseph (Joe), 147, 216
Cambodia, 36–37, 41
Camp Kilmer, New Jersey, 46
Canada, 193–94, 242
Carey, Hugh, 130, 131–32, 233
Carter, Jimmy, 133*f*; background
  of, 126–27; and Baldwin, 17; and
  Brezhnev, 143–44; at dedication of
  JFK's Presidential Library, 140; and
  human rights, 138; Iranian hostage
  crisis and, 142–43, 144–45; and MLK,
  126, 128; in presidential election of
  1976, 126, 127–32; in presidential
  election of 1980, 139, 140, 144; and
  RFK, 140; and Wiesel, 187–88
Carter, Lillian, 128
Carter, Rosalynn, 132
Cary, Eve, 118
Castro, Fidel, 196
Celler, Emmanuel, 171
Chappaquiddick incident, 140, 142
Chavez, Cesar, 88
Chennault, Claire, 35
Cherne, Leo, 43, 45
Chiang Kai-shek, 34–35
China: civil war in, 43–44; Communist,
  concerns about, 35, 36; Japanese
  invasion of, 168, 205; and Korea, 35,
  36, 229; and Malaysia, 37; OSS in, 32;
  and Vietnam, 37, 39, 41
Chinese Nationalist forces (KMT): in
  Taiwan, 33–34, 35; in Thailand,
  33–34, 34*f*
Church, Frank, 130, 131
Churchill, Winston, 8; and FDR,
  175, 190, 208; on Hitler, 166; on
  Holocaust, 164; and Theodore

Roosevelt, 207–8; during World War II,
  137, 165–66, 174, 182
*Citizens United v. Federal Election
  Commission,* 241
Civilian Conservation Corps, 213
civil rights: JFK and, 73; LBJ and, 231;
  RFK and, 61, 62, 83, 87, 94
Civil Rights Act of 1964, 65
civil rights revolution, 60–62; in Prince
  Edward County, Virginia, 70–73.
  *See also* desegregation
Civil War, 240; alternative scenario for,
  207–8; last battle of, 70
Clifford, Clark, 229
Clinton, Bill: and FDR memorials,
  193, 235; and Iraq Liberation Act,
  151; luncheon with, 147–48; refugee
  policies of, 246n3
Cohen, Benjamin, 173
Cold War: Hungarian Revolution and,
  58; United Nations during, 145, 154
Cole, Fred B., 75
*Columbia Journalism Review,* article for,
  116–25
Communism: in China, 35, 36; collapse
  of, 215; cornerstones of, 57; FDR's
  views on, 154; Hungarian Revolution
  and, 53, 55, 56, 57, 58, 109; RFK's
  views on, 64; in Vietnam, 41;
  worldwide spread of, 41, 43–44.
  *See also* Soviet Union
Communist International, 33
Connally, John, 227
Connally, Nellie, 227
Connally, Tom, 219
Coolidge, Calvin, 167, 220, 221
Cooper, Duff, 1
Corcoran, Thomas, 223, 226
*Cornell Law Review,* 13, 23
Cornell University, 2, 12, 15, 23
corruption: in age of Theodore
  Roosevelt, 210; in current age, 240–41;
  FDR on defense against, 232; as
  threat to democracy, 237, 240; UN as
  instrument of defense against, 156

Cortelyou, George, 206
Costanza, Midge, 127
courts: problems with, 109–10. *See also*
    criminal justice system; Supreme
    Court
Cox, James, 200
Cox, William H., 62, 64
criminal justice system, 95; inequities in,
    20, 97–98, 103–5, 108, 112, 120–21,
    122; problems with, 109–10; racism
    in, 97–98, 119. *See also* prison(s)
Cuba: Bay of Pigs debacle, 196; Jewish
    refugees in, 173
Cuban missile crisis, 94, 130, 154
Cuomo, Andrew M., 235
Cushman, Robert, 12
Czechoslovakia, Nazi occupation of,
    164, 169, 174, 205

Daniel, Robert P., 75
Darden, Colgate, 66, 67*f*, 69, 74–75, 76,
    77, 82, 83
Darrow, Clarence, 21
Davis, Angela, 104
Davison, Jo, 233
Dawes, Charles G., 203
Dayan, Moshe, 138
D-Day invasion, 181, 182
Deak, Istvan, 182
Dean, Arthur, 35
Dean, John, 89
de Castries, Christian, 40, 245n2
Declaration of Independence, 33, 239
Deep Springs College, 2, 10–11, 12*f*
de Gaulle, Charles, 38, 89
de Jong, Louis, 172
democracy: America's commitment to,
    95, 161, 192, 199, 233; current threats
    to, 59, 189, 237–42; defense of, 2, 5,
    25, 175, 210, 211, 232; fear as threat
    to, 152, 156; Great Depression and
    threat to, 156, 211, 216; media's role
    in, 119, 123; wealth as threat to, 210,
    237, 240–41; World War II and threat
    to, 156, 164, 175, 192, 232

Democratic National Convention: of
    1924, 191; of 1932, 220; of 1940,
    207; of 1960, 63*f*; of 1964, 86; of
    1976, 132, 133*f*
Democratic Party: Carter and, 129, 131;
    Eleanor Roosevelt and reform of,
    195–96; FDR and, 206; RFK and, 89,
    92; vanden Heuvel and, 23, 62
De Sapio, Carmine, 195, 196
desegregation: *Brown v. Board of*
    *Education* and, 60, 61, 71; Carter
    and, 126; Eisenhower and, 69; Prince
    Edward County Free Schools and,
    66–69, 68*f*, 73, 75–84; resistance to,
    61, 64–65, 69–74
d'Estaing, Valéry Giscard, 89
Dewey, John, 43
Dickstein, Samuel, 171
Diem, Ngo Dinh, 40, 42
Dien Bien Phu, battle of, 39, 40–42, 229
Dies, Martin, 219, 227
Dipple, John, 172
disabilities, people with, FDR's legacy
    for, 193–94
Dishman, J. D., 76
Dole, Vincent, 103
Dominican Republic, 168
Donn, Linda, 200
Donovan, Anna, 24
Donovan, Tim, 24
Donovan, Vincent, 24
Donovan, William J. "Wild Bill," 23–59;
    as ambassador to Thailand, 23, 32–42,
    229; death of, 58; and Eisenhower, 23,
    32, 33, 36, 42, 47, 58; and FDR, 23,
    24, 26, 31, 43; as hero and mentor, 14,
    25, 242; Hungarian Revolution and,
    45, 47, 48, 58, 96; and IRC, 43, 44;
    observatory trips by, 42–43, 44; and
    OSS, 23, 31–32, 43; in World War I,
    23, 25, 26–32, 38
Donovan Commission report, 48–57
Dostoyevsky, Fyodor, 118, 125
Doswell, Rudolph, 77
Douglas, William O., 207

Douglass, Frederick, 7, 14
Douglass, Robert, 111
*Dread Scott* decision, 222
drug addicts, in prison, 103, 112–13
Dubinsky, David, 174
Duffy, Father Francis, 29, 30
Dulles, John Foster, 35, 38, 39, 197
Dunn, Susan, 198, 199

Eastern Europe: immigrants from, quotas
    for, 167; Jewish population in, 169,
    179, 183; Soviet occupation of, 58.
    *See also specific countries*
Eastland, James, 62–64
Eastman, George, 5
Eden, Anthony, 182
education: Free Schools, 66–69, 68*f*,
    73, 75–84; National Teacher Corps,
    proposal for, 83; racism and denial
    of opportunities in, 240; resistance
    to desegregation in, 61, 64–65, 69–74;
    vanden Heuvel's, 2, 10–13, 14, 15
Egypt, Suez Canal crisis and, 44–45,
    47, 58
Eichmann, Adolf, 183, 185
Einaudi, Luigi, 12, 13
Einstein, Albert, 43, 174–75
Eisenhower, Dwight: and desegregation, 69;
    and Donovan, 23, 32, 33, 36, 42, 47, 58,
    229; in election of 1956, 44; Hungarian
    Revolution and, 47; Korean War and,
    35; Vietnam policies of, 39; visit to Nazi
    concentration camp, 186, 187
Eizenstat, Stuart, 132
election(s): of 1912, 142, 212; of 1932,
    218, 220; of 1936, 5–6, 8, 221; of
    1938, 205; of 1940, 227; of 1948, 13;
    of 1952, 23; of 1956, 44; of 1960, 62,
    96, 195; of 1964, 85–88, 230; of 1968,
    91–92; of 1976, 126; of 1980, 139–41;
    of 2016, 237
Ellis Island, 4–5
Emerson, Ralph Waldo, 19
Evian Conference, 168–69
Eychaner, Fred, 234

Farley, James, 222
Ferdinand, Franz, 24
Ferrara, Alphonse, 6
Feynman, Richard, 2, 12
Field, Arthur, 82
Finletter, Thomas, 203
First Amendment, 242
Ford, Gerald, 126, 132
Ford Foundation, 78
Founding Fathers, 239
Four Freedoms Award, 233–34, 242,
    247n14
Four Freedoms Park, New York City,
    231, 234–36, 235*f*
France: colonial empire in Asia, 33,
    37–38, 42; Evian Conference in,
    168–69; during Gulf War, 155;
    Jewish refugees in, 173; military
    campaign in Vietnam, 39–42, 229;
    RFK's visit to, 89, 90*f*; and Suez
    Canal crisis, 44–45; during World
    War I, 24–25, 26; during World War II,
    38, 43, 174, 176, 181, 205
Franco, Francisco, 174
Frankel, Marvin, 117, 132
Frankfurter, Felix, 173, 192
Franklin, Benjamin, 108
Franklin Delano Roosevelt
    Memorial Park, 231, 234–36,
    235*f*
Freedom Riders, 60, 62
Free Schools, Prince Edward County,
    66–69, 68*f*, 73, 75–84
Fry, Varian, 43, 176
Fulbright, J. William, 229

Gable, John, 248n39
Galbraith, John Kenneth, 62, 147
Gandhi, Mahatma, 21
Gantry, Elmer, 140
Gardner, Richard, 127
Garner, John Nance, 225, 226
General Agreement on Tariffs and Trade
    (GATT), 134
Geneva Mission, UN, 132–38

Germany: in Gulf War, 155; immigrants
to U.S. from, 168; Jews in, 166–67,
169, 171; in World War I, 4, 24–25,
26; after World War II, 44. *See also*
Nazi Germany
Gero, Erno, 51
Geyl, Pieter, 165
Gilbert, Martin, 183
Gillespie, Pete, 29
Goebbels, Joseph, 163, 171, 187
Goethe, Johann Wolfgang von, 97
Gold Clause Cases, 220, 221
Golden Triangle, 33
Goldman, Emma, 15, 20
Goldsmith, Oliver, 241
Goldwater, Barry, 22, 87
Gomulka, Wladyslaw, 49
Goodman, Fritzi, 127, 162
Good Neighbor Policy, 88, 242
Goodwin, Doris Kearns, 216
Gorbachev, Mikhail, 145, 234
Gould, Jay, 209
Graham, Katherine, 233
Grant, Ulysses, 70
Great Britain: Atlantic Alliance with, 208;
colonial policies in Asia, 37; in Gulf
War, 155; Holocaust and, 178, 185;
immigrants to U.S. from, 168; Jewish
refugees in, 170; Mandate in Palestine,
180; RFK's visit to, 89; and Suez Canal
crisis, 44–45; in World War I, 24–25,
27; in World War II, 32, 174, 175
Great Depression: FDR's response to,
5, 156, 167, 175, 215, 218, 220;
and immigration policies, 168;
personal experience of, 4; as threat to
democracy, 156, 211, 216
Great Society programs, 215, 223,
230, 231
Green, Robert, 78
Gregory, Dick, 65
Grey, Sir Edward, 25
Griffin, Francis, 66, 67*f*, 69, 71, 72–73,
75, 76, 77, 81, 83
Gulf War, 155–56

Hagel, Chuck, 151
Hajdok, John, 45, 46*f*
Hajdok, Mary, 45, 46*f*
Halprin, Lawrence, 193
Hampden-Sydney College, 69–70, 82;
keynote address at, 70–84
Hand, Learned, 82
Hanna, Mark, 199, 202, 203
Hansberry, Lorraine, 62
Hard, James A., 6
Harding, Warren G., 167, 201,
202, 220
Harlem Four, 120–21
Harriman, Averell, 195
Harrison, Albertis S., Jr., 67*f*, 69, 74, 75
Heaney, Seamus, 242
Heath, Donald, 38
Hebrew Committee on National
Liberation (HCNL), 180
Henderson, Thomas, 75
Henry, Patrick, 69
Hentoff, Nat, 117
Heritage Foundation, 147
Hess, Rudolph, 135–37
Hessel, Stéphane, 132
Hillman, Sidney, 174
Hiss, Alger, 15
Hitler, Adolf, 8, 158; deputy chancellor
under, 135; FDR's opposition to, 5, 31,
163, 165, 166, 171, 175, 185–87, 192;
hatred of Jews, 164, 166–67, 168, 169,
176, 177, 180; and nuclear weapons,
175; occupation of European countries
by, 167, 169, 174, 176–77, 205; rise
of, and creation of IRC, 43; and Stalin,
174. *See also* Nazi Germany
Ho Chi Minh, 33, 37, 38; search for
alternative to, 39, 40
Hogan, Frank, 104
Holocaust, 164–65, 174–87; American
Jews' response to, 166, 179–80;
America's response to, accusations
regarding, 162–63, 165, 177–78,
181–83, 187–89; Churchill on, 164;
inability to foresee, 169, 170, 172, 176;

knowledge about, 178, 183, 184; prelude to, 174. *See also* Auschwitz
Holocaust Memorial Museum, Washington, DC: exhibit on bombing Auschwitz in, 181, 182; lecture at, 163
Hoover, Herbert: and Donovan, 31; and FDR, 220; and immigration policies, 168; and Supreme Court, 220
Hoover, J. Edgar, 84
Horthy, Miklós, 58, 185
Howard, Christopher, 69
Howe, Louis, 201
Howe, Mark DeWolfe, 30
Hughes, Charles Evans, 206, 223
Hughes, John, 122
Hull, Cordell, 173
human rights: Baldwin and, 15, 21; Carter and, 138, 143; Eleanor Roosevelt and, 195–98, 214–15; FDR and, 212, 233; Free Schools program and, 70, 84; vs. property rights, 211, 212; United Nations and, 160. *See also* Universal Declaration of Human Rights
Humphrey, Hubert, 86, 92
Hungarian Revolution (1956), 44–58, 96, 109
Hungary: murder of Jews in, during World War II, 183–85; Nazi invasion of, 183, 185; refugees from, 45–47, 46f, 52–53, 54–56, 96, 109
Hyde Park, New York, 10, 194, 200, 205; Eleanor Roosevelt's residence in, 195, 197; FDR's Presidential Library in, 162, 189

Ickes, Harold, 221, 223
immigration, to U.S.: Congress and limits on, 170, 171; Jewish, 170, 172, 173; personal connection with, 4–5; restrictions on, during World War II, 173; rules and regulations on, history of, 167–68
India, independence of, 37

International Atomic Energy Commission, 160
International Court of Justice, 21, 159–60
International Labour Organization (ILO), 134–35
International League for Human Rights, 21
International League for the Rights of Man, 15
International Red Cross, 134
International Rescue Committee (IRC), 43–44, 59; Donovan and, 43, 44; Donovan Commission report to, 48–57; Eleanor Roosevelt and, 43, 168, 176; Hungarian Revolution and, 45, 47, 48, 54–56, 96; Nazi persecution of Jews and, 168, 176; vanden Heuvel and, 5, 48–57, 245n4
International Telecommunication Union, 134
Iran: hostage crisis in, 142–45; Iraqi invasion of, 144–45
Iraq: invasion of Iran, 144–45; invasion of Kuwait, 148, 155; U.S. invasion of, 145, 148, 149–53, 157, 238; weapons of mass destruction in, UN concern about, 148–49
Iraq Liberation Act, 151
IRC. *See* International Rescue Committee
Irgun Zevai Leumi, 180
Irish Americans: classical story of, 24; RFK's appeal to, 87; in World War I, 27, 31
Iron Curtain, 43, 57, 58
isolationism, U.S., 167, 175; FDR's opposition to, 175–76
Israel: on FDR's response to Holocaust, 189; in Gulf War, 155; and Suez Canal crisis, 45; and UN politics, 138, 144; U.S. invasion of Iraq and, 152
Italy, during World War II, 174, 181, 183

Jackson, George, 120
Jackson, Henry "Scoop," 129, 130

Japan: in Gulf War, 155; invasion of
China, 168, 205; in World War II, 175,
176, 181, 186
Javits, Jack, 195
Jefferson, Thomas, 19, 108
Jewish Council, Vrba-Wetzler report and,
184–85
Jews: American, response to genocide
in Europe, 166, 179–80; Bulgarian,
183; Dutch, 176; FDR's relations
with, 163, 165, 166, 168, 169–70,
173–74, 179; German, 166–67, 169,
171, 172–73, 174, 176; Hungarian,
183–85; immigration to U.S., 170,
172, 173; Polish, 168, 174, 176, 178;
posthumous accusations of FDR,
162–63; Romanian, 168, 183; Russian,
176; as targets of Hitler's hatred, 164,
166–67, 168, 169, 176, 177–79, 180;
Zionist movement and, 163, 174, 176,
180. *See also* anti-Semitism; Holocaust
John Paul II, Pope, 135
Johns, Barbara, 71
Johns, Vernon, 71
Johnson, Lyndon B.: assumption of
presidency, 84–85; decision not to run
for second term, 92; at Democratic
National Convention of 1960, 63*f*;
as FDR's disciple, 215–31; Great
Society of, 215, 223, 230, 231; legacy
of, 230–31; and National Youth
Administration (NYA), 218–19;
personality of, 216–17; political career
of, 217–19, 222–23, 224, 227–28; in
presidential election of 1964, 85–88,
230; and RFK, 85, 86, 88, 89–91; as
storyteller, 226; Vietnam policies of,
39, 89–91, 92, 154, 228–30
Jordan, Hamilton, 128, 129, 130,
131, 132
Juliana (Princess of the Netherlands), 233

Kadar, Janos, 52
Kahn, Louis, 234, 235
Kastner, Rudolf, 185

Katzenbach, Nick, 84
Keating, Kenneth, 85
Keegan, John, 246n5
Kefauver, Estes, 23
Kempton, Lawrence, 11
Kennedy, Edward (Ted), 141*f*; and
Chappaquiddick incident, 140, 142;
and MLK, 65; opposition to invasion
of Iraq, 149–53; and presidential
election of 1976, 127; in presidential
election of 1980, 139–41, 142, 144;
RFK's presidential campaign and,
91*f*, 92
Kennedy, Ethel, 67*f*, 82, 140
Kennedy, Jackie, 86
Kennedy, Jean, 85, 86
Kennedy, John F.: and Alliance for
Progress, 88; assassination of, 81, 84,
87, 140; and civil rights, 64, 72, 78,
81; and Cuban missile crisis, 154; at
Democratic National Convention of
1960, 63*f*; and Eleanor Roosevelt, 195;
and FDR's legacy, 230; Four Freedoms
Medal awarded to, 233; and New
Frontier, 215; obsequies honoring, 85;
Presidential Library in Boston, 140;
and reorganization of judiciary, 64;
visit to Vietnam, 39
Kennedy, John F., Jr., 86
Kennedy, Robert F., 93–94; and African
Americans, 62, 87, 94; appeal of,
87, 93; assassination of, 135, 140;
as attorney general, 61, 64, 196;
campaign for U.S. Senate, 85–87;
and Carter, 140; decision to run for
president, 89–92, 91*f*; at Democratic
National Convention of 1964, 86;
first meeting with, 62, 64; JFK's
assassination and, 84, 85; and LBJ,
85, 86, 88, 89–91; in presidential
election of 1968, 92; and Prince
Edward County school desegregation,
64, 66, 67*f*, 69, 72, 74, 75, 78,
82, 83; prophetic politics of, 94;
as senator, 88–89; special assistant

to, 64–65, 66, 67*f*, 86, 88–89, 90*f*;
Vietnam crisis and, 88–89, 91; visit to
Willowbrook, 120
Keppel, Francis, 72, 74, 75
Kéthly, Anna, 45
Khachaturian, Aram, 13
Khomeini, Ayatollah, 143, 144
Khrushchev, Nikita, 44, 49, 57
Kilmer, Joyce, 30–31, 32
Kimmelman, Michael, 235
King, Coretta Scott, 103
King, Martin Luther, Jr., 60, 93*f*;
assassination of, 92; Baldwin
compared to, 21; Carter and, 126,
128; and Free Schools, 76; on northern
segregation, 65
King, Martin Luther, Sr., 128
Kirkland, Lane, 134
Kleberg, Richard, 218
KMT. *See* Chinese Nationalist forces
Korean War, 13, 23, 35–36, 154, 229
Kristallnacht, 167, 169; international
reaction to, 169, 170
Kubowitzki, Leon, 181
Kun, Béla, 58
Kuomintang. *See* Chinese Nationalist
forces (KMT)
Kurosawa, Akira, 65
Kuwait, Iraqi invasion of, 148, 155

Lafollette, Robert, 212
Laos, 41
Lasker, Mary, 196
Lasker, Morris, 102
Latin America: Good Neighbor Policy
toward, 88, 242; RFK's trip to, 88
League of Nations, 32, 167, 213
Lee, Beauregard, 79
Lee, Robert E., 70, 207
Le Hand, Missy, 226
Lehman, Herbert, 87, 195, 203
Lend Lease, 175
Leuchtenberg, William, 220
Levy, Richard, 188
Lewis, John L., 225

Lichtheim, Richard, 179
Lincoln, Abraham, 70, 85, 208, 220,
231, 240
Lindbergh, Charles, 8
Lindsay, John V., 48, 96, 97*f*; in
congressional election of 1960, 62,
96; New York City prison crisis and,
95–96, 98, 102, 103, 114, 125; and
Roosevelt Island, 234
Lodge, Henry Cabot, 213
Loeb, William, 206
Long, Breckenridge, 170
Longworth, Alice, 201
Louis, Joe, 61
Lukacs, John, 163

MacArthur, Douglas, 15, 31, 228
MacDonald, John, 12
MacDonald, Malcolm, 37
MacDonald, Ramsay, 37
Machiavelli, Niccolò, 148
Malaysia, 37
Malcolm, Benjamin J., 103, 119–20
Maleter, Pal, 51
Manac'h, Etienne, 89
Mandela, Nelson, 234, 242–43
Manhattan Detention Pens. *See* Tombs, the
Manhattan Project, 175
Mann, Gerald, 227
Mann, Thomas, 166
Mansfield, Mike, 39–40
March of Dimes, 191, 194
Marsh, Henry, 67*f*
Marshall, Burke, 61, 72
Marshall, George, 186
Marshall, Thurgood, 71, 233
Marshall Field Foundation, 78
Marshall Plan, 44
Mason, Alice, 127
Maverick, Maury, 218–19, 225–26
Mays, Willie, 103
McCain, John, 237
McCarthy, Eugene, 91, 92
McCarthy era, 15, 38
McClenney, Earl H., 75

McCloy, John, 181, 182
McGovern, "Earthquake McGoon," 41
McHenry, Donald, 139, 143
McKinley, William, 198–99, 202–3
Meany, George, 134
media: prison coverage by, need for, 116–25; regulations reducing access of, 116–17, 118; responsibility of, 242
Mendes-France, Pierre, 42
Merkel, Angela, 234
Mexico, relations with, 155, 242
Miliband, David, 59
Mindszenty, Jozsef, 52
Mitford, Jessica, 119
Monnet, Jean, 32, 89
Montgomery, Alabama, bus boycott, 60
Montgomery, James, 115
Moore, Raymond Lavon, 100
Morgenstern, Joseph, 99
Morgenthau, Bob, 84
Morgenthau, Henry, Jr., 173, 183
Moss, Dickie, 79
Moss, Gordon, 73–74, 79
Moton High School, Virginia, 70–71, 76, 83
Mudd, Roger, 142
Murrow, Edward R., 178

NAACP, 60, 66, 72; and civil rights revolution, 71; and Free Schools program, 76; and press access to prisons, 118, 119
Nagy, Imre, 50, 51, 52
Napanoch State Prison, 113
Nasser, Gamal Abdel, 47
National Association for the Advancement of Colored People. *See* NAACP
National Education Association (NEA), 78
National Park System, 213
National Rifle Association (NRA), 147
National Teacher Corps, proposal for, 83
National Youth Administration (NYA), 218–19
NATO, creation of, 44

Navarre, Henri, 40
Nazi Germany: FDR as shield against, 5, 31, 163, 165, 166, 171, 175, 185–87; mass murders by, 164; military force of, 175; occupation of European countries by, 167, 169, 174, 176–77, 183, 205; persecution of Jews by, 166–67, 169, 170, 171, 176, 177–79, 180; and refugee flows, 43, 167, 168–73, 174, 176–77, 183. *See also* Hitler, Adolf; Holocaust
Netanyahu, Benjamin, 189
Netherlands: Four Freedoms Award in, 233–34, 247n14; Jewish population in, 176; Jewish refugees in, 173, 176; Roosevelts' ancestry in, 199; vanden Heuvel's ancestry in, 4, 8; in World War II, 8, 174, 175, 176
New Deal, 208, 218; attacks on, 163, 191, 220–22, 223; personal impact of, 5; protection of, 205, 224, 226, 231
Newfield, Jack, 118, 121
New Nationalism, 210
Newton, Verne W., 162
New York City: Four Freedoms Park in, 234–36, 235f; prison crisis in, 95–96, 98–102; St. Patrick's Day parade in, Carter at, 129; Tammany Hall in, 195, 196, 203
New York City Board of Corrections, 96; accomplishments of, 98–105, 118, 125; appointment as chairman of, 96, 97–98
New York State: Attica prison riot in, 105–6, 108, 110–14, 118; Board of Corrections in, 114; Carter's campaign in, 127, 129, 130–32; Hyde Park in, 10, 162, 189, 194, 195, 197, 200, 205; Oyster Bay in, 200
Ngo Dinh Diem, 40, 42
Niebuhr, Reinhold, 12, 43
Niles, David, 173
Nixon, Richard: racist strategies of, 142; resignation of, 126; Vietnam War and, 39, 230

Nobel Peace Prize: for International Labour Organization (ILO), 134; for Theodore Roosevelt, 213
Noonan, Peggy, 151
Norodom (King of Cambodia), 36–37
North, U.S.: civil rights revolution in, 61; racism in, 65
North Africa: Allied invasion in World War II, 150; French colonies in, independence of, 38; Jewish refugees in, 183
North Korea, 229. *See also* Korean War
Novick, Peter, 165
Nunn, L. L., 12
Nuremberg Laws, 166
Nuremberg trials, 137, 185
Nyswander, Marie, 103

Obama, Barack, 69, 83–84
O'Connor, Donald, 13
O'Daniel, "Iron Mike," 38
O'Daniel, Lee "Pass the Biscuits Pappy," 227, 228
Office of Strategic Services (OSS), 23, 31–32, 43, 229; in Asia, 32, 33, 36
Ohrdruf Nord concentration camp, 186, 187
O'Neill, Dick, 29
Operation Desert Storm, 148
OSS. *See* Office of Strategic Services
Ostermann, Joseph, 171
Oswald, Lee Harvey, 87
Oswald, Russell, 116
Oyster Bay, New York, 200

Paine, Thomas, 19
Palestine: American Jewish communities' divisions over, 179, 180; Jewish commonwealth in, FDR on, 174; Jewish community in, response to Holocaust, 178, 181
Palestinian Liberation Organization (PLO), 134, 138
Parks, Rosa, 60
Patton, George, 186–87

peace: definition of, 238; search for, 238–39
Peace Corps, 77, 81, 128
Pearl Harbor, 176, 228
Pearson, Drew, 227
Pei, I. M., 140
Pell, Claiborne, 48, 245n5
Pepper, Claude, 193
Peres, Shimon, 234
Perez, Jose, 96
Perkins, Frances, 2
Perle, Richard, 156
Pershing, John J., 26
Platt, Thomas, 202
*Plessy v. Ferguson,* 71
Plunkitt, George W., 203
Poindexter, Grace, 83
Poland: Jews in, 168, 174, 176, 178; partition of, 174; protests against Soviet rule in, 44, 49; Solidarity movement in, 135
Polen, Han, 233
Polier, Justine, 174
polio, 6, 191
Portugal: U.S. military strength compared to, 175, 228; during World War II, 176, 183
poverty: FDR and struggle against, 226, 230, 232; and imprisonment, 108; LBJ and struggle against, 226, 230; personal experience of, 3, 4; in Prince Edward County, Virginia, 80, 83; RFK and struggle against, 88, 94
Powell, Colin, 152, 155
Powell, Jody, 132
press: prison coverage by, need for, 116–25; regulations reducing access of, 116–17, 118; responsibility of, 242
Price, Leontyne, 7
Pridi Phanomyong, 32
Prince Edward County, Virginia, 64–84; civil rights revolution and, 70–73; Free Schools in, 66–69, 68*f,* 73, 75–84; resistance to desegregation in, 61, 64–65, 69–74; RFK's concern about, 64, 66, 67*f*

prison(s): bail system and, 103–4, 108,
109–10, 120; Baldwin in, 17, 20; as
community facilities, 107; drug addicts
in, 103, 112–13; inmate deaths in, 96,
98–100; libraries in, 104; locations
of, 115; media coverage of, need for,
116–25; overcrowding in, 101–2,
106–7; poverty and, 108; public
address regarding, 106–16; reforms of,
102–5, 108, 113–14, 115, 122; riots
in, 95–96, 105–6, 108, 110–12, 117,
118; statistics on, 95
Proskauer, Joseph, 180

racism, 239–40; and criminal justice
system, 97–98, 119, 240; and
education, 61, 64–65, 69–74, 240;
in North vs. South, 65; in South,
and Nixon's political strategy, 142;
struggle against, 230, 240; as threat to
democracy, 237
Radford, Arthur, 39
Rafshoon, Jerry, 132
Rajik, Laslo, 49
Rakosi, Matyas, 49
*Rashomon* (film), 65–66
*Rashomon* approach, 66, 99
Rayburn, Sam, 219, 224, 225, 227
Reagan, Nancy, 194
Reagan, Ronald: admiration for FDR,
193, 194; and RFK medal, 140
refugees: FDR's policies on, 168, 169,
183, 186; Hungarian Revolution and,
45–47, 46*f*, 52–53, 54–56, 96, 109;
Nazi persecution and, 43, 167, 168–73,
174, 176–77, 183; today, 58–59;
U.S. immigration policies and, 168;
after World War II, 43–44. *See also*
International Rescue Committee (IRC)
Reich, Alan, 193
Reigner, Gerhart, 178
Reis, Don, 13
Reston, James, 217
Rice, Grantland, 31
Rich, Frank, 151

Rickover, Hyman, 127
Riegner, Gerhart, 178
Rikers Island prison, 96
Ripple, F. D. G., 75
Rivera, Geraldo, 120
Robert Moton High School, Virginia,
70–71, 76, 83
Robinson, Jackie, 81
Rochester, New York: childhood in, 3, 5,
6–7, 14
Rockefeller, Nelson, 96, 128; Attica
prison riot and, 105, 111, 114;
criticism of, 107, 111; and Roosevelt
Island, 234; and Willowbrook
institution, 120
Roldan, Julio, 96, 98, 101; investigation
into death of, 98–100
Romania: Jewish population in, 168,
183; in World War II, 181
Roosevelt, Anna Eleanor, 234, 235
Roosevelt, Eleanor, 194–98; at
Democratic National Convention of
1940, 207; and Democratic Party
reforms, 195–96; early encounters
with, 6, 10, 194–95; Four Freedoms
Medal awarded to, 233; and
human rights, 195–98, 214–15; and
International Rescue Committee,
43, 168; and Jewish refugees, 173;
and LBJ, 219; legacy of, 197–98,
199, 212, 214–15; marriage to FDR,
200; vs. New York party bosses,
203; as personal hero, 6, 14, 23; vs.
reactionary politicians, 208; relations
with cousins, 200–201; and Theodore
Roosevelt, 200, 202; at UN, 196–98,
214; and Universal Declaration of
Human Rights, 196, 197, 214–15
Roosevelt, Elliott, 200
Roosevelt, Elliott, Jr., 222
Roosevelt, Franklin Delano, 190–91,
217; and Baldwin, 15; childhood
memories of, 5–6, 8; and Churchill,
175, 190; Clinton compared to, 147;
on colonial era, 33; and conservation

movement, 213; vs. corporate interests, 210, 211; court reorganization plan of, 220, 222, 223–24; death of, 186, 217; and Donovan, 23, 24, 26, 31, 43; early support for, 8, 10; Einstein's letter to, 174–75; on fear, 152, 156, 218; fiftieth anniversary of death of, 147; first anniversary of death of, 10; on Four Freedoms, 175, 214, 231–33; Good Neighbor Policy of, 88, 242; Great Depression and, 5, 156, 167, 175, 215, 218, 220; and Holocaust, posthumous accusations regarding, 162–63, 177, 187–89; on Holocaust, warning regarding, 185–86; and human rights, 212, 233; and International Labour Organization (ILO), 134; and invasion of North Africa, 150; LBJ as disciple of, 215–31; legacy of, 43, 189, 191–93, 199, 212, 215, 216; and Manhattan Project, 175; and March of Dimes, 191, 194; marriage to Eleanor, 200; memorials to, 192–93, 231, 234–36, 235*f*; mortgage moratorium declared by, 5, 190; and New Deal, 5, 163, 191, 205, 208, 218, 224; vs. New York party bosses, 203; opposition to Hitler, 5, 31, 163, 165, 166, 171, 175, 185–87, 192; opposition to isolationism, 175–76; as personal hero, 14, 242, 243; vs. reactionary forces, 205, 220–22; reaction to Kristallnacht, 169; reelection in 1936, 5–6, 8, 221; reelection in 1940, 227; refugee policies of, 168, 169, 183, 186; relations with Jews, 163, 165, 166, 168, 169–70, 173–74, 179; second inaugural address of, 148; and State Department, disagreements with, 38; as storyteller, 226; succession to presidency of, 207; and tax reform, 210; and Theodore Roosevelt, 200, 202, 203, 204, 208–10; and Theodore Roosevelt's children, 200–201; third term as president, 175, 204–6, 225,

227; and United Nations, 153, 154, 190, 214; during World War II, focus on victory in, 179–80, 228
Roosevelt, Franklin Delano, Jr., 195, 247n14
Roosevelt, Mrs. Franklin Delano, Jr., 235
Roosevelt, P. J., 247n14
Roosevelt, Theodore, 199; 100th anniversary of presidency, speech for, 198–215; children of, 200–201; and conservation movement, 212, 213; vs. corporate interests, 208–10; death of, 201; decision to seek third term, 204; and Eleanor Roosevelt, 200, 202; in election of 1912, 142, 212; and Franklin Roosevelt, 200, 202, 203, 204, 208–10; legacy of, 199, 202, 215; and New Nationalism, 210; vs. New York party bosses, 202–3; Nobel Peace Prize for, 213; possible reelection in 1912, impact on history, 207–8; and Square Deal, 202, 208; and succession to presidency, 206–7; and tax reform, 209–10; vs. Woodrow Wilson, 213
Roosevelt, Theodore, Jr., 200–201
Roosevelt Institute, 162, 188, 194, 233, 234
Roosevelt Island, 234
Roosevelt Memorial Park, 231, 234–36, 235*f*
Root, Elihu, 206
Rosenberg, Anna, 173–74
Rosenman, Samuel, 173
Rosevelt, Claes Martenson van, 199
Rosevelt, Nicholas van, 199
Ross, Steve, 194
Rowe, James, 217
R. T. French Company, 4, 8
Rubenstein, Howard, 131
Rublee, George, 169
Rumsfeld, Donald, 151
Russell, Bertrand, 243
Russell, Richard, Jr., 229
Russia: oligarchs in, 240–41; in World War I, 24–25. *See also* Soviet Union

Sabin, Albert, 191
Saddam Hussein, 148, 149, 151, 155
Salk, Jonas, 191
Schacht, Hjalmar, 169
Schlesinger, Arthur, Jr., 62, 85, 147, 163, 189, 205, 231, 247n29
Schlesinger, Rudolph, 12
Schwartz, Herman, 118
Schwartzkopf, Norman, Jr., 155
Scowcroft, Brent, 152
SEATO (Southeast Asia Treaty Organization), 42
Seeger, Alan, 30
segregation, 64–65. *See also* desegregation; racism
Selective Service Act, 228
Selma, Alabama, race riots, 231
September 11 attacks, 152, 156, 198
Shaw, George Bernard, 21
Sheppard, Morris, 219, 227
Shipp, Madge, 81
Silver, Abba Hillel, 180
Sinclair, Sir Archibald, 182
Sirhan, Sirhan, 135
Slavs, as target of Hitler's hatred, 164
smallpox, eradication of, 135, 159
Smathers, George, 193
Smith, Alfred E., 191, 201
Smith, Jerome, 62
Smith, Steven, 86, 91*f*
Snow, Richard, 163
*Sobel v. Reed,* 117
Social Security Act, 221, 223
Sokolov, Ray, 101
Sorenson, Gillian, 127
Sorenson, Ted, 85, 91*f*, 126, 127, 147
South, U.S.: "Black Belt" in, 70; Carter's victory in, 129–30; civil rights revolution in, 60–62; racism in, 64–65, 142; as Republican stronghold, Nixon's strategy for, 142; resistance to desegregation in, 71–72, 73. *See also* Prince Edward County, Virginia
South Africa, 22, 242

Southeast Asia Treaty Organization (SEATO), 42
"Southern Manifesto," 240
South Korea, 229. *See also* Korean War
Soviet Union: Carter's policies on, 143–44; collapse of, 145; and Germany after World War II, 44; Hungarian Revolution and, 44–58; and International Labour Organization (ILO), 134; invasion of Afghanistan, 143; refugees from, 168; Stalin-Hitler Pact, 174; and United Nations, 145, 196, 214; in World War II, 154, 164, 176, 181
Spaatz, Carl, 182
Spain, during World War II, 174, 176, 183
Square Deal, 202, 208
*SS St. Louis* (ship), 172–73
Stalin, Joseph, 44, 174
State Department: FDR's disagreements with, 38–39, 170; French campaign in Indochina and, 33, 36, 37, 38; and immigration policies, 170
states' rights, 65, 73, 211, 240
Steinkraus, Herman, 48, 245n5
Stevenson, Adlai, 44, 195, 198
Stevenson, Coke, 228
Stevenson, Robert Louis, 18, 30
St. George's Church, New York City, address at, 106–16
Stone, Harlan Fiske, 24, 31, 221
Strauss, Bob, 131
Sturz, Herb, 103
Suez Canal crisis, 44–45, 47, 58
Sullivan, "Big Tim," 203
Sullivan, Ed, 45
Sullivan, Neil, 66, 69, 75, 76, 78, 80
Supreme Court: *Brown v. Board of Education,* 60, 61, 71, 240; *Citizens United v. Federal Election Commission,* 241; *Dread Scott* decision, 222; FDR and, 220, 222, 223–24; Gold Clause Cases, 220, 221; *Plessy v. Ferguson,* 71; on Prince Edward County schools, 69, 82;

reactionary forces in, 211, 212, 220–22
Swing, Joseph, 48, 96
Switzerland: Geneva Mission to UN in, 132–38; Jewish refugees in, 176, 185; TWA airliner hijacking in, 135–38; World Jewish Congress in, 178, 179
Syrian civil war, 238

Tabor, John, 13
Taft, William Howard, 142, 206–7, 210, 220
Taiwan, 34; Chinese Nationalist soldiers (KMT) in, 33–34, 35; Donovan's visit to, 34–35
Tammany Hall, 195, 196, 203
Telluride House, 2, 12–13
Templer, Sir Gerald, 37
Tet Offensive, 91
Tew, Mrs. William, 79
Thailand: Chinese Nationalist forces (KMT) in, 33, 34*f*; Donovan as ambassador to, 23, 32–42, 229
Theodore Roosevelt Association, 247n14, 248n39
Thompson, Jim, 36
Thompson, Llewellyn, 47
Thoreau, Henry David, 19, 21
Tito, Josip Broz, 183
Tittman, Harold, 56
Tombs, the (detention center), 106–7; Harlem Four in, 120; inmate deaths in, 96, 98–100; library in, 104; overcrowding in, 101, 106–7; poor inmates in, 108; reforms in, 102; riots in, 96, 118
Troyanovsky, Oleg, 145
Truman, Harry: and Berlin airlift, 44; and Eleanor Roosevelt, 196; in election campaign of 1948, 13; in election campaign of 1960, 63*f*; and FDR's legacy, 230; at first anniversary of FDR's death, 10, 195; Four Freedoms Medal awarded to, 233; Hungarian Revolution and, 58; and Theodore Roosevelt, 207

Tunney, John, 141
Turkey: in Gulf War, 155; U.S. invasion of Iraq and, 152
TWA airliner hijacking, 135–38

Udall, Mo, 127, 129, 130
United Kingdom. *See* Great Britain
United Mine Workers, 225
United Nations: appointment as ambassador in Geneva, 132–38; appointment as deputy permanent representative in New York, 139, 139*f*; Arab-Israeli relations at, 138, 144; attack by Trotskyites at, 145, 146*f*; Baldwin and, 15, 21; Charter of, 153, 214, 239; Cold War and, 145, 154; creation of, 153; discussions on importance of, 147–48; Donovan and, 32; early days of, 43; Eleanor Roosevelt at, 196–98, 214; FDR and, 153, 154, 190, 214; Franklin Delano Roosevelt International Disability Award at, 193–94; Gulf War and, 155–56; Hungarian Revolution and, 53, 56; Iranian hostage crisis and, 143, 144; Iraqi weapons of mass destruction and, 148–49, 150; lack of knowledge regarding, 154–55; mandate to end war, 238, 239; Nation Building Commission at, proposal for, 158; as scapegoat, 138; sense of fatalism at, 238; support for, need for, 157–61; U.S. financial contributions to, 135, 155, 157; U.S. role in, 148, 157, 160–61, 197
United Nations Commission on Human Rights (UNCHR), 134, 160
United Nations High Commissioner for Refugees (UNHCR), 46, 58
Universal Declaration of Human Rights, 153, 160; Eleanor Roosevelt and, 196, 197, 214–15; Roger Baldwin and, 15

Vance, Cyrus, 131, 132, 137, 144
vanden Heuvel, Alberta (mother), 1, 3, 4–5, 6, 7–8, 9*f*, 11, 25

vanden Heuvel, Camille (brother), 9
vanden Heuvel, Jennie (sister), 3, 6, 7
vanden Heuvel, Joost (father), 1, 3–4, 5,
    7–8, 9, 9f
vanden Heuvel, Katrina (daughter), 135,
    136f, 137, 145
vanden Heuvel, Leo (brother), 7, 9
vanden Heuvel, Melinda (wife), 243
vanden Heuvel, William J.: as
    ambassador to UN in Geneva, 132–38;
    as ambassador to UN in New York,
    139, 139f, 143, 144, 145, 146f;
    and Carter's presidential campaign
    of 1976, 127–32; childhood of, 3,
    5–10; in congressional election of
    1960, 62, 63f, 96, 195; and Donovan
    Commission report, 48–57; as
    Donovan's assistant, 23–24, 25,
    34–35, 34f, 43, 96; early interest in
    politics, 6, 8, 242; education of, 2,
    10–13, 14, 15; heroes and mentors of,
    14, 23, 24, 132, 242, 243; Hungarian
    Revolution and, 45, 46f, 48–57, 96;
    and International Rescue Committee,
    5, 48–57, 96; military service of, 13,
    23, 64; and New York City Board
    of Corrections, 96, 97–105; parents
    of, 1–2, 3–5, 7–8, 9f, 242; in Prince
    Edward County, Virginia, 64–69, 67f,
    68f, 72–84; as RFK's special assistant,
    64–65, 66, 67f, 86, 88–89, 90f; and
    Roosevelt Institute, 188, 194, 234;
    in Southeast Asia, 34–37; values and
    political beliefs of, 242–43; as young
    lawyer, 13, 23, 195
vanden Heuvel, William Jacobus
    (grandfather), 3, 7, 8
Vera Foundation, 103
Vidal, Gore, 195, 196
Vietnam: and Cambodia, 37; and China,
    39, 41; French military campaign in,
    39–42; OSS in, 32; refugees in/from, 44;
    U.S. policies in, 39–40; visits to, 37–38
Vietnam War, 39; de Gaulle on, 89; LBJ's
    policies on, 89–91, 92, 154, 228–30;

RFK on, 88–89, 91; Tet Offensive, 91;
    UN during, 154
Vinson, Carl, 224
Vinson, Fred, 224
Virginia: resistance to desegregation in,
    61, 71–72. See also Prince Edward
    County, Virginia
Vishinsky, Andrei, 196
Voorhees, Tracy, 47
voting rights, 231, 240
Vrba, Rudolf, 183–85, 189

Wagner, Robert, 81, 85, 86
Wagner Act, 221, 223
Walesa, Lech, 135
Wall, Barrye, 73, 76
Wallace, George, 129, 130
Wallace, Henry, 207
Wallenberg, Raoul, 185
Wannsee Conference, 176
war: struggle to prevent, 32, 238–39;
    as threat to democracy, 237. See also
    specific wars
Warfield, Murphy, 7
Warfield, William, 7
Warm Springs Foundation, 191
Warner, Mark, 83
War Refugee Board, 183, 185
Warren Commission report, 87
Washington, George, 108
Watergate, 126
Watson, Jack, 132
Watson, Willie Mae, 77
wealth, as threat to democracy, 210, 237,
    240–41
Weinberg, Gerhard, 167, 168, 179
Weinstein, Jack, 139f
Weizmann, Chaim, 180
Welles, Sumner, 170, 178
Wetzler, Alfred, 183–84
Wheeler, Burton, 8
White, William Allen, 232
Whitehead, John, 48, 245n5
Whitney, Simon N., 11
Wiesel, Elie, 184, 187–88

Wilhelmina (Queen of the
Netherlands), 233
Williams, Aubrey, 219
Willkie, Wendell, 206, 224
Willowbrook (institution), 120
Wilson, Harold, 89
Wilson, Woodrow, 213–14; Churchill's
vision for, 208; election for president,
142, 207; and League of Nations, 32,
213; World War I and, 25, 26, 207
Wirtz, Alvin, 220
Wise, Stephen, 163, 166, 174, 178, 180
Wolfe, Robert, 188
Wolgast, William, 11
Woollcott, Alexander, 31
World Health Organization (WHO),
134, 135, 159
World Intellectual Property
Organization, 134
World Jewish Congress, 178, 179, 181
World Meteorological
Organization, 134
World War I, 24–26; conscientious
objectors to, 16–17, 20; de Gaulle
in, 38; Donovan in, 23, 25, 26–32,
38; isolationism after, 167; mother's

experience in, 4, 25; Theodore
Roosevelt during, 213
World War II: African Americans during,
61; Allied bombing strategy in,
181; Allied victory in, 10, 154, 181;
beginning of, 205; civilians as victims
of, 164; D-Day invasion in, 181, 182;
Donovan's prediction of, 32; FDR's
focus on winning, 179–80, 228; France
during, 38, 174, 176, 205; impact on
vanden Heuvel family, 8–9; proposals
to bomb Auschwitz in, 181–83;
scenario avoiding, 207; Soviet Union
in, 154, 164, 176, 181; and threat to
democracy, 156, 164, 175, 192, 232;
and United Nations, creation of, 153.
*See also* Holocaust; Nazi Germany
Wyman, David, 165

Young, Andrew, 127–28, 138–39
Young Democrats, 228
Yugoslavia, 183

Zeferetti, Leo, 105
Zimmerman, Moshe, 189
Zionist movement, 163, 174, 176, 180